# The Book of ACTS

EARLY CHURCH HISTORY
AND THE MINISTRY OF THE HOLY SPIRIT

KEVIN J. CONNER

City Bible Publishing
9200 NE Fremont
Portland, Oregon 97220

Printed in U.S.A.

City Bible Publishing is a ministry of City Bible Church and is dedicated to serving the local church and its leaders through the production and distribution of quality restoration materials.

It is our prayer that these materials, proven in the context of the local church, will equip leaders in exalting the Lord and extending His kingdom.

*For a free catalog of additional resources from City Bible Publishing, please call 1-800-777-6057 or visit our web site at www.citybiblepublishing.com.*



ISBN 1-886849-02-1

Unless otherwise noted, all Scripture references are taken from the King James Version of the Bible. In some Scripture references italics have been added by the author for emphasis.

## Other Resources Available by Kevin J. Conner

### *Kevin J. Conner*

The Epistle to the Romans
The Church in the New Testament
The Book of Acts
Interpreting the Book of Revelation
Interpreting the Symbols & Types
The Feasts of Israel
The Foundations of Christian Doctrine
The Tabernacle of Moses
The Tabernacle of David
The Temple of Solomon

### *Kevin J. Conner & Ken Malmin*

The Covenants
New Testament Survey
Old Testament Survey
Interpreting the Scriptures

*Ask for these resources from your Local Christian bookstore.*

CITYBIBLE
PUBLISHING

City Bible Publishing
9200 NE Fremont
Portland, OR 97220
(503) 253-9020 1-800-777-6057
www.citybiblepublishing.com

## INDEX

## FOREWORD

IN THESE DAYS of the outpouring of the Holy Spirit upon "all flesh," the Book of Acts is being viewed again in new light and meaning.

The Church generally has suffered many, many years under ultra-dispensationalism, and the book of Acts has been looked upon simply as being a "transition period" from Judaism to Christianity in which the supernatural in the Book of Acts was simply to establish Christianity as a Divine Religion and to confirm the Early Church in its faith.

It has been taught that once the "Canon of Scripture" and Church Truth was completed, then the supernatural and miraculous elements of the preaching of the "Gospel of the Kingdom" passed away as having served their purpose, being superceded by another Gospel, called the "Gospel of the Grace of God."

Church History disproves such teaching. There is but ONE Gospel. God has always had a faithful remnant in every generation, regardless how little the light may have shone.

God never leaves Himself without a witness.

The close of this Age is seeing a renewal of all that was in the Acts of the Apostles.

The Book of Acts is a book which has no "Amen" to it, for it is still being written in the Ministry of the Ascended Lord in and through His Church.

The Church is to be restored to all its early glory and power, and greater, for the promise is "The glory of the Latter House shall be greater than the Former." Hag. 2:9.

Christ shall return to present unto Himself a glorious Church without spot or wrinkle or any such thing. It will be a Church like unto Himself and suitable to Him as His Bride. Ephesians 5:23-32.

A word as to the following Notes:

The writer makes no pretence to any literary presentation as this is not the purpose of this Commentary.

These Notes were given over a period of two years of Bible Studies in Melbourne, Australia, at the Local Church, and were simply designed to give emphasis on Early Church History and the Ministry of the Holy Spirit.

They have been a Textbook and Commentary for a number of Ministers in Local New Testament Churches in New Zealand, and there is much material for teaching and expansion for the diligent student.

They are sent forth as they are, with all their imperfections, to give "Handfuls of Purpose" (Ruth 2:16) to the Ministry and to the Church, the Body of Christ.

It cannot be overemphasized that "The Book of Acts" should be read, along with additional Scriptures, as well as the comments.

It is THE WORD itself which is the incorruptible Seed of God, and is the creative power in the Church to bring the Church to the Divine Standard.

While Nations and Cultures may vary, the Divine Principles as seen in the Acts will work in all the world. God can only fully bless and seal with His Glory that which measures up to His Pattern.

May "The Acts Of The Holy Spirit" come to fulness in these last of the Last Days.

Kevin J. Conner

# BOOK OF ACTS

## INTRODUCTORY

### THE TITLE

The Book of Acts is called "The Acts of the Apostles," but more truly could it be called "The Acts of the Holy Spirit in the Church."

The secret to the whole Book is the glorious Person, Work and Ministry of the Holy Spirit in the Church which is revealed as the mystical and spiritual Body of Christ in the earth.

There are about 50 references to the Person of the Holy Spirit in this "sketch history" of the Early Church.

All that is said and done, by means of preaching and teaching the Word of the Lord, declaring the resurrection of the Lord Jesus Christ in power, signs and wonders, and the phenomenal growth and development of the Church numerically, plus the Doctrine, Grace and Gifts and Word — all is found in the operation of the HOLY SPIRIT. He is "the key" to the Book of Acts!

The Early Church recognized its helplessness, inability, frailty and weakness without the Holy Spirit.

The believers recognized their daily need of utter dependence on the Spirit for working and witnessing. They realized they were absolutely powerless in themselves for the great Commission and purpose for which Christ had called them. They equally realized the fact that all their needs of Grace, Gift and Power were in the Holy Spirit, the Comforter. The Lord Jesus had taught them that the Comforter would be in them, all that He Himself was with them, in localized form. John 14:17.

The truth of these statements will be abundantly evidenced in these comments on the Acts.

It is here we hear the voice of the risen Lord, by the Spirit, in the Church and then through the Church to the world.

The Book has variously been called:

1. The Acts of the Apostles.
2. The Acts of the Ascended and Glorified Lord
3. The Gospel of the Resurrection
4. The Acts of the Holy Spirit
5. The Gospel of the Holy Spirit

### THE AUTHOR

Luke, the Beloved Physician, is recognized as the author and writer of the Acts, as also the Gospel after his name. Compare Acts 1:1 with Luke 1:1-4.

The Divine Author however is the Holy Spirit. The Acts is part of that all-Scripture which is God-breathed and is profitable for doctrine, reproof, correction, and instruction. II Timothy 3:14-17. II Peter 1:19-21.

Luke's first treatise concerns Christ in His Earthly Ministry, covering details from His birth to His crucifixion and ascension. The Gospels reveal "The Christ after the flesh."

Luke's second treatise concerns Christ in His Heavenly Ministry, and reveals Him in ministry since His Ascension and Exaltation to the very Throne of God.

The Book of Acts reveals "The Christ after the Spirit." Note: II Corinthians 5:16-18.

## THE POSITION

Its position in the New Testament is placed rightly after the Gospels and before the Epistles to the Church.

In the four Gospels we see the Corn of Wheat falling into the ground and dying; while in the Acts we see this Corn bringing forth much fruit. The Lord Jesus as the Corn of Wheat fell into the ground and died, but in His death He has brought to life the Church. John 12:24.

The Book of Acts is the "fruit" of the "seed" sown. The Church is brought to birth through Christ's death and resurrection.

In the Gospels we have the promise and prophecy that the Lord would "build HIS Church" and the Gates of Hades would not prevail against it, (Matthew 16:-20) and in the Acts we see this Church being built.

In the Gospels we see Christ purchasing this Church with His own Blood and in the Acts we see this Church, so purchased, rising into actual existence, marching forth, conquering and to conquer!

The Acts establishes for us the foundation truths and principles of the Church "in Word and in Deed," while the Epistles declare and define the liberties and limits of "Doctrine and Practice" for the Church.

The Standard of Doctrine and Practice is set here for the Church from the ascension of Christ to His second advent when He receives the Church unto Himself forever.

## THE SCOPE

John 21-25 tells us that "The world itself could not contain the books that should be written."

It shows that the Gospels are but "sketches" of the life and ministry of Christ, and so the Acts of the Apostles is but a "sketch history" of the glory and ministry of the Early Church.

If everything said and done was recorded, numerous would be the Books. The Holy Spirit has drawn upon various facts and truths and incidents that are standard for the Church Era.

Acts is the only unfinished Book of the Bible! Hence it has no "Amen" to it. Its history is still being recorded in the Books of Heaven. It will only be finished when the Church has finished her earthly ministry and the "End will be much better than the beginning." Ecclesiastes 7:8.

## THE CHALLENGE

If traditions of men, false ideas and concepts could be erased from the "Modern-day Church"; and the Acts could be read in the light and illumination of the Spirit, we would see that there is nothing to compare with that early glory of that Early Church.

Acts is God's design, God's standard of principles, for His Church TODAY! It was then. It is now. God does not change, as man does.

"Jesus Christ — THE SAME — yesterday, today and forever." Hebrews 13:8; Malachi 3:6.

The Book of Acts is the New Testament in action!

May we return to the Bible, to God, to the Lord Jesus Christ, and to utter dependence upon the Holy Spirit, and we shall see the Acts of the Holy Spirit repeated again.

## GENERAL OUTLINE AND ANALYSIS

**KEY VERSE** "And ye shall receive power after that the Holy Spirit is come upon you, and ye shall be witnesses unto me." Acts 1:8.

### ORDER OF WITNESS

1. **Jerusalem** Acts 1:8; 1:4; Luke 24:47.
2. **Judea** Acts 2:9, 14; 8:1, 40; 9:31-43; 10-11 chapters; Acts 1-7.
3. **Samaria** Acts 8-10 chapters.
4. **Uttermost part** Acts 11:19-26; Acts 13-28 chapters.

This was the general order of the Commission of Jesus, and also the order of fulfilment, giving a general outline of the Book of Acts.

## PETER AND PAUL

Though it was called "Acts of the Apostles," it particularly centers around two Apostles, namely, Peter and Paul.

1. **PETER** — The Apostle to the Jews, the Apostle of the Circumcision. Gal. 1:7.
   Ministry — Acts 1-12 chapters.
2. **PAUL** — The Apostle to the Gentiles, the Apostle of the Uncircumcision. Galatians 2:7-9.
   Ministry — Acts 13-28 chapters.

The following outline gives a brief summary of the Book in relation to these two Ministries of the Lord in the Church.

### GENERAL OUTLINE

| | | | |
|---|---|---|---|
| Acts 1:1-11 | The Lord Jesus Christ | ) | **The Son of God** |
| | The Crucified-Resurrected One | ) | |
| Acts 1:12-26 | The 120 in the Upper Room | ) | |
| | Before Pentecost | | **Jerusalem — The** |
| Acts 2:1-13 | The First Feast of Pentecost | ) | **City and Center** |
| Acts 2:14-47 | The First Sermon and Converts | ) | |
| Acts 3-4 | The First Miracle and Opposition | ) | |
| Acts 5 | The First Divine Judgment | ) | |
| Acts 6 | The First Deacons Chosen | ) | **Peter** — Apostle |
| Acts 7 | The First Martyr, Stephen | ) | to the Jews, the |
| Acts 8:1-4 | The First Great Persecution | ) | Circumcision |
| Acts 8:5-40 | The First Evangelist, Philip | ) | |
| Acts 9 | The Visitation of Local Churches. Under Peter | ) | |
| Acts 10-11 | The First Outpouring on the Gentiles | ) | Writer of two |
| Acts 12 | Final Mention of Peter | ) | Epistles |

Acts 12 is the last mention we have of Peter in Acts particularly, and brings the scene to a close on the activities of the Church in Jerusalem which had reached out from Jerusalem, to Judea and to Samaria.

Now the rest of the Acts deals especially with Paul and the Ministry of the Church from Antioch, unto the Uttermost part of the then-known world — unto the Gentiles.

| | | | |
|---|---|---|---|
| Acts 9:1-31 | The Conversion of the Apostle Saul | ) | |
| Acts 12:24-26 | Barnabas and Paul Together | ) | |
| Acts 13 | Barnabas and Paul Separated for the Ministry unto the Gentiles | ) | **Antioch — The City and Center** |
| Acts 14 | Various Churches Established | ) | |
| Acts 15 | The First Council in Jerusalem | ) | |
| Acts 16-17 | Missionary Journeys of Paul | ) | |
| Acts 18-19 | | ) | |
| Acts 20 | The 2nd and 3rd Missionary Journeys of Paul | ) | **Paul** — The Apostle to the Gentiles, and |
| Acts 21-22 | Paul at Jerusalem | ) | the Uncircumcision |
| Acts 23-24 | Paul's Witness Before Kings & Rulers | ) | |
| Acts 25-26 | | ) | |
| Acts 27 | Paul's Voyage to Rome | ) | Writer of 14 |
| Acts 28 | Paul in Rome — The Gospel Established | ) | Epistles |

PETER in his Ministry reaches from Jerusalem, to Judea and Samaria. PAUL in his Ministry reaches the Uttermost Part of the Earth.

Note the following comparison between Peter and Paul. The Holy Spirit sealed both Apostolic Ministries almost identically in their respective fields of witness.

The Church needs both Peter and Paul! I Corinthians 3:4-6; 21-23.

| **PETER** | **PAUL** |
|---|---|
| (Acts 1-12 chapters) | (Acts 13-28 chapters) |
| An Apostle to the Jews, the Circumcision | Apostle to the Gentiles, Uncircumcision |
| Foundation Ministry | Foundation Ministry |
| Apostolic Revelation to the Church | Apostolic Revelation to the Church |
| To the Jew First | To the Synagogues First |
| Then to the Gentiles | Then to the Gentiles |
| Lays Hands on the Samaritans | Lays Hands on the Ephesians |
| Outpoured Holy Spirit | Outpoured Holy Spirit |
| Healed a Lame Man | Healed a Lame Man |
| Raised a Person from the Dead | Raised a Person from the Dead |
| Signs and Wonders | Signs and Wonders |
| Deals with a Sorcerer | Deals with a Sorcerer |
| Witnessed before the Sanhedrin | Witnessed before the Sanhedrin |
| Seven Addresses Recorded in Acts | Seven Addressed Recorded in Acts |
| Established Local Churches | Established Local Churches |
| Imprisoned for Witnessing | Imprisoned for Witnessing |
| Angel of Lord Delivers from Prison | Angel of Lord Sends Earthquake |
| Arrested in the Temple | Arrested in the Temple |
| Chains Fell Off | Chains Loosed |
| A Man of Heavenly Visions | A Man of Heavenly Visions |
| Religious and Political Opposition | Religious and Political Opposition |

| | |
|---|---|
| Beaten for the Name of Jesus | Beaten and Stoned for the Lord |
| Jerusalem, Judea, Samaria | The Uttermost Part of the Earth |
| Writer of 2 Epistles | Writer of 14 Epistles |
| **JERUSALEM** | **ROME** |

Note: I Corinthians 15:1-10; II Corinthians 11:5; 12:11-12
For these comparisons, note especially the Book of Acts.

## ALTERNATIVE ANALYSIS

**INTRODUCTION** — Acts 1:1-3

1. **JERUSALEM — "Home Missions"**

| | | |
|---|---|---|
| a. | The City and Center<br>Mission of the Holy Spirit<br>Equipment of the Apostles | Acts 1:4 to 2:13 |
| b. | Peter (with others) Apostle to the Jews, the Circumcision<br>Ministry in Jerusalem, and Land, Acts 2:14 to | Acts 2:14 to chapter 8 |
| c. | Jerusalem — Peter's Imprisonment<br>Subsequent Abode (Caesarea)<br>Close of Ministry | Acts 12:1-23 |
| d. | Ministries — Peter, John, Stephen, Philip | |
| e. | Witness — Jerusalem, Judea, Samaria | |

2. **ANTIOCH — "Foreign Missions"**

| | | |
|---|---|---|
| a. | The City and Center<br>Mission of the Holy Spirit<br>Equipment of the Apostles | Acts 12:24 to 13:3 |
| b. | Paul (with others) Apostle to the Gentiles, the Uncircumcision<br>Ministry apart from Jerusalem and the Twelve to other Nations<br>The Uttermost Parts | Acts 13:4 to 14:28 |
| | Paul's Ministry in association with the Twelve | Acts 15:1 to 19:20 |
| c. | Jerusalem — Ephesus — Paul's arrest and imprisonment<br>Subsequent abode (Rome)<br>Close of Ministry | Acts 19:21 to 28:29 |
| d. | Ministries — Paul, Barnabas, Silas, Apollos | |

**Conclusion** — Acts 28:30-31 (Extract. "Companion Bible")

Thus the Gospel begins in Jerusalem, the Religious hub of the world. It ends in Rome, the Political hub of the world.

How significant!

ROME, the World Kingdom which crucified Jesus of Nazareth, the despised Carpenter and Jew.

ROME, who declared and boasted her justice, yet condemned the Christ of God, the Innocent One, to the Religious Leaders of Jerusalem to be crucified.

ROME, who stamped her seal on the Tomb of Jesus to prevent the resurrection. ROME working with JERUSALEM against the Lord and His Anointed.

Thus the Gospels begin!

But the Acts of the Apostles reveal the resurrected Christ, working from Heaven upon earth through His Church, His Body.

JERUSALEM buried Him!
ROME sealed Him in the Tomb!
GOD raised Him!

Now from Jerusalem — "Beginning at Jerusalem" — the Gospel of the Crucified-Resurrected-Ascended-Glorified-Exalted Son of God, the LORD JESUS CHRIST, goes into all the world, and it ends in Rome, in Caesar's Court, by Paul, a JEW!

Religious and Political Powers are conquered by the Lord Jesus Christ.

ROME and JERUSALEM linked together. As it was then, so shall it be in the end of the Age.

## ACTS CHAPTER 1

### THE LAST WORDS OF THE LORD JESUS UPON EARTH. Acts 1:1-9

a. **Christ's Continued Ministry** — vs. 1.

"All that Jesus began both to do and to teach," Acts 1:1; Mark 6:30.
This statement divided the work of Christ into two main streams, i.e., the Gospels and the Acts.
Before and after the Ascension.
The Gospels concern that which Christ BEGAN to do and teach.
The Acts concerns His continued doing and teaching, by the Holy Spirit, through the Church, His Body.
BOTH doing and teaching! Not one without the other!
It was the beginning and not the end of His Ministry. Christ is still doing and teaching today.
Christ Jesus had many things to teach His disciples by the Spirit.
The New Testament revelation had not as yet been given. John 16:12-15.

The difference between the Gospels and the Acts is seen here.

The Gospels — Christ comes from the Father, descends to earth, and earthly ministry begins.
Christ crucified and dying for us.
The Finished Work of the CROSS.

The Acts — Christ returns to the Father, ascends to Heaven, and Heavenly Ministry begins.
Christ living, and glorified for us.
The Continued Work from the THRONE.

The "doing and teaching" of Jesus is what He said, and what He did. His words and His works were of the Father. John 12:49; 14:10. He wants to continue to "do and to teach" in and through the Church.

b. **Christ and the Holy Spirit.** vs. 2.

In vs. 4, The Father is spoken of. )
In vs. 1, The Son is spoken of. ) The Eternal Godhead
In vs. 2, The Holy Spirit is mentioned. )
Father, Son and Holy Spirit. The Triune God. One God revealed in Three Persons. Matthew 28:19.

"He gave commandment by the Holy Spirit unto the Apostles. . ." This is the last mention of the Holy Spirit in relation to the earthly Ministry of the Lord Jesus.

Note that His whole life was one of utter dependence upon the Holy Spirit. If He, as the sinless, perfect Son of God had to depend on the Spirit, how much more shall His disciples, His Church, also need to depend upon the same Spirit.

Note the Holy Spirit in the life of the Lord Jesus.

1. He was born of the Spirit. Luke 1:35; Matthew 1:18-20.
2. He was anointed of the Spirit. Matthew 3:16-17.
3. He was filled with the fulness of the Spirit. John 3:34.
4. He was led of the Spirit. Matthew 4:1.

5. He spoke and taught by the Spirit. Luke 4:18.
6. He cast out devils by the Spirit. Matthew 12:28.
7. He healed the sick by the Spirit. Matthew 12:28; 8:16.
8. He was offered on Calvary by the Spirit. Hebrews 9:14.
9. He was resurrected by the Spirit. Romans 8:11.
10. He gave Commandments by the Spirit. Acts 1:2.
11. He baptized and empowered His Church by the Spirit. Acts 1:5, 8. Pouring out His Spirit.
12. Directs and governs His Church by the Spirit. Revelation 1-2-3 "Hear what the Spirit saith to the Churches."

Thus the Head of the Church, Christ Jesus, was utterly given over to and yielded to the Holy Spirit, and all His life and ministry was by the power and ability of the Spirit.

This power and ability of the Spirit is what He intended His Church, His Body, to have, in the Acts of the Apostles and in this Dispensation of the Church Age.

Note these Scriptures, as fulfilled in the Church and the believer. John 3:1-5; Ephesians 3:17-19; I Peter 1:11-12; Acts 8:5-7; II Corinthians 1:21; Romans 8:2, 13; John 5:19; 12:49.

c. **Christ's Resurrection.** vs. 3.

"He shewed Himself ALIVE, after the PASSION, by many INFALLIBLE PROOFS." The crucified-resurrected Saviour.
His Passion — His complete suffering from Gethsemane to Calvary.
Many infallible proofs — positive, convincing, and unmistakable proofs.

On the fact of Christ's resurrection hangs the whole structure of Christianity, and the Plan of Redemption and the Atonement. Without it, Christianity is but another religion founded on a dead man.

The RESURRECTED Christ is the foundation stone of the Church. I Corinthians 15. The Resurrection Chapter states this fact.

The Resurrected Christ is the power and center of every Sermon in Acts. It is the power of every miracle, sign and wonder, and the foundation of all teaching in the Early Church.

God raised Him from the dead and shewed Him to chosen witnesses only. Acts 10:38-41.

The last the world saw of Him was upon the Cross — crucified!
The last the believers saw of Him was on Mt. Olivet — Resurrected!

The 11 Apostles saw Him at various times.
The women were the first witnesses of His resurrection.
Christ ate and drank with His disciples.
Doubting Thomas touched Him, saying, "My Lord and my God!"
For 40 days He made appearances to His own. They were not deceived.

None could account for the Roman soldiers falling asleep, which was punishable by death.
Who would dare to break the Seal of Rome on the Tomb?

Who rolled the stone away for the women? Who caused the earthquake?
Who stole the body of Jesus, and why could none fine it?
Why was the napkin about His Head folded in a place by itself, and the clothes about His body left in the shape of a 'cocoon'?
How did His body get out of these grave-clothes?
Why did the Priests pay the soldiers money to keep the resurrection story quiet?

**CHRIST IS ALIVE!**

He gave many infallible proofs of His bodily resurrection.

Study these Scriptures: I Corinthians 15:1-8; Matthew 27:62-66; John 20; Mark 16:1-7; Luke 24:16-24; Matthew 28:11-15.

There would be no Book of Acts, no Christianity, no Salvation, no signs or wonders, without the resurrected Christ.

d. **Christ and the Kingdom of God.** vs. 3.

Compare vs. 3 with vs. 6.

"The Kingdom of God" or "The Kingdom to Israel."

John the Baptist, Jesus, and the Apostles all preached the Kingdom of God. Matthew's Gospel especially is the Book of the King and the Kingdom. In it we see the Birth and Ministry of the King. The King rejected and crucified. The King resurrected, returns to the Father — to receive the Kingdom. In this Gospel there are twelve Kingdom of Heaven parables.

It is this Gospel which declares, "Upon this Rock I will build My CHURCH, and I will give unto thee the Keys of the KINGDOM." Matthew 16:13-20.

Thus the Church and the Kingdom are vitally connected.
The Kingdom is the theme of the Gospels and the Church is the theme of the Acts and Epistles.
Because Jewry had a wrong concept of the Kingdom of God, confining it in a Nationalistic, Materialistic and Physical sense, they crucified Christ when He did not establish that type of a Kingdom.

The History of World Gentile Kingdoms is foretold in order in Daniel 2 and in Daniel 7.
The History of the Kingdom of Israel is foretold in Old Testament Prophecies also.

The only Kingdom God is concerned about is HIS KINGDOM. The Kingdom of God — the New Testament Kingdom — by means of The CHURCH — will be declared in power by the Gospel of the Kingdom until the Kingdoms of this world become the Kingdom of our God and His Christ for 1000 years. Matthew 24:14; Revelations 11:15.

His Kingdom is Heavenly, Spiritual, Eternal — not of this earth. John 18:36-37.

e. **Times and Seasons.** vs. 7.

Compare these Scriptures: Ecclesiastes 3:1-8, 17; Acts 1:7; I Thessalonians 5:1.

Jesus as a Man did not know the Times and Seasons until His Ascension and Glorification. Mark 13:32. He received them then from His Father (Revelation 1:1) and gave them to John, and also to Paul, concerning the Times and Seasons pertaining to the End of the Age. Matthew 24:36.

f. **The Promise of the Father.** vs. 4.

This is a wonderful title of the Holy Spirit. Luke 24:49; John 15:26; Ephesians 1:13.

On the basis of the Everlasting Covenant made in Eternity between the Persons of the Godhead (Father, Son and Holy Spirit), the Father covenanted with the Son that when the work of Redemption was accomplished, He would give the Holy Spirit to be poured out on all who would accept the Sacrifice of the Son and who would come to the Father through Him; thus enabling them to be born of the Spirit, filled with the Spirit and preserved by the Spirit until the Day of Full Redemption.

This was the Father's Promise to the Son in this Covenant. Hebrews 13:20. Thus Jesus spoke of the Promise of My Father.

This was also called "The Holy Spirit of Promise," which means that God has made many promises to the saints in and through Christ and these promises are brought to pass, to fulfilment, by the Holy Spirit. He is the Father's Promise to us and He fulfills the Father's Promise in us.

g. **The Baptism of the Holy Spirit.** vs. 5.

This expression is a Scriptural one.
It is used by 1. John the Baptist. Matthew 3:11.
2. The Lord Jesus Himself. Acts 1:5.
3. By Peter the Apostle. Acts 11:16.
A threefold witness of this expression.

Verse 5 links the two Baptisms in one.
In the Book of Acts we see Water Baptism and Holy Spirit Baptism together, forming ONE Baptism.
There is ONE Baptism. Ephesians 4:1-5.
There is the Doctrine of Baptisms (plural.) Hebrews 6:1-2.

The Lord Jesus is the perfect pattern. He was baptized in water and in the Spirit at the same operation. Two, yet one. Matthew 3:16-17.

h. **The Power of the Holy Spirit.** vs. 8.

There are two Greek words for "power."

1. "Exousia," meaning, "privilege, authority,"
used in John 1:12; Matthew 10:1.

2. "Dunamis," meaning, "Power, ability,"
used in Luke 4:14; Acts 1:8. (Dynamite)

"Ye shall receive ABILITY after that the Holy Spirit is come upon you."
The authority is ours, through Christ.
The ability is His, by the Spirit.
Each chapter in Acts is a demonstration of the ability of the Holy Spirit. Not man's ability.
Ability, or lack of it, does not count with God. Often human ability is a hindrance to God.

Moses was stripped of his ability and his might in word and wisdom and deed in the 40 years in the backside of the desert, and then God gave him HIS ability. Acts 7:22; Exodus 3:1-15.

Peter and Paul, and other Apostles and Saints were stripped of their ability, in order to depend upon the ability of the Holy Spirit.

Jesus said, "I do nothing of Myself." John 5:19; 12:49; 14:10.
Jesus said, "Without Me ye can do nothing."

What is the ABILITY of the Spirit? He is able to do all things. He is GOD — Deity.

The Holy Spirit is co-equal in majesty, power, glory, honour and attributes with the Father and the Son.
All that the Father is, the Son is.
All that the Son is, the Spirit is, and He is able to be all that in the Church, which is the Body of Christ.

He is Omnipotent — All Powerful. He can do all things.
He is Omniscient — All Seeing. He sees all.
He is Omnipresent — All Present. He is always present in all places.

The 9 Gifts of the Spirit reveal these attributes of the Holy Spirit in the Church. I Corinthians 12:1-12.

The Church would know to depend upon the ability of the Spirit.

i. **Witnesses unto Me.** vs. 8.

The Greek word for "witness" is "martyr."
It includes opposition, persecution and tribulation for the Name and cause of Christ.

Stephen, James and others were martyred in Acts for their faith in Christ. Millions have been martyrs today, in other countries. True witnesses never testify of themselves.

As the Son witnessed of the Father and declared the Father, so shall true witnesses speak of the Risen Christ. John 5:30-40; 15:26-27.

j. **The Great Commission.** vs. 8.

The following Scriptures should be read together, for they give the complete 'Great Commission' of the Lord Jesus.

| | | |
|---|---|---|
| Matthew 28:18-20 | ) | |
| Mark 16:14-18 | ) | |
| Luke 24:46-49 | ) | The Great Commission |
| John 20:21-23 | ) | The Charge to the Church |
| Acts 1:8 | ) | |

For Order of Fulfilment, refer to notes on the Introduction.

These Scriptures tell us how Christ commanded His disciples to preach and teach, and take the Gospel to every creature in every nation. He commanded them to make disciples of all nations, baptizing the believers, and preaching the Gospel with signs following.

*If we want to know how the disciples interpreted the Commission of Christ, then the only Divine record we have is that found in the Book of Acts.*

Acts stands in its own Divine light as the interpretation of the Great Commission.

If we want to understand what Jesus meant by preaching the Gospel, teaching repentance and remission of sins in His Name, then we may study the Sermons and preaching in the Acts.

If we want to know what Jesus meant by signs following them that believe, in His Name, then we must turn to the Book of Acts.

If we want to understand and appreciate what Jesus meant by speaking with new tongues, by healing the sick, casting out of devils, and taking up deadly serpents, etc., then again we turn to the Book of Acts.

*All must be interpreted in the light of the Acts of the Holy Spirit.*

Consistency of interpretation follows, that, if we want to know and understand what Jesus meant by baptizing into the Name of the Father, and of the Son, and of the Holy Spirit, then again we must turn to the Acts of the Apostles.

Acts is the interpretation and demonstration of Christ's words.

The Commandments of the Great Commission were given by Jesus through the Holy Spirit. Acts 1:4. Acts is the Acts of the Holy Spirit fulfilling and obeying that Commission.

The Commission remains unchanged. The means of fulfilling it and obeying it is the same. The interpretation, as seen in the Acts and the Epistles is the same.

Unbelieving believers may argue over "speaking with tongues, healing, casting out of devils," as "not for today," or "this does not mean that," and others may argue over water baptismal formulas and words, but THE ACTS stands in its own Divine light as the answer to what Jesus meant in the Commands of the Great Commission as given in the Gospels.

Both the Acts and the Gospels must go together. One cannot use one against the other.
The Gospels are the COMMANDMENTS of Jesus, and the Acts are the FULFILMENT of those Commandments.
It says what it means, and means what it says!

k. **The Ascension of Jesus.** vs. 9.

The Scripture says, concerning His ascension:

1. He was "taken up." Acts 1:9
2. He was "carried up." Luke 24:50-53
3. He was "received up." Mark 16:9

His translation. Earthly ministry finished. Heavenly ministry begins.

The Son of God, as Second Person of the Godhead, had to return to the Father before the Third Person, the Blessed Holy Spirit, could descend from the Father and be poured out upon all flesh.

This is the last glimpse of the "Christ after the flesh," until He comes the second time. II Corinthians 5:16.

The Gospels show the disciples walking BY SIGHT of THE MAN on this earth. II Corinthians 5:7.
The Acts reveal the disciples walking BY FAITH of THE MAN in Heaven.

The Ascension is the closing action of the 40 days' ministry after Christ's resurrection.

Note some of the most important events of the 40 days' ministry.

**Seen of them 40 days.** vs. 3.

The events of this 40-day period fulfilled a number of typical and prophetic things of the Law.
Note Matthew 5:17-18; 11:13.
Christ came to fulfill all that was in the Law and the Prophets.

1. The resurrection of Christ. I Corinthians 15.
2. The Presentation of Himself as the Sheaf of Firstfruits. Leviticus 23:9-15; I Corinthians 15:20-23.
3. The presentation of the Blood and Body of Jesus Christ at the Throne of the Father. Hebrews 9:12-15; 6:19-20; Leviticus 16; John 20:11-18. Entrance within the Veil.
4. The New Birth of the Disciples. John 20:22-23; John 3:1-8; Cf. Gen. 2:7. The Resurrection Day.
The Firstfruits of the "New Birth" company — the Church. As Adam received the breath of life, so did the disciples here. Became quickened spirits.
Old Testament saints were saved by faith in the coming of Messiah. New Birth in the New Testament made possible through Messiah's death and resurrection.
The Veil was rent at Calvary. Thus there remained no Law, no Priesthood, no Temple, no Old Covenant, as all was fulfilled and abolished in His perfect once-for-all sacrifice. Only His Blood is acceptable to God under the New Covenant. Though the disciples were "born of the Spirit," yet Jesus commanded them to wait and be "baptized in the Spirit."
5. Various "appearances" of Christ to His own. John 20: Luke 24:13-35; Mark 16.
Acts 10:38-41; John 21:1, 14. The Lord Jesus shewed Himself in a number of appearances in these 40 days to His own.
6. Opening of the understanding in the Scriptures. Luke 24:44-46. Giving spiritual insight into the Prophets, the Law and the Psalms. Prophecy and fulfilment. Interpretation given.
7. Speaking of the Kingdom of God.
Acts 1:3, 6; Matthew 21:41-44; I Peter 2:1-9; Revelation 1:6; 5:9-10.
The Kingdom as revealed in the Church.
8. The Great Commission given. Refer to Scriptures above.

**Jesus Ascends.** vs. 9.

The disciples beheld Him as A CLOUD (cf. Matthew 17:1-7) receives Him out of their sight.

The following Scriptures reveal the exaltation and glory of Jesus THE MAN, as He enters Heaven to the Father's Throne.

He enters as the King of Glory. Psalms 24.
He enters and sits down as KING-PRIEST. Psalms 110.
He sits at the right hand of the Majesty on High. Revelations 3:21.
He receives the exalted Name. Philippians 2:5-11; Acts 2:33-36.
He ascends far above all. Ephesians 4:8-16; Hebrews 1:3-14; Hebrews 2:9.
He sat down — after a finished work. Mark 16:19-20; Hebrews 10:12-13; Revelation 1:1.

Thus JESUS, is crowned with Glory and Honour. He is given the Oath of the Melchisedek Priesthood, and is given THE NAME ABOVE EVERY NAME, seated at the Father's Right Hand of power. Here He receives the Revelation (Revelation 1:1) and receives the Holy Spirit from the Father, to be poured out on the waiting disciples.

Here he begins His Heavenly Ministry, confirming His Word on earth. Here He sits and reigns until all enemies are made His footstool. The MAN in Glory. Incomparable!

(Note. **Jonah** the Prophet, was 3 days and 3 nights in the heart of the fish, and then experienced 40 days, in which he preached to the Gentile City of Ninevah, bringing it to repentance. Jonah 1-4 chapter. So **Jesus Christ**, buried and resurrected from the heart of the earth, after which He speaks to His disciples for 40 days, and then the message of repentance goes to the Gentile Cities. Matthew 12:40-41. Thus 3 days and 3 nights; then 40 days; then Gentiles come to repentance.)

1. **Two Witnesses at the Ascension.** vs. 10-11.

"**Two MEN** (not Angels) stood by them in white apparel."

It is significant that all through the life of Jesus there were at least Two Witnesses (Men, or Angels) at the most important events.

1. At His Birth there were wise men; at least two of them, possibly three. Matthew 2:1-2.
2. At His Temptation Angels (messengers) ministered unto Him. Matthew 4:11.
3. At His Transfiguration two men — named as Moses and Elijah — minister to Christ of His coming exodus by way of the Cross. Luke 9:28-35; Matthew 17:3-12. They were dressed in shining garments, white apparel, and glory.
4. At His Gethsemane an angel (messenger, Greek) strengthens Him. Luke 22:43.
5. At His Resurrection two men were in shining garments. Luke 24:4; John 20:12.
6. At His Ascension here again there stands two men, Acts 1:10. They declare the fact of His Second Advent. vs. 11.
7. At His Second Advent there will be two witnesses who perform wonders and bring about plagues, which only Moses and Elijah did in Old Testament days. Both had an unfinished ministry. Revelation 11.
   They are called HIS WITNESSES.
   In Zechariah they are spoken of as the two Anointed Ones, the Sons of Oil. Zechariah 4.

   The Scripture demands the Testimony of two or three witnesses. Deuteronomy 17:6; Matthew 18:16.
   A true witness must be one who has actually seen and heard the facts. Acts 22:15; I John 1:1-3; Acts 4:20.

   Moses and Elijah could not be true witnesses unless they had seen and heard the above events. They will declare these things in power and authority to Jewry-Israel, that Jesus is the Messiah and that He is about to return to set up His Kingdom for 1000 years.

(Some Expositors interpret these two men as "Moses-Elijah" Company. Others interpret the same two men as Enoch and Elijah, or Moses and Elijah).

m. **The Disciples gazing up.**

Even as Elisha gazed up and saw the translated Elijah, waiting for his Mantle and the Double Portion of the Spirit to fall upon him, to carry on his ministry; so the disciples gaze upon the translated Christ here.

n. **This Same Jesus**

Note II Corinthians 11:1-4. Many are preaching "another Jesus" and "another Gospel," and "receiving another spirit" today. It will be the same Jesus — The Virgin Born, Sinless, Spotless, Crucified, Resurrected, Glorified, Ascended Son of God who will come again the second time. The same yesterday — today — forever. Hebrews 13:8.

o. **In Like Manner.**

He will return in the exact manner as He went away. That is, He went in a cloud, He went bodily, Personally, Literally, Visibly, Gloriously, as the God-Man; and He will return the same way. Revelation 19; I Thessalonians 4:15-17.

p. **The Upper Room — before Pentecost.** vs. 12-14.

1. **The Disciples**

The 11 Apostles named. The Apostles of the Lamb. Matthew 10:1. The Unnamed Women also. A new day was dawning. The Holy Spirit to be poured out on "all flesh." Men and women! Mary — Mother of Jesus here. Last mention of Mary. No voice, no command, no authority. Christ's half-brethren. Eternal difference between Christ and His brethren is that Christ had but one Father, (God). All others have two (human and Divine.)

All from various walks of life. Different natures, different temperaments, yet all in the One Christ. No matter what their past experience, all needed the Spirit.

2. **The 120 Disciples**

Note I Corinthians 15:6. Over 500 brethren witnessed the Ascension but only 120 got to the Upper Room, for the Day of Pentecost.
A significant number.
Moses' life divided into 3 × 40 = 120 years.
Christ's life stamped with 3 groups of 40 days upon it.
i.e. 40 days in His circumcision
40 days in His temptation
40 days in His resurrection

Solomon's Temple, dedicated in the 7th month in the Feast of Tabernacles had 120 trumpeters. II Chronicles 5:11-14.
Here at the dedication of the Church, the true and spiritual Temple, there are 120 disciples.
In the days of Noah, the Holy Spirit strove with men for 120 years before the flood came. At the end of 120 years, Noah ceased to preach the word and the Spirit ceased to strive with men. All ungodly flesh was judged by the flood.

The number 120 signifies "the end of all flesh and the Spirit supreme."

The Holy Spirit strives with men for 120 Jubilees (120 × 50 = 6000 years,) at the end of which all ungodly flesh will be destroyed. Genesis 6:3.

In this instance it signifies the end of the Law-Man, the Flesh-Man Ministry, and the Holy Spirit being supreme as the Shekinah Glory in the New Covenant Temple. Ephesians 2:20-22.

3. **One Accord.** vs. 14.

Of one accord both before and after Pentecost. They did not go there to become of one accord, but because they were already of one accord. They were there for the same thing, the one thing. Unity of desire. One heart, one mind, one purpose, one accord. UNITY. John 17; Psalms 133. The Anointing Oil of the High Priest could only flow down to the Body where unity was. Philippians 1:27.

This "one accord" was a secret of power and blessing in Acts. Acts 2:1, 46; 4:24, 32; 1:14; II Chronicles 5:11-14.

No fighting, bitterness, criticism, strife, etc., amongst the disciples. Unity among men and women in the Upper Room.

4. **Prayer and Supplication.** vs. 14.

Supplication — means humble (self abasement) and earnest prayer in worship.
"To kneel down, to entreat, implore, call upon humbly."

Prayer — to petition.

Constant, continual prayer. Not listlessness, carelessness, indifference. Persistent in prayer and supplication. Earnest, sincere heart-prayers based upon the word of promise. Realized their need of Power from on High. Realized uselessness, helplessness, inability of self to preach in Jerusalem, etc., win men to Christ.

Although they had ministered before (Matthew 10,) yet they understood this Power was distinct in its operations as a soul-convicting, soul-convincing, soul-converting power.

5. **Praise and Faith Obedient.** Luke 24:44-53; Acts 5:32.

"He gives the Spirit to them that obey Him."
They waited until the Spirit came. They believed. They obeyed. They received the promise in the appointed time. They did not just claim "by faith."

6. **Praise and Blessing.** Luke 24:44-53.

They were in the Temple praising and blessing God.

7. **Sense of Responsibility**

The disciples understood the great Commission, and a sense of responsibility came upon them.
They were to be witnesses of the resurrected Christ in all the world and make disciples of all nations. Matthew 28:18-20.

q. **The Fallen Apostle, Judas, replaced.** vs. 15-26.

The Holy Spirit devotes 11 verses to this incident of the replacing of Judas, the fallen Apostle.

Was Judas ever saved or was he a devil from the beginning? Was he foreordained or predestined to do what he did? Did he have no choice in the matter, or did he sell Christ out in order to fulfill the Scriptures?

These and other questions immediately come into the mind of believers in this matter of Judas.

There are two lines of Scriptures which only meet in God. Those that pertain to Divine Sovereignty and those that pertain to Human Responsibility.

There are several words mentioned in the Bible which help us to understand these things, in the measure that finite minds can understand the Infinite.

1. **Foreknowledge.** Romans 8:29; Acts 15:18.

   God is Omniscient. He knows all things at all times. He knows the end from the beginning. He is the I AM.
   He Foreknows. I Peter 1:2.
   He Foresees. Acts 2:25, 31.
   He Foreordains. Ephesians 1:4; I Peter 1:20.
   He Foretells. This is Prophecy. I Peter 1:10-12; II Peter 1:20-21.

2. **Election.** I Peter 1:2.

   The act of choosing. Chosen on or according to foreknowledge. Ephesians 1:4. In Grace.

3. **Predestination.**

   Bringing to pass of Election. Election looks back to Foreknowledge. Predestination looks forward to the destiny. Predestination linked with God's love. God will never do anything with His creatures which is inconsistent with His own Nature. Predestination has to do with the future destiny of those who believe. Romans 8:29; Ephesians 1:5.

   NOTE— PROPHECY is not Predestination but FOREKNOWLEDGE. God Foreknew, He Foresaw, and thus, through the mouth of the Prophets He FORETOLD!

   Thus Judas fulfilled the Scriptures because God foreknew all things, and foretold the same. Acts 1:16.
   Note the following general outline of the history of Judas.

The Lord Jesus chose 12 Apostles to represent the 12 Tribes of Israel. Matthew 10:1-4.
Judas is listed among the Apostles, as a Sent One. He came of the same Tribe as Jesus came from, the Tribe of Judah.
Jesus gave them power over unclean spirits to cast them out, and also power over all sickness and all disease.

Jesus ordained these 12 Apostles and sent them forth to preach the Gospel of the Kingdom. Mark 3:13-19.

The whole of Matthew Chapter 10 should be read in connection with the choice of the 12 Apostles.
Judas is ordained to be an Apostle, ordained to preach the Gospel, by Jesus Himself. He is given power over devils, over sickness and disease; all of which are works of the Devil. He is a Sent One, one of the Twelve. Matthew 11:1.

Jesus said to the Twelve: "I send you forth as SHEEP in the midst of wolves." Matthew 10:16. Not 11 Sheep and 1 Devil. Judas is also included here as a "sheep" as well as the other 11 Apostles.

Jesus again says to the Twelve: "It is not you that speak but the Spirit of your Father which speaketh in you." Matthew 10:19-20. Thus the Holy Spirit spoke through the Twelve in their ministering and preaching.
We cannot exclude Judas from this any more than any other of the Twelve.

Again Jesus speaks to the Twelve saying, "He that endure to the end, the same shall be saved." Matthew 10:22.

The Twelve were chosen and ordained to bring forth fruit. John 15:16. The Twelve were sent forth two by two. So Judas worked with one of the other Apostles. Mark 6:7.

If Judas were "a Devil from the beginning" then it is questioned as to why Jesus gave him (a Devil) power over all sickness and disease, which are works of the Devil.

Why did Jesus give him (a Devil) power to cast out devils? Why was a Devil ordained to preach as a Sent One for Christ? Why was a Devil chosen to preach the Gospel of the Kingdom?

Does Satan cast out Satan, and rise up against himself? Mark 3:22-23, 26.

The Scripture tells us: "That Jesus knew from the beginning who they (plural) were that believe Him not, and who (singular) should (was about, Amp. N.T.) to betray Him."

The "many" and the "one" are included here.

In verse 66, we are told that many of His disciples went back and walked no more with Him. Jesus turns and asks the Twelve whether they would go away too.

In verses 70-71, Jesus then said, "Have not I chosen you Twelve and one of you is (not was!) a Devil . . . He spake of Judas . . . for he it was that should (Amp. N.T. 'was about to') betray Him."

The time element is nearing the close of the Lord's public ministry.

All 4 Gospels declare that Christ had the Passover with the Twelve Apostles, which included Judas. Matthew 26:17-25; Mark 14:17-26; Luke 22:14-23; John 13.

The Disciples called Him "Lord" and "Master." Matthew 26:22, 25. John 13:13; I Corinthians 12:3.

Judas had the Passover. He became the first one to be guilty of the Body and Blood of Christ. I Corinthians 11:27.

"Jesus loved His own (even Judas) unto the end." John 13:1.

Jesus hid from the other disciples what Judas was about to do.

"**The Devil having now put it into the heart of Judas to betray Him.**" John 13:2.
Here the hellish thought of betrayal is put into the heart of Judas.

The Lord Jesus washes the disciples' feet. He says that they are not all clean, for Judas had just previously been to the Priests to sell Christ out. Jn. 13:3-17; 10-11; Matthew 26:14-16.

Jesus now quotes from the Psalms. "Mine own familiar friend, in whom I trusted, which did eat of My bread, hath lifted up his heel against Me." Psalms 41:9; John 13:18; Genesis 3:15.

"A Devil surely was not Christ's familiar friend, in whom He trusted."

In the Garden of Gethsemane, when Judas betrayed Him with a kiss, Jesus called him "Friend." Matthew 26:47-50.

The tragedy of it all is found in John 13:27-30, "After the sop SATAN ENTERED INTO him (Judas) . . . and he went out, and it was NIGHT."

If Judas was a Devil from the beginning, would Jesus call a Devil to preach His Gospel, give him power over the works of the Devil, and over evil spirits?

Would Jesus minister the Table of Communion to a Devil, wash the Devil's feet, call the Devil a familiar friend, in whom He trusted, etc.?

How could a Devil put something into the heart of a Devil, and then the Devil (Satan) enter into a Devil?

The answer is found for us in Acts 1:18-20. "Judas by TRANSGRESSION FELL."

Not by predestination! As the Archangel became a Devil, so the sheep Judas became incarnate of the Devil. John 10:1-16; 26-29; Isaiah 53:6. As a sheep he went astray. He ceased to follow the Shepherd, left the fold, and followed the voice of the Stranger, even Satan.

His transgression and fall was over the love of money. Matthew 26:6-9; John 12:1-6; I Timothy 6:10.

He fell from his Ministry as an Apostle of the Lord Jesus. One cannot fall from a place one has not been. He fell through transgression.

God as Creator will do nothing with His Creatures which is inconsistent with His Holy Character. To teach that Judas was predestined, and foreordained, against his own will, to betray Christ and sell Him out is to insult the Moral attributes of God in His holiness, justice, righteousness and love.

God foreknows all things, and thus He foretold these things. God knew that Judas would fall through love of money, and caused His Prophets to foretell the same.

Satan desired to sift Peter also, as well as all the others. Matthew 16:23; Luke 22:31.

As Joseph was sold by Judah to the Ishmaelites for 20 pieces of silver and into the hands of the Gentiles, so was Christ sold by Judas (same Tribe!) to the Priests for 30 pieces of silver, and then into the hands of the Gentiles.

Judas repented to the Priests, but not to Jesus. Matthew 27:3-10. It is possible that Judas had expected Jesus to escape the mob, as He had in previous times. But Judas had the weakness for money. His sin became exceedingly sinful in the light of His Ministry as an Apostle, and his 3½ years being with the Lord Jesus with all that this meant in word and deed and ministry.

Note how Judas fulfilled the prophecy of Zechariah 11:10-14. Judas' blood was spilt, and he became a broken vessel beyond redemption, after he hung himself. A vessel marred in the Potter's House.

In Acts 1:15-26, we see him being replaced by another.

**The Holy Spirit foretold** concerning Judas. vs. 16, 20.
Psalms 69:25-28; Psalms 109:8. These two Psalms are especially "The Judas Psalms." Imprecatory Psalms.
Peter quotes these several verses.

The Apostles had their understanding of the Scriptures opened by the Lord Jesus. Luke 24:44-46.

Who could have applied these Scritures to Judas but the Holy Spirit Himself?

This Psalm concerning Judas shows that his Name would be blotted out of the Book of the Living. Cf. Exodus 32:32-33 and Revelation 3:5 with Psalms 69:28. Such could not be unless it had once been written in.

**The Suicide of Judas.** vs. 18-20.

Judas hung himself upon a Tree, even as Ahithophel hung himself on a Tree after conspiring against David. II Samuel 17:23.

"Cursed is every one that hangeth on a Tree." Deuteronomy 21:22-23.

Christ hung on the Tree of Calvary that man might not hang on a Tree. Galatians 3:13. He was accursed of God for us. Man sinned by the Tree of Knowledge of Good and Evil, hence the Lord Jesus suffers on a Tree to redeem us.
Calvary now becomes the Tree of Eternal Life.
Jesus hung on the Tree. Judas hung on his own Tree.

Judas went to "his own place." vs. 25. Cf. Luke 16:28; John 14:2; Heaven or Hell is open for all to choose.

Judas lost his Bishopric. vs. 20. Literally, his Office, Charge, Ministry, Overseership.

**The Choice of Matthias by lots.** vs. 22-26.

It is to be remembered that the Holy Spirit had not yet been outpoured. The disciples are still in the transition period emerging from the Old Covenant into the New Covenant era. The choice of Matthias was by lot, and was of the Lord. According to ancient custom of writing names on paper and then placing these names in the lap or a vessel, which was shaken to and fro and the first name cast out of the lap or vessel was recognized as the choice of the Lord.
Note: Leviticus 16:8; Jonah 1:3-7; Numbers 26:55-56.

*"The lot is cast into the lap but the disposing thereof (the choice or decision) is of the Lord."* Proverbs 16:33.

Remember their prayer in verses 24-25, that the Lord would show who He had chosen of these two men.

Matthias is here recognized as one of the Twelve, in verse 26.

Matthias was numbered with the 11 Apostles. Before Pentecost. He was counted with the 11 Apostles after Pentecost. Acts 2:14. Paul recognized Matthias as among the Twelve also in I Corinthians 15:5.

No Apostles have the unique place as do these Twelve Apostles, for they are expressly called "The Twelve Apostles of the Lamb." Revelation 21:14.

The fact that Matthias is not mentioned again in Acts cannot be used as an argument against his choice as of the Lord, for very few of the original Twelve are mentioned in the Book of Acts.
The main Apostles mentioned are Peter, James and John, and then the Apostle Paul.

Apostles are never again chosen by lot in the New Testament once the Holy Spirit was poured out. The Lord Jesus chose and ordained and equipped the Ministries from this time on, by the Spirit.

The Apostle Paul has a unique position in the Early Church, but his choice is sovereignly proven, by the Lord Jesus Himself.
The choice of Paul is dealt with in Chapter 9.

**SUMMARY of Chapter 1**

Notice the main characters in Acts, Chapter 1.
The Godhead spoken of as Father, Son and Holy Spirit.

The 12 Apostles named.
Judas, the Fallen One of the Twelve Apostles. Replaced by Matthias.
Mary, the Virgin Mother, and other women named amongst the 120 disciples.
The Two Witnesses who foretell the Second Coming of Jesus.

Judas becomes a terrible warning and type of the Spirit of Anti-Christ. He was the Fallen One of the Twelve Apostles.

It is significant that the Ministries of the Apostle and Prophet, which are the Foundation Ministries of the Church, have been rejected by the Church generally today.
These Ministries are to be restored to the Church. The Bible also shows that there will be false Apostles and Prophets, and in them will be revealed the Spirit of Anti-christ. Revelation 13; I John 4:1-3.

A great company will fall with these False Ministries. The Bible shows that there will be two streams of prophecies being fulfilled in the last days.

1. A great Outpouring of the Spirit, bringing restoration, and revival and awakening. Isaiah 60:1-2; Hosea 6:1-2.

2. A great Apostacy and Falling Away.
   II Thessalonians 2:1-12; Hebrews 6:1-8; 10:25-31; II Peter 2:20; Luke 12:43-46; Hebrews 3:12-14; Matthew 7:15-23; Ezekiel 18:19-32; 24-26.

   "Many will say to Me in that day, Have we not prophecied in Thy Name, and cast out devils and done many wonderful works, in Thy Name? Then He will say unto them, I never knew you, depart from Me ye that work iniquity," Matthew 7:15-23.

   Judas foreshadows that company of Apostates.

   A careful study of Ezekiel, chapters 3, 18 and 33 reveal that the Lord will forget all their righteousness which they have done, and remember their iniquities because of their apostacies.

   All these 'seeds' are found in the beginning of the Book of Acts.

## ACTS CHAPTER 2

a. **The Day of Pentecost.** vs. 1.

"And when the Day of Pentecost was fully come . . ."
Literally, the 50th Day.
There were 40 days of Christ's post-resurrection Ministry, then 10 days of waiting. Acts 1:3; 2:1.

There was a set time for the Holy Spirit to come, even as there was for Christ Jesus to die on Calvary. Galatians 4:4.

Jehovah appointed 3 Feasts in the Old Testament for the Nation of Israel. Leviticus 23. Deuteronomy 16:16-17.

1. The Feast of Passover. Exodus 12. Fulfilled in the Gospels.
2. The Feast of Pentecost. Fulfilled in Acts and Epistles.
3. The Feast of Tabernacles. Fulfilled in Hebrews and Revelation.

Israel as "The Church in the Wilderness" (Acts 7:38), kept the Feast of Pentecost at Mt. Sinai 50 days after the Passover Lamb had been slain and the deliverance from the Egyptians at the Red Sea.
The New Testament Church follows the same pattern, keeping the Feasts of the Lord, in spiritual reality, in Mt. Zion, Heavenly Jerusalem. Hebrews 12:22-24.

The following diagram illustrates that which is set forth in the Feasts of the Lord in relation to the unfolding New Testament fulfilment.

The Old Testament is the type and prophecy and shadow.
The New Testament is the antitype, and fulfilment and substance.

| Passover<br>1st month | Pentecost<br>3rd month | Months<br>4th – 5th – 6th | Tabernacles<br>7th month |
|---|---|---|---|
| The Lamb<br>Unleavened<br>Bread<br>Sheaf of<br>Firstfruits<br>3 40 + 10 = 50 | The Two<br>Wave Loaves<br>Leavened<br><br><br>Days<br>Early Rain | No Rain Period<br>Dry Months | Trumpets<br>Atonement<br>Ingathering<br>or Booths<br><br>Latter Rain |
| THE GOSPELLS | THE ACTS | EPISTLES | HEBREWS<br>REVELATION |

b. **The Law Covenant**

Under the Old Testament Pentecost, the Law was written on Tables of Stone, and the Tabernacle of Moses, the Aaronic Priesthood Order is given, and the Church in the Wilderness was established. Exodus 19:1-6; Exodus chapters 20-40.

Under the New Testament Pentecost, the Law is written on Tables of the Heart, by the Spirit. Here the New Testament Order of the Church is established. II Corinthians 3.

While the Priests and the Jewish Nation kept the Ceremonials of the Feast of

Pentecost at the Temple, which Temple God had now finished with as demonstrated in the rent Veil, the Disciples of Jesus in the Upper Room kept the True and Spiritual Feast in the New Temple, even the Church.
Jewry kept the Letter, the Shadow, the Form, the Type, the Promise and Prophecy.

The disciples kept the Spirit, the Substance, the Reality, the Antitype and the Fulfilment.

c. **Supernatural Manifestations**

At Pentecost there were Divine Signs. "A sound came from heaven." The Spirit was being outpoured. The Spirit descending from God.

1. **The mighty rushing wind.** Filled the house.
2. **The cloven tongues like as fire.** Sat on each of them.
3. **The speaking with other tongues,** as the Spirit gave them the utterance. They were all filled with the Spirit.

The WIND and the FIRE were both Old Testament symbols of the Holy Spirit. The Invisible Person was seen and heard in the symbols of His own Nature and Person.
These signs touched the senses of "seeing" and "hearing."
They SAW and they HEARD.
These things are the only evidence of a true witness and testimony.

There were similar manifestations in the Old Testament for:

1. Moses and Israel, at Mt. Sinai, Feast of Pentecost. Exodus 19.
2. Elijah, at Mt. Horeb, as God spoke to him in the still small voice after the earthquake, wind and fire. I Kings 19:8-13.
3. The Church, in the New Testament Pentecost experiences the rushing wind, the fire, and the new tongues.

The Lord caused the earthquake, wind and fire. All were Divine manifestations of His power, yet He was not in them, but He was in the still small voice which followed.
The still small voice of the Spirit.

So it was on the Day of Pentecost.

THE WIND of the Spirit. John 3:8; 20:22; Ezekiel 37:9. The breath of God.

THE FIRE of the Spirit. Matthew 3:11-12. To burn up the chaff.

In contrast to the Church, the Lord Jesus had the Dove of the Holy Spirit upon Him, for He was the only sinless and perfect Man. Matthew 3:14-17.

There was but ONE SOURCE of the Divine Fire, but it became cloven tongues of fire upon the head of each disciple. Many flames were lit from that fire.

**"Tongues of Fire."** Spiritually this was the lighting of the lamps upon the Golden Candlestick as fulfilled in the New Testament Church so that the Lord would have the witness of LIGHT in the world, in and through the Church. Revelation 1:12-20; Matthew 8:12.

**"The Burning Bush."** Hebrews 1:7; Exodus 3:1-15.

As God arrested Moses and spake to him from out of the Burning Bush and Glory of His Holiness, so God would make the New Testament Church a Burning Bush; "Burning yet unconsumed," to arrest the unbelieving world, causing His fire, His voice, His Holiness, His Name, to be revealed in convicting, convincing, converting power.

Fire is ever the symbol of God's holiness. The symbol of conviction against sin, unrighteousness.
The Word of God and the Spirit of God are likened to fire. This fire would be seen and heard in the Church.

Purging, purifying, cleansing, warming, and revealing the Glory of the Risen Christ in the Church, His Body.

d. **All filled with the Spirit.** vs. 4.

Jesus had previously spoken to His disciples of the necessity of His leaving them and returning to the Father, in order that the Spirit could come and dwell in them as He had been with them. John 14:17.

He had given them much teaching on the ministry, work and power of the Holy Spirit in John's Gospel. John, chapters 14, 15 and 16.

As long as He remained with them, He was "straitened," limited by the physical, and localized in one place. He could be with them, walking and talking with them, but the only way He could be in them, "His Spiritual Body," was to return to the Father and then come again to His disciples in the Person of the Holy Spirit.

For this reason He said to them, "I will not leave you comfortless: I will come to you." John 14:17-18.

This necessitated His leaving them and leaving this earth.

In Acts, Chapter 1, we see Him returning to the Father, and in Acts, Chapter 2, we see the Holy Spirit coming to them.
In the Gospels it was "Christ with them."
In the Acts and Epistles it is "Christ in them."

True Christianity is Christ re-living His life in His own, saying and doing in and through them exactly what He said and did while He was here with them. This is the glorious Mystery, "Christ IN you, the Hope of Glory." Colossians 1:27.

In the Book of Acts and the Epistles, and throughout the New Testament, we find different expressions all speaking of one and the same experience.

Each different term or phrase used is bringing out some different facet of truth concerning the Baptism of the Holy Spirit.

Consider the following different expressions, describing the glory of the Baptism of the Spirit.

1. **Baptized with the Spirit.** Acts 1:5; 11:15-17; John 1:33.
   Symbolic of immersion into the Spirit.

2. **Filled with the Spirit.** Acts 2:4; 4:41; 6:5; Ephesians 5:18; Acts 9:17.
   Filled as an empty vessel would be.
   "One Baptism, but many fillings" is New Testament order. Or, "Be continually filled with the Spirit."

3. **Receiving the Spirit.** Acts 2:38; 8:15-17; 10:47.
   As receiving or taking a Gift from a Giver.
   It is worthy to note that there was only ever one "tarrying meeting" in the Book of Acts, and this was before Pentecost had come. None could be baptized in or with the Spirit until the Day of Pentecost had fully come. God's Spiritual

Calendar and Time-piece was involved. All other records were "Receiving meetings."

4. **Falling upon them.** Acts 8:15-19; 10:44-45; 11:15.
   Or, the Spirit came upon them. Acts 19:6.
   The thought here is of coming upon one from above, from the Lord in Heaven.

5. **The Holy Spirit given.** Acts 2:38; 8:18-19; 11:16-17.
   Related to number 3.
   The Holy Spirit was given as a GIFT. Not earned by works or merit of the receiver.

6. **Poured out upon them.** Acts 10:44-45.
   Poured out on the disciples, as Outpoured Rain, Early or Latter Rain, or as Living Waters upon the thirsty ground. Under this expression is noticed the symbolic characteristics of the Holy Spirit as being able to be "poured out." Rain, Waters, Rivers, Dew, and Oil — all are symbols of the Person of the Holy Spirit.

7. **Endued with power.** Luke 24:47-49.
   Literally, to be "clothed with power from on high."
   As with a Garment.
   In the Old Testament, the Spirit of the Lord came upon (or, clothed Himself with, or upon) Gideon, or Samson, or various of the Judges, etc., and so the believer receives a Garment of Priestly Ministry unto the Lord in the clothing from above.

e. **They began to speak with other tongues.** vs. 4.

"These Signs shall follow them that believe . . . they shall speak with New Tongues." Mark 16:17; Acts 2:4.

Note the progression in the Bible concerning "tongues."

1. **Tower of Babel.**
   Origin of tongues. Genesis 11:1-10. The origin of all languages, of all Nations. The Languages here were a sign of judgement on mankind for disobedience to the Word of God.

2. **Pentecost.**
   Acts 2:4. Here at Pentecost, Babel is reversed. God gave the sign of tongues as a sign of grace. A Gift available for all mankind, through faith in the Lord Jesus Christ.
   It came as a result of obedience to the Word of God, and as a blessing. Here salvation is opened to all nations, kindreds, tongues and tribes.

3. **Heaven.** Revelation 5:9-10; 7:9.
   John beholds an innumerable multitude gathered out of every kindred, every tongue, every tribe and nation, worshipping the Lamb of God. A sign of glory and redemption here. Their language here is "Worthy is the Lamb."

Let us notice the contrast between Babel and Pentecost.

| **BABEL** | **PENTECOST** |
|---|---|
| Nimrod — the Spirit of Satan | Christ — the Spirit of God |
| Rebellion and blasphemy | Obedience and worship |
| To glorify man here | To glorify God here |

| | |
|---|---|
| Bitumen bricks and slime | Living stones of believers |
| False unity, centralize | True unity, to be sent forth |
| Confusion and division | Order and unity |
| Tongues of confusion | Tongues of unity |
| Let us make US a Name | To magnify and reveal God's Name |
| The Babylon of earth | The Heavenly Jerusalem |
| Obedience to Nimrod, Rebel | Obedience to the Lord Jesus Christ |

The Disciples were not preaching the Gospel to the heathen nations in these new tongues.
They were not merely using "sanctified new tongues," as believers.
The record is very clear on the fact that the Disciples spake with tongues.
"They began to speak with tongues." Acts 2:4. Cf. Acts 1:1.
The Greek word for "tongues" is "languages."

"They began to speak in other (different, foreign) languages as the Spirit kept giving them clear and loud expression in each tongue in appropriate words." Amp. N.T. Acts 2:4.

Jesus promised believers that they would speak in NEW tongues. Mark 16:17. The disciples own native tongue would not be a 'new tongue.' They spake with other tongues. Not their own Jewish or native tongues. The Spirit gave them utterance, expression and words to speak.

The hearers heard them speak in the various languages. Verses 6-8. The disciples were declaring the wonderful works of God. Verse 11. This speaking in tongues was a miracle of speech, not a miracle of hearing. The disciples were not speaking in their own Jewish language while the hearers hear their own national languages in their minds!

It was a miracle of speech, by the Spirit, in and through the believers. They were speaking languages they had never learned, and languages they did not understand.
The hearers, in this record, were their own interpreters. It was the ability of the Holy Spirit, giving the disciples the words.
The hearers heard and understood naturally by their own native birth what the disciples spoke supernaturally, by the Spirit.

It was a convincing and convicting sign to some, as they realized that these ignorant Galileans were speaking languages never learned by them.
It was a convincing sign of the Baptism of the Spirit.
So was every other record in the Acts of the Apostles.

The hearers were not Gentiles, but JEWS OUT OF EVERY NATION under heaven, who had gathered for the Feast of Passover and Pentecost, who had their own Jewish language, plus the language or tongue of the nation wherein they were born.
The 17 places named covered the 4 corners of the then-known earth.

The Grace of the LORD was to be manifested to ALL NATIONS, because of the MAN Christ Jesus, who was born and died a JEW, but was then raised as THE NEW MAN! I Timothy 2:5-6.
His Body was Jewish Body, but His Blood was Divine Blood, not Jewish Blood. Acts 20:28.

f. **The Sign of Tongues in the Old Testament.**

There are several foreshadowings of the "sign of tongues" in the Old Testament, all of which find their fulfilment in the Church and the New Testament. God had used this 'sign' in the Old Testament, but never expressly through human voice.

1. **To Balaam.** Numbers 22; II Peter 2:15-16.
God used a dumb ass to speak in a tongue never learned, unknown to the speaker, but understood by the hearer. The animal here rebuked the Prophet for his iniquity. The Prophet was his own interpreter. The sign was "a speaking with tongues."
This miracle of speech was similar to the Day of Pentecost sign.

2. **To Belshazzar.** Daniel 5.
God wrote by the Hand in an unknown tongue over against the Candlestick on the Walls of Babylon. God used Daniel to interpret it. This was the Sign of Judgment on the Fall of Babylon, and it is prophetic of the Lord speaking by His Church against Spiritual Babylon today!

3. **To Israel.** Isaiah 28:9-13; Deuteronomy 4:31-35.
God spoke in the Hebrew tongue to the Chosen Nation at the Feast of Pentecost in Mt. Sinai. In the New Testament Pentecost, God spoke by many tongues for all nations! Isaiah foretold that God would use the "stammering lips and another tongue to speak to this people, yet people would not hear!" I Corinthians 14:21.

The reaction to this Sign of Tongues then is the same today! Acts 2:6-7; 12-13. They were *confounded, amazed, doubted* and *mocked!*

g. **Why did God choose Speaking in Tongues?**

1. **His love for all nations.**
At Pentecost He reversed the sign of judgment of tongues at Babel, and the Door of Salvation opened to all nations.

God originated all languages! God can speak any and all languages! He can understand, at the same time, all languages! It has pleased God to choose 'tongues' as the distinct New Testament sign of Pentecost and the evidence of receiving the Baptism of the Holy Spirit.

2. **The Tongue Tamed.**
Note James 3, the chapter on "The Tongue." NO MAN can tame the human tongue.

James 3:6. "And the tongue is a fire, a world of iniquity; so is the tongue among our members, that it defileth the whole body, and setteth on fire the course of nature; and it is set on fire of hell."

On the Day of Pentecost, when the Holy Spirit came, He tamed the untamable, and the uncontrollable human tongue.

He sat upon each of them, men and women, as a "Tongue of Fire — set on Fire of Heaven." The tongue of fire sat on each of them in order to purify them, burning up the dross and chaff that they might become the fuel of the Divine Fire, that men may see them as a Tongue of Fire, in witnessing, convicting and converting power.

As God was seen in the Sign of Tongues at Babel, spoke to the Prophet Balaam, and convicted the King Belshazzar, so God would be seen in the Sign of Tongues here; to those who believe and to those who believe not!

3. **The Evidence of the Baptism of the Spirit in Acts.**
In the Book of Acts "speaking with other tongues" was the distinct and unique sign, and evidence of the Baptism of the Holy Spirit.

If the Church today had but the record of the Book of Acts, and cast aside the traditional teaching and books of men, we would have to admit that The Evidence in Acts of the reception of the Spirit was this sign! Why must we go outside of the Scripture?

Note in every case in Acts that it gives or suggests this evidence.

a. **Acts 2:1-4.**
Speaking in tongues was the evidence to both the individual and the hearer on the Day of Pentecost that they had been filled with the Spirit.

b. **Acts 8:5-13, 14-24.**
The Samaritans received the Holy Spirit through the Laying on of Hands. There must have been some distinct visible or audible evidence and sign that made Simon desire this power, yet not desire the power that Philip had manifested in previous miracles, healings, etc.

c. **Acts 9:17-19.**
Paul, the Chosen Apostle, received the Holy Spirit through the Laying on of Hands. Though it is not recorded in Acts that he spoke in tongues, we have his testimony concerning the use of this Gift in I Corinthians 14:18, "I thank my God, I speak with tongues more than ye all."

d. **Acts 10:44-48; 11:15-17.**
The Gentiles, received the Holy Spirit as Peter ministered the Word of Salvation to them. Peter's testimony to the Council at Jerusalem was that the Holy Spirit "fell on them as on us at the beginning." This outpouring was a number of years later than Pentecost.

How did Peter know that the Gentiles had received the Spirit? Because they heard them speak with tongues!

e. **Acts 19:1-7.**
The Ephesian disciples received the Holy Spirit through the Laying on of Hands by Paul. How did Paul detect they had not received the Spirit?

When they did receive the Spirit, they spake with tongues and prophecied; the sign and evidence to speakers and hearers that the Holy Spirit had come.

f. **Acts 18:1-11; I Corinthians 14.**
Although it is not recorded in the Acts, it is evident that the Corinthians received the Holy Spirit and the Sign and Gift of other tongues was manifested there in the believers and the Local Church.

Thus we have three (a perfect Scriptural testimony and witness) distinct cases in Acts, and three others that may be accepted in the light of other Scriptures.

The sign of 'New Tongues' followed them that believe and received. Mark 16:17. It was the accepted witness and evidence of the Spirit's reception in Acts, and Acts is the Divine Pattern for the whole of this Church Age!

Note: Acts 1-2 is the ONLY RECORD of any "tarrying for the Holy Spirit." In three of the above cases God used the Laying on of Hands and the other two cases were Sovereign acts, i.e. at Pentecost and on the Gentiles! Not "tarrying for the Spirit" but "receiving the Spirit" is

God's will!

It is worthy to note that the signs of the Rushing Wind and the Tongue of Fire are not repeated in any of these records, but the sign of Speaking with Tongues is!

The Ability to speak with tongues was of the Spirit. Acts 1:8; 2:4. They (the disciples) spake with tongues.

How? — "As the Spirit gave them the utterance." It was and is the ability of the Spirit, not man's. Not the flesh. It is not of the human mind but it is of the Spirit.

Evil spirits may counterfeit this sign, as other gifts of the Spirit, yet the Lord said in Luke 11:9-13 that if we ask The Father for The Holy Spirit He will not give us A Serpent (Devil)

It must always be remembered, however, that though "speaking with tongues" is the evidence of the Spirit's reception, Holy Living is the evidence of the Holy Spirit filled life. The Holy Spirit comes to make us Holy!

It is sadly possible to receive the Spirit, yet not walk in and live in the Spirit. Consider Samson and other Old Testament Saints and believers in the Corinthian Church.

**Do all speak with Tongues?** I Corinthians 12:30.

A careful study of each record in Acts shows that THE SIGN of speaking in tongues accompanied believers, according to the Word of Jesus in Mark 16:15-17, and this, without Interpretation to the Church.
Thus all did and may speak with tongues today, in receiving the Baptism of the Spirit.

In the Epistle to the Corinthians, Paul is dealing expressly with the Gifts of the Spirit, and especially deals with THE GIFT of speaking with tongues with INTERPRETATION, as in the function of a New Testament believer's meeting. Without interpretation, then the person must keep silent.
All do not have this public function.

THE SIGN of tongues is for personal edification.
The GIFT with INTERPRETATION is for edification of the Church.

h. **The First Pentecostal Sermon.** vs. 14-35.

Peter, the Apostle to the Jews (the Circumcision) uses the Keys to open the Door of the Kingdom to 3,000 converts. Galatians 2:7-8; Matthew 16:19.

There are tremendously important facts in this First Pentecostal Sermon, which fall into two main divisions:

1. Joel
2. Jesus!

It is the pattern sermon for all preaching. The Early Church preached CHRIST!

1. **Joel — The Prophetic Word.**
Acts 2:16-17. "But this is that which was spoken by the prophet Joel; And it shall come to pass in the last days, saith God, I will pour out of my Spirit upon all flesh . . ."

**The Last Days.**
What did the prophets mean by the "Last Days?" Note these Scriptures: Isaiah 2:1-3; Genesis 2:17; Psalms 90:4; II Peter 3:8. ". . . that one day is with the Lord as a thousand years, and a thousand years as one day."

The Last Days of the Dispensation of Time are allotted to man, i.e., the Last 2 Days of the Lord of 2,000 years. Refer to diagram.

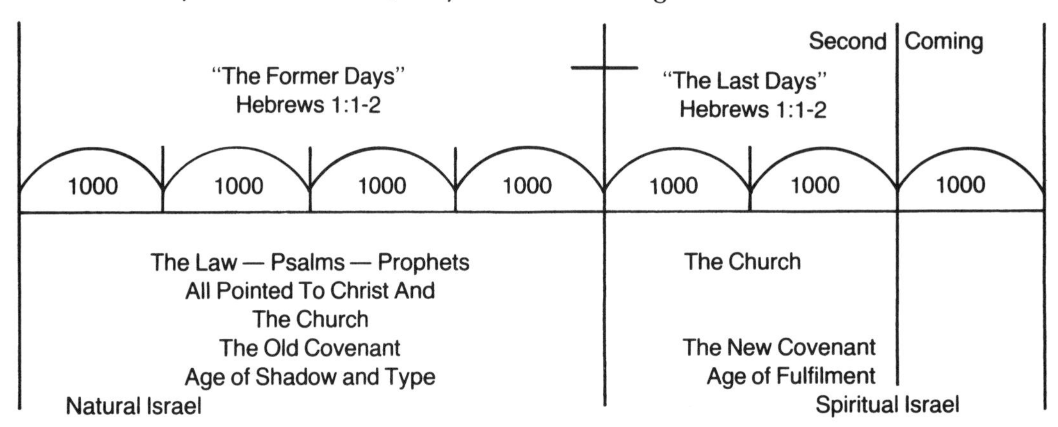


The Early Church had no "New Testament," hence we see their constant appeal to the OLD TESTAMENT PROPHETS for everything that God was doing in their time.

Their understanding had been opened to the truth that the Prophets not only spoke to their time but also to the generations in this present era. I Peter 1:10-12; II Peter 1:20-21.

2. **Jesus — The Living Incarnate Word!**
Note the 8 important facts Peter declares concerning Jesus of Nazareth. These facts are the truths brought out in every Sermon in the Book of Acts.

a. **His Sinlessness**
Jesus — The Sinless Man. vs. 22.
Jesus "Saviour" — He shall save His people from their sins. Matthew 1:21.
Only save others from sin if He were sinless.
Jesus of Nazareth. This involves His Sinless Birth, His Virgin Birth or Incarnation, His Humanity, His Nazarite vow and consecration to Jehovah's will and service. This title was used by man, devils, and on the cross. Mark 1:24; 14:67; John 1:45; Matthew 2:23.

b. **His Life Ministry.**
Jesus — The Perfect Man. vs. 22.

He was approved of God by miracles, signs and wonders. God did them by and through Him. Never had God worked through any other as He did His Only Son; — not Moses, not Elijah or Elisha, and not the Judges. NONE could compare with the Ministry of the Lord Jesus in word, deed, or claim. God was with Christ.

Acts 10:38. "How God anointed Jesus of Nazareth with the Holy Ghost and with power: . . . for God was with Him."

John 8:28; 9:4; 14:10. Healings, Miracles, Revelation, Casting out Satan and demons.

c. **His Crucifixion.**
Jesus — The Crucified Man. vs. 23.

The Divine Side — God's plan, counsel and foreknowledge of Calvary. The Human Side-Man's Lawlessness and wickedness fulfilled above. Acts 13:27. "... because they knew Him not, nor yet the voices of the prophets which are read every sabbath day, they have fulfilled them in condemning Him."

d. **His Resurrection.**
Jesus — The Resurrected Man. vs. 24-32.

The central fact of all Pentecost sermons is the RESURRECTION for on it hangs all the previous and following facts. I Corinthians 15.

Peter uses David's Psalms to show they could not, and did not, find their fulfilment in David himself, as his tomb was still with them. Therefore David spoke of the Messiah, Jesus, in whom alone these Scriptures find their fulfilment.

e. **His Exaltation**
Jesus — The Exalted Man. vs. 33.

No other man ever received the Spirit in full measure as Jesus had. John 3:34. "... for God giveth not the Spirit by measure unto Him." Again, it was the distinct office of Messiah to receive this Divine Fulness and pour out the Spirit upon all flesh, the Father's Promise. Isaiah 44:3; Joel 2:28.

f. **His Ascension.**
Jesus — The Ascended Man. vs. 34.

"What is it but that He first descended, then ascended?"
No other Man had ever descended from the bosom of the Father, except the Eternal Son. The Son begotten after He descended!

All others were born of man, of the flesh and of the earth. He is the Lord–The Man from Heaven–The Man in Heaven. Proberbs 30:4. "Who hath ascended up into heaven, or descended? . . . what is His Name, and what is His Son's Name, if thou canst tell?" Ephesians 4:8-11.

g. **His Enthronement.**
Jesus — The Enthroned Man. vs. 34-35.

Hebrews 1:3; 10:13; Matthew 22:41-46; Psalms 110:1
"The Lord said unto my Lord, Sit thou at my right hand, until I make thine enemies thy footstool." Promise to Overcomer. Revelation 3:21.

This is a most important verse. It speaks of the Finished Ministry and the Perfect Sacrifice, setting forth Christ as the Perfect and Heavenly Priest. He is a Priest Enthroned.

Zechariah 6:12-13. "... and He shall bear the Glory, and shall sit and rule upon His throne; and He shall be a priest upon His throne: and the counsel of peace shall be between them both."

No other man, no angel, dares to sit in the Fahter's Throne, only the Divine Son.

h. **His Glorification.**
Jesus — The Glorified Man. vs. 34-36.

He is the Man in God's Image, the Last Adam, through whom a race of people would come to this same image. (Genesis 1:26) Heaven had never received a Man like this! The glorification of JESUS — AS MAN — was the reception of THE NAME of God His Father. God's Glory is His Name! "The Triune Name" is the glorious climax of this Sermon, or in other words, LORD JESUS CHRIST.

Acts 2:36. "Therefore let all the house of Israel know assuredly, that God hath made that same Jesus, whom ye have crucified, both Lord and Christ."

Three ways in which God revealed His will under the Old Testament to Prophets, were by:

Prophecy )<br>
Dreams ) Numbers 12:6-8. The Prophetic Spirit to be upon<br>
Vision ) all flesh now!

**ALL FLESH!** Joel 2:28-29

1. Sons and Daughters! Legal Heirs.
2. Young men and Old men! Age does not count. The Priests began ministry at 30 years of age and retired at 50 years.
3. Servants and Handmaids! Class distinction over. The Spirit is now available for all, regardless of position, age, sex or race.

A New Day had dawned! The Holy Spirit had been poured out only upon the Chosen Israel Nation and the selected ones in that Nation; such as Prophets, Priests, Kings, Judges, etc. The Spirit is now available, through Christ, for all flesh and all mankind!

Joel's prophecy covers the whole of this age as the Age of Pentecostal Outpouring! Not just the early church in its beginning, but it consumates at the Second Advent of Christ, amidst Signs in Heaven and Earth before the Notable Day of the Lord. Revelation 6:12-17.

The signs spoken of by Joel were not fulfilled at Pentecost, i.e., the sun was not darkened, the moon was not turned to blood, there was no vapour, fire and pillars of smoke. None of these phenomena took place.

The fulfilment of Joel's prophecy reaches down to the events in the Book of Revelation. All this goes to confirm that the "time element" of Joel's prophecy reaches from Pentecost to the Coming of the Lord Jesus the Second Time.

i. **What Constitutes a New Testament Church?** vs. 37-47.

The result of Peter's preaching 'with the Holy Spirit sent down from Heaven' (I Peter 1:12), and the revelation and declaration of the Triune Name in verse 36, was deep conviction of the Spirit upon the hearers.

The conviction was promised by the Lord Jesus in John 16:8-11. "And when He is come, He will reprove the world of sin, and of righteousness, and of judgment: Of sin because they believe not on me: Of righteousness, because I go to My Father, and ye see me no more: Of judgment, because the prince of this world is judged."

It brought forth the question, "What shall we do?"

Note that the hearers were religious, devout Jews. vs. 5.

Peter gave the answer in verse 38, in which is laid down God's standard from then unto the end of this age, the conditions of Church membership! His Word changes not!

1. **Repentance.**
   Refer to the Studies on 'First Principles' concerning the 'Doctrine of Repentance.'

   John the Baptist's first message was Repentance. Matthew 3:1-2.
   Christ's first message was Repentance. Matthew 4:17.
   The Apostles preached Repentance. Acts 20:21; 26:20.
   The first message on the Day of Pentecost was Repentance.
   Repentance is the first principle of the Doctrine of Christ. Hebrews 6:1-2.
   It is the first word of the Gospel, then faith. Mark 1:14-15; Acts 20:21.

2. **Water Baptism.**
   Water Baptism, by immersion, was not optional in the Early Church, but A COMMAND of Christ and the Apostles. Matthew 28:19-20; Acts 1:4; 20:48.
   This is the first Pentecostal sermon and has these principles laid down by the Spirit.

   Before the Cross and crucifixion, John's Baptism was ordained of God. John 1:19-34; Matthew 3:13-17.
   After the Resurrection and Ascension, Christ's Baptism is ordained of God. Matthew 28:19; Acts 2:36-38.

   Water Baptism was commanded to be into the Name of the Father, and of the Son, and of the Holy Spirit, and this Name was revealed in the Triune Name of "LORD JESUS CHRIST!"

   There are about 7 records of Water Baptism in the Book of Acts and 7 records in the Epistles to Water Baptism. Every record speaks of Water Baptism as being into the Name of the Lord, or Lord Jesus, or Jesus Christ.

   By consulting earlier manuscripts and other translations it is seen that Water Baptism was into the triune Name of the Lord Jesus Christ. For centuries, the Church has been torn by division and strife over modes and formulas of Water Baptism. The Epistles have been used against Acts and Acts against the Epistles. What Jesus said has been used against what the Apostles did. The only reconciliation between what Jesus said and what the Apostles did is to bring both together. There is no conflict, contradiction between the commandment of Jesus and the obedience of the Apostles.

   No doctrine of Scripture can be built on one verse only. Every Scripture pertaining to this subject should be placed together so that the whole truth can be viewed in the light of all the verses and not just one verse. There is nothing wrong with Matthew 28:19, and there is nothing wrong with the record in the Book of Acts. Both are correct. Both belong to each other, the one is the interpretation by the Spirit of the other.

   There is no record in Acts or the Epistles of the disciples merely quoting the command of Matthew 28:19. No one fulfills a command by quoting it. The disciples did not quote the command, they obeyed it. The command of Jesus is to baptize into the Name (not Names) of the Father, and of the Son, and of the Holy Spirit. This is the Name of the Godhead bodily and it finds its glorious fulfilment in the Name of the Lord Jesus Christ. A Triune Name for the Triune God.

A formula of the very Scripture itself is:

a. **Quote the Command** of Jesus of Matthew 28:19.

b. **Invoking the Name** of the Lord Jesus Christ as in Acts.

c. **Declaring the spiritual truth** of water baptism as set forth in Romans 6:3-4.

Acts 2:36-38; 8:12-16; Romans 6:3-4; Galatians 3:27; Acts 19:1-8; I Corinthians 1:10-15.

3. **Receive the Gift of the Holy Spirit.**

The emphasis in Acts, after the Day of Pentecost, is "Receiving" the Gift of the Holy Spirit.

The one and only record of "Tarrying for the Spirit" is in Acts 1, and the reasons for this were:

a. **The Set Time** for the Feast of Pentecost, as foreshadowed in the Old Testament Feast, was not yet come.

b. The Holy Spirit could not be given until Jesus Christ was glorified. John 7:37-39.

All other records speak of "Receiving the Spirit." The Holy Spirit came from Heaven and is here in the earth now, available to all the repentant and obedient. Acts 5:32; Acts 2:38; 9:17-18; 10:44-48.
Acts 19:2, "Have ye received since ye believed?" Paul asked. Jesus spoke of the Holy Spirit which they that believe on Him should receive. John 7:39.

Refer to comments on Acts 2:4 on The Baptism in the Holy Spirit.

4. **The Apostles Doctrine.**

The new converts continued stedfastly in the Apostles Doctrine.

What a contrast to many today. The SEED OF THE WORD had fallen on 'good ground' and brought forth fruit. Matthew 13:1-24.

The Apostles Doctrine is simply defined in Hebrews 6:1-2 in Seven steps, and all are revealed in operation in the Book of Acts, except the Doctrine of Perfection which is dealt with in the Epistle to the Hebrews.

a. Repentance from Dead Works,

b. Faith toward God,

c. Doctrine of Baptisms,

d. Laying on of Hands,

e. Resurrection of the Dead,

f. Eternal judgment,

g. Perfection of the Saints.

The Early Church recognized the importance of Sound Doctrine. In the Last Days many shall depart from the Faith, being seduced by Doctrines of Devils. I Timothy 1:10; I Timothy 4:1; I Timothy 4:6, 13, 16; Hebrews 13:9.

**5. Fellowship**

I Corinthians 1:9; Ephesians 3:9; 5:11; Philippians 3:10.
I John 1:3, 6, 7. "... that ye also may have fellowship with us: and truly our fellowship is with the Father, and with His Son Jesus Christ." Fellowship with one another. Not organization-fellowship, or sectarian-fellowship.

All who walk in the light — as He is in the light — should have fellowship with each other. If we are in fellowship with the Father, and the Son, we should be in fellowship with each other as believer-priests.

6. **Breaking of Bread.**

Matthew 26:26; I Corinthians 10:15-21; 11:23-34.

The Early Disciples met the First Day of the week to "break bread together." Acts 20:7, "Upon the first day of the week, the disciples came together to break bread." The Table of the Lord.

This is symbolized in the Table of Shewbread in the Tabernacle. The bread was arranged every 7th day. Leviticus 24:1-9. It was with The Bread of His Presence. Manifest Communion. The Discerning of the Body of Christ. Symbols of the New Covenant. The Children's Bread. Divine Healing and Divine Health and Cleansing. The Unity of the Body of Christ. John 17.

In not discerning the Lord's Table — His Body and the Church, which is His Spiritual Body — we bring judgment to ourselves in sickness, weakness and death. The opposite is also true. As we discern "The Body of Christ," we receive blessing in health, strength and life.

7. **Prayers.**

Note: At least 17 chapters in Acts have some reference to prayer. The Prayers of the Saints are the incense upon the Golden Altar, ascending to God, the Father, through the ministry of the High Priest, Jesus Christ. Revelation 5:8; Psalms 141:1, 2; Hebrews 7:25. "Wherefore he is able also to save them to the uttermost that come unto God by him, seeing He ever liveth to make intercession for them."

**A Prayerless Church is a Powerless Church.** Jude 20.
I Thessalonians 5:17. The Church was born in Prayer. Prayer in the Spirit. His house is to be called "A House of Prayer." Matthew 21:13.

**This is how the Lord "added to His Church."**
His standard for Church membership has not altered!

**Note:— For the Student,** there is a wealth of truth in relating the above comments relative to membership in the Early Church to that which is typically set forth in the Tabernacle of Moses. Exodus 25 to chapter 40.

1. The Triune Name of the Triune God, as revealed in the Lord Jesus Christ. Relate to the Triune Cherubimed Mercy-Seat upon the Ark of the Covenant. The Holiest of All.
2. Repentance (and Faith,)
   Relate to the Gate of the Court and Brazen Altar. Blood Atonement.
3. Baptism in Water. Relate to the Brazen Laver. Blood first, then Water.
4. Baptism in the Holy Spirit. Relate to the "clothing" of the Priestly Garment to enter the Sanctuary.
5. The Apostles Doctrine. Comparable to the 7 Lamps on the 7 Branched Golden Candlestick. The Holy Place.
6. Breaking of Bread. Related to the Table of Shewbread, in the Holy Place.
7. Prayers. Comparable to the Golden Altar of Incense, just before the Veil.

   **FELLOWSHIP** — Believer Priests in Fellowship in the Presence of the Lord.

## ACTS CHAPTER 3

1. **The Healing of the Lame Man.** vs. 1-11.

In this chapter we have the first recorded miracle of healing in the Book of Acts.

a. Peter and John at the hour of prayer are going up to the Temple. vs. 1.

The Temple had been cleansed by the Lord Jesus and had seen His wonderful Ministry.
The Priests had rejected this cleansing of the Temple. God had rent the Veil of the Temple in two at the crucifixion of Jesus. Matthew 27:51.
This testimony of God had been rejected, hence the Temple was to be destroyed in a number of years, in A.D. 70.

Contrast the Healing of the Lame man at the Pool of Bethseda, by Jesus Himself, in John 5:1-11, and the Healing of this Lame man at the Gate called Beautiful.

The Healing of the Lame man was "an act of the Holy Spirit" through the Apostles.
It was the manifestation of the Gifts of the Spirit, in Healing and Miracles and Faith. I Corinthians 12:6-9.

b. **Compare** verse 4 and verse 12.

To the man in need, Peter says, "Look on us."

To the questioning people, Peter says, "Why look ye on us, as though by our own power and holiness this man stands here whole."

The Lame man did not expect to receive healing, nor did he seem to have immediate faith for such. vs. 5.
He undoubtedly had been here for many years, yet Jesus had not healed him, during His earthly ministry.

c. "**Silver and gold have I none** . . . but such as I have give I thee." vs. 6.

This is in great contrast to the rich Laodicean Church, which was rich and increased with goods, and had need of nothing. Laodicea is the Church which has a form of godliness, and denies the power thereof.

Though the disciples had laid money at the feet of the Apostles, yet Peter and John could say they had no silver and gold.

The power of money versus the power of God! Many times a rich Church becomes a powerless Church.

"Such as I have" — Matthew 10:1; Luke 9:1. The Lord Jesus had given them power over all sickness and disease, and power to cast out devils.

Peter did not tell the Lame man to "attend a few meetings, keep on believing, wait until he received faith, and continue to pray and look to the Lord," etc.

Here the Lord Jesus confirmed His Word "with signs following." Mark 16:15-17, 18-20.

d. Verse 6. "**IN THE NAME** of Jesus Christ of Nazareth, rise up and walk."

This is the first distinctive use of "The Name" in healing power after the ascension and glorification of the Lord Jesus Christ.

A particular study of John 14:12-14, 26; 16:23-24, 25-28 shows this truth.

The Lord Jesus had said to them "Hitherto ye have asked nothing in My Name, but now, whatsoever ye shall ask the Father in My Name, He shall give it to you."

Here the Lord gave the disciples the legal right to use His Name.

Peter had declared the Triune Name in Acts 2:36.
He had commanded them to be baptized into the Name of the Lord Jesus Christ. Acts 2:38.
Here we see the power and the operation of The Name of Jesus in healing. Acts 3:6, 16.

The disciples understood the power in the Name of Jesus. He was at the back of His Name.
His Name took His place in the Early Church.

"The Name" was not just a magic formula, or a mere theory, or doctrine to argue over.

"The Name" meant the Lord Jesus Christ Himself. "Himself is His Name and His Name is Himself" — such is an old Hebrew saying concerning God and His Name.

As Peter took the lame man by the right hand, immediately the power of the risen Christ flowed into his being, and his ankle bones received strength, causing the man to leap and walk.

The people saw the man leaping and walking and praising God, and greatly wondered over the miracle. vs. 7-10.

This took place in Solomon's Porch. Verse 11. Solomon's Temple had never witnessed such 'glory' as this.

2. **Peter's Sermon to the People.** vs. 12-26.

The rest of this chapter gives Peter's sermon to the wondering people gathered at the Temple.
It is Peter's second sermon in the Book of Acts.

The Sign of speaking in tongues was the basis for the first Pentecostal sermon, by Peter, in Acts 2.

The Sign of the healing of the Lame man is the basis for this Sermon in Acts, Chapter 3.

Every miracle in Acts was actually 'a sermon' to those who had ears to hear what the Spirit was saying.

a. **Not by our power or holiness.** vs. 12.

Peter here affirms and declares a real truth. It was not by his power (what he could do), or by his holiness (what he was), that the man had been healed.

It was by the POWER and HOLINESS of the Risen Christ. Acts 1:8.

It is possible to have "power without holiness," or "holiness without power," but God desires that both holiness and power be manifested in His people, and in the Church.

HIS power, and HIS holiness!

Samson, and others of the Old Testament Judges, were men who were equipped with power but lacked the Divine Holiness. Judges 16:20; I Samuel 16:14; Psalms 51:10.

b. **The Triune God.** vs. 13.

"The God of Abraham, of Isaac and of Jacob." Cf. Exodus 3:14-15.
This is one of the richest and most significant Divine Titles in the Bible. Its first revelation was to Moses at the Burning Bush, at which God revealed Himself to be "I AM WHO I AM."

These are the only THREE MEN after which God has been pleased to call Himself the God of, even the "God of Abraham, the God of Isaac and the God of Jacob."

Three typical and symbolical men. These Three Men are symbolical of the Fulness of the Godhead Bodily.

Each of these men manifest certain characteristics and operations pertaining to the Godhead, as Father, Son and Holy Spirit.

Abraham —typifies the Father God. The foundation, the source, the beginning. The covenant-holder, and source of the promises of salvation. Father of all who believe.

Isaac —typifies the Only Begotten Son of God. Born as the result of a miracle, and typically sacrificed and resurrected (Hebrews 11:17), he becomes a magnificent type of the New Testament Only Begotten Son, Jesus Christ. Genesis 22.
He also was born as the result of a miracle, and then in due time, was actually sacrificed and resurrected.

Jacob —typifies the Holy Spirit. Jacob was the third person of this trinity of men, who proceeded from the Father Abraham, through the Begotton Son.
He is the first one to anoint the rock (Bethel) with oil. Genesis 28:18.

Jesus Himself declared that this was a Divine Title illustrative of the Resurrection and the Life.
Mark 12:26-27. He is not the God of the dead, but of the living.
John 8:56-59. The Lord Jesus Christ is the I AM.

This Name, "The God of Abraham, Isaac and of Jacob" is a Triune Name or Triune Title.

It is the Old Testament type of that Triune Name as revealed in the Lord Jesus Christ.
Genesis 48:15-16. Compare with Acts 2:36.

In Him dwells all the Fulness of the Godhead BODILY. Colossians 1:19; 2:9.

c. **Sermon facts.** vs. 13-15.

Jesus delivered up. His arrest.
Jesus denied. His trial.
Jesus innocent. His innocence declared by Pilate.
Jesus the Holy and Just One. The Holy and Righteous One.
Jesus killed. His death.
Jesus — The Prince of Life, i.e., The Author of Life.

A murderer granted to the people, even Barabbas, who was released instead of Jesus.

Jesus raised up from the dead. His resurrection.
Jesus glorified. His ascension and glorification.

The apostles are witnesses of these facts. Witnesses who have both seen and heard the resurrected Christ.

d. **The Power of His Name.** vs. 16.

Refer to comments on verse 6.

Note the emphasis here, by Peter, on "FAITH, through FAITH in His Name does this man stand here whole."

Faith comes by hearing the Word of God. Romans 10:17.
Jesus Christ Himself is THE WORD. John 1:1-3, 14-18; Psalms 138:2.

This healing of the Lame man is spoken of as:

1. A Healing.
2. A Miracle.
3. Through Faith.
   Compare I Corinthians 12:6-9, and the operation of the Gifts of the Spirit in faith, healings and miracles, as evidenced here. Acts 4:22.

e. **The Sin of Ignorance.** vs. 17.

The crucifixion was a sin of ignorance for many in Jewry, and for some of the Rulers of the people.

For sins of ignorance God had provided a blood-sacrifice. Study Leviticus Chapter 4, especially.

For sins of presumption there was no sacrifice for sins.

Note those who declared this terrible sin of ignorance which was manifest in the crucifixion, for many in Jewry. Not all were ignorant of this sin. Jesus said, "Father, forgive them, they know not what they do." Luke 23:34. Paul said, "Had they known it they would not have crucified the Lord of Glory." I Corinthians 2:8; I Timothy 1:13.

Peter says, "Through ignorance ye did it . . ." Acts 4:17.

Notice the difference between the sins of ignorance, and the sins of presumption, as set forth in Numbers 15:22-29 and Numbers 15:30-31.

The greatest sin of presumption is to die without Jesus Christ and to presume upon the grace of God in rejecting the one and only Saviour of the world, and sacrifice for sin.

Sins of presumption resulted in the person being "cut off" from Israel, under the Law Covenant.

Under the New Covenant of Grace, Christ's sacrificial blood covers our sins of ignorance. I John 2:1-2.

The sin of presumption becomes the unpardonable sin. Hebrews 6:1-6; Hebrews 10:25-31.

f. **The Old Testament Prophets.** vs. 18-23.

Consider in this section Peter's use of the Prophets in the Old Testament. It must be continually remembered that the Early Church had no New Testament, and thus they continually appealed to the Old Testament Writings and the Prophets, as witness and confirmation of all that God was doing in their midst.

The declaration of diverse and numerous prophecies, given by various persons over several thousands of years, over different generations, yet all finding their fulfilment in the ONE MAN, even Jesus Christ — all this proves absolute inspiration, and the infallibility of the Sacred Scriptures.

These facts prove the Deity of Jesus Christ, as the Son of God, and the long-promised and foretold Messiah of God.

Note the use of the word "Prophets" in verses 18, 21, 22, 23, 24, 25.

The Lord Jesus had opened their understanding to that which was hidden in the Law, the Psalms and the Prophets, concerning Himself. Luke 24:27, 44-46.

The Law, Psalms and Prophets were a "sealed book" until the risen Lord unlocked and broke these seals, opening their eyes, and their understanding to see Him.

"In the Volume of the Book it is written of Me." Hebrews 10:5-7.

The Prophets spoke not only to their own generation, but also to our generation, upon whom the ends of the ages are come. I Peter 1:10-12; II Peter 1:10-21; Matthew 13:17.

**The Restoration of all things spoken by the Prophets.** vs. 19, 20, 21.

These verses can correctly be written as follows:

"Seasons (or Times) of Refreshing shall come from the Presence of the Lord; and He (the Father) shall send Jesus Christ, which before was preached unto you, whom the heaven must retain (receive) UNTIL the RESTORATION (restitution) of all things, which God hath spoken by the mouth of all His Holy Prophets, since the world began."

In these verses we have:

1. Repentance. Compare with Acts 2:38, also.
2. Blotting out of sins.
3. Conversion. Right about face, about turn.
4. Refreshing from the Presence of the Lord.
   Particularly the thought of "Rain, Early and Latter Rain".
   Outpouring, which brings refreshing, and reviving from the effects of heat and drought. Isaiah 28:12; Deuteronomy 11:10-21. Amp. N.T.
5 The first coming of Christ. God the Father sent Him the first time.
   John 7:28-29; 17:18; 1:6. The Sent One.
6. The heaven has received Him again. His ascension to the Father's Throne. Acts 1:9.
   The Heavens will retain (or hold Him back) until a certain period of time, spoken of as "The restitution."

7. Restitution, or restoration. Joel 2:25.

   Note — The restoration of all things is limited to that which is spoken of in and by the Prophets.

   Nowhere do the Prophets speak of any restoration of the Devil, Fallen Angels and unrepentant and unregenerate sinners of mankind.

8. The Restoration is that which pertains to the CHURCH, to SPIRITUAL ISRAEL.

   Whether Jew, Israelite, or Gentile — the Scriptures teach that God's restoration is not just material, nationalistic, and certainly not a restoration of carnal ordinances in a Temple, or Priesthood or animal sacrifices, but it is a SPIRITUAL RESTORATION which can only be fulfilled by faith "in Christ." Romans 11.

9. The Second Coming of Christ in the end of the age.

**The Prophet like Moses.** vs. 22. Refer to Deuteronomy 18:15-22.

Jesus Christ was the Prophet like unto Moses, who received the words of the Father God, and spoke in the Name of the Lord, and He was the one to whom Moses pointed.

Moses was the foundation of all the Old Testament Prophets. All who spoke were measured according to that revelation given to Moses.

Moses foretold that Christ would "come from the midst of thy brethren." This was prophetical of the incarnation in the virgin Mary, and His being born of the Tribe of Judah and of the House of David.

"Like unto Moses" — In His birth, ministry, signs, wonders and miracles. In His glory, greater than Moses.

Jesus fulfilled the Mosaic economy, of the Tabernacle, the Priesthood, the Sacrifices, the Feasts of Israel.

He fulfilled the Law; Moral, Civil and Ceremonial.

Moses said all that he was commanded to, but Jesus spoke the Father's words: "But I say unto you." Matthew 5. The voice of authority.

Israel could not stand the Glory or the Voice of God at Mt. Sinai, and asked God to give them a Man, a Mediator, and thus God spoke through Moses to them. Exodus 20:18-21; Deuteronomy 4:10-13, 32-40; Hebrews 12:18-21.

Moses spoke all that he was commanded to, in the Name of the Lord.

Thus Moses was a remarkable type of the Lord Jesus Christ.

Christ is the "greater than Moses." The One to whom Moses pointed, the One of whom Moses was but a type.

Moses was the SERVANT in the House.
Jesus was the SON and made the House. Hebrews 3:4-6.

He spoke the Father's Words, in His Father's Name. John 8:26-33, 37-47, 56-59; 12:47-50.

It is eternal judgment to reject the One to whom Moses pointed. Hebrews 12:25; Acts 3:22-23; Acts 7:35-38. Moses, type of Lord Jesus Christ, as the MEDIATOR of Old Covenant Church in Wilderness.

**Samuel, and all the Prophets who have spoken,** vs. 24.

Peter brings in Moses in verses 22-23.
Peter brings in Samuel in verse 24.
Then he mentions ALL THE PROPHETS, as many as have spoken — all foretold of "these days."

That is to say, ALL THE PROPHETS foretold of the Last Days, "these days," the days in which we live, which "Last Days" began with the Early Outpouring of the Spirit at Pentecost.

It is worthy to note briefly the use of the Old Testament as seen in the Book of Acts. These quotations from the Prophets show us clearly how the Early Apostles understood, interpreted and applied the utterances of the Old Testament Prophets, to that which was being fulfilled in the Church.

"The New Testament writers become the infallible interpreters of the Old Testament Prophets, and Scriptures."

Following is a brief list of Prophets who were referred to or quoted in the Book of Acts. They are continually applied to the CHURCH, to spiritual Israel, and to that which takes place to those who are "in Christ.

| | | |
|---|---|---|
| 1. | Acts 1:15-20. | The Psalms, spoken by the Spirit in David. |
| 2. | Acts 2:14-21. | The Prophet Joel, foretold of the Spirit. |
| 3. | Acts 3:19-23. | Moses, as a Prophet, foretold of Christ. |
| 4. | Acts 3:22-25. | Samuel, and all the Prophets who spoke. |
| 5. | Acts 2:22-36. | David, in the Psalms, spoke of Christ. |
| 6. | Acts 4:23-30. | David. |
| 7. | Acts 8:28-37. | Isaiah the Prophet spoke of Christ. |
| 8. | Acts 10:43. | All the Prophets. |
| 9. | Acts 13:15, 38-41. | The Prophet Habakkuk; 13:33-35, David; 13:47, Isaiah. |
| 10. | Acts 17:2-3. | Paul opened the Scriptures to them. |
| 11. | Acts 28:23-31. | The Law and the Prophets.<br>Moses and Isaiah. |
| 12. | Acts 15:15-18. | The Tabernacle of David, foretold by Amos. |

The whole of the New Testament is the revelation of that which was in the Seed-form in the Old Testament.

The Gospels, the Book of Acts and the Epistles abound with quotations, allusions and interpretative revelation of that which is hidden in the Law, the Psalms and the Prophets.

**The Children of the Prophets.** vs. 25.

Peter tells them that they were the children of the Prophets, and also the children of the Covenant which God made with Abraham, Isaac and Jacob.

Jesus Christ was THE SEED of David, and SEED of Abraham, in whom all nations were to be blessed.

This "SEED" to bless all nations is that "many-membered Seed" revealed in

Christ and the Church.

Galatians 3:16, 28-29. "To Abraham and his Seed were the promises made . . . to thy Seed, which IS CHRIST . . . and if ye be Christ's, then are ye Abraham's SEED AND heirs according to the Promise."

The New Testament teaches unmistakably that the Seed of Abraham now is Christ and His Church.
It is not that Seed after the Natural, or the national, or that birth which is of and after the flesh, but it is the Seed which is after the spiritual, the heavenly, and that New Birth which is of the Spirit of God.

To exalt the natural or the national is to exalt the flesh above the Spirit, and this God will not accept. John 3:1-5; 1:9-12.

Christ and His Church will bless ALL the Nations, through the Gospel of the Kingdom, as in operation in the Book of Acts.

**To the Jew First.** vs. 26.

God sent His Son TO THE JEW FIRST, to bless them and turn them from their iniquities.
The Gospel was preached TO THE JEW FIRST (Romans 1:16-17). Everywhere that Paul went, he went TO THE JEW FIRST, into the Synagogues. The tragedy is that the Jew rejected the Gospel as a whole (although thousands were saved), and then the Gospel was sent to the Gentiles.

JEW AND GENTILE may both be grafted into the Good Olive Tree, Spiritual Israel, through faith in Christ Jesus. Romans 11.

Blind unbelief read and heard the Scriptures every Sabbath day, yet fulfilled them in condemning the Christ of God. Acts 13:27.

## ACTS CHAPTER 4

THIS CHAPTER is a continuation of the events pertaining to the healing of the lame man in Acts Chapter 3.

Every witness and sermon in Acts concerns the Resurrected Jesus.

a. **Jesus the Resurrection.** vs. 1-2.

The signs and wonders in Acts were the proof of the resurrected Christ.
Proof of His risen power.
God worked with the disciples in spite of all opposition.
The Priests, the Captain of the Temple, and the Sadducees were grieved that they preached through "Jesus the resurrection from the dead."

Christ's special enemies were religious enemies! The same enemies against the Church, His Body.

b. **Religious Leaders oppose.** vs. 1, 4-6.

The disciples are imprisoned. vs. 3.
About 5000 Jews believe on the Lord Jesus Christ. vs. 4.
The Election of Grace. Romans 11:1, 5.
Pentecost was a great harvest time, and fulfilment of this. We see the great harvest of souls.
It was the Feast of Firstfruit, under the Early Rain Outpouring of the Holy Spirit.
First the Natural, then the Spiritual. I Corinthians 15:46-47.

c. **The Sanhedrin.** vs. 5-6.

The Priests, the Rulers, the Elders, the Scribes, and Annas and Caiaphas and kindred gather together, in council.

The council actually consisted of being the Sanhedrin. The Great Council of the Jews consisting of at least 70 members, with the High Priest as President.

The Sanhedrin had power, under Rome, to condemn, but not to put to death.

The Word of God had by-passed Annas and Caiaphas, under John's Ministry. Luke 3:1-6.
Both these High Priests shared in the trial of Jesus, and had Him condemned to death by the testimony of false witnesses.

Caiaphas had even prophesied the death of Jesus for the whole nation. John 11:47-54; 18:13-24, 28; Matthew 26:3-5, 57-68.

Caiaphas had actually condemned himself when he rent his Priestly robe, which was forbidden by the Law. Leviticus 10:6.

The Sanhedrin and the Leaders violated law after law in order to get Jesus crucified, thus bringing themselves under the death penalty.

These religious leaders had condemned Christ because of envy. Matthew 27:18.

The voice of the Priests were loudest at the trial of Jesus. Luke 23:13, 23-25.

The Sadducees were the Modernist of that day, and did not believe in Angel or Spirit, or the Bodily Resurrection. Acts 23:8.

Yet all these things are evidenced in the Gospels and the Acts.
There is seen the Ministry of the Holy Spirit, the Ministry of the Angels and Bodily

Resurrections, all upon the foundation of the resurrection of the Lord Jesus.

Refer again to Acts 13:27. These Religious Leaders had had the witness of John the Baptist as the Prophet and Forerunner of Messiah. Then they had the Ministry of Jesus Christ, the Son of God, for 3½ years, and here once again is the witness and testimony of the Apostles Peter and John in the miracle healing of the lame man.

The tragic thing is that they had not a love for the truth, and they believed the lie, thus rejecting and falsely condemning the innocent.

How far their hearts were from God in that they could not recognize the Christ of God.

This was the new moving of the Spirit of God; the time of their visitation and they knew it not.
It eventually ended outside of Judaism because Judaism had degenerated into hypocritical fundamentalism, and ritualistic formalism, bound by Talmudic traditions and interpretation of the Scriptures.

d. **The Challenge.** vs. 7.

"By what power or by what Name have ye done this?"

A man who had been lame for 38 years has been miraculously healed, yet the religious leaders, instead of rejoicing and praising God for this miracle and giving God the glory, question the disciples by what power or name they had done this.

History repeats itself. They opposed the Name of Jesus.

There is no greater blindness than religious blindness. It is the worst type of blindness. Note John 9:39-40.

The words of Jesus in Mark 13:9-13 would come to the disciples. Jesus had foretold the time would come when the disciples would be taken before Councils, and cast out of the Synagogue, but they were not to be concerned about what they would speak, for the Holy Spirit would give the answer in the same hour.

They were to be hated for "HIS NAME'S sake." Matthew 10:20; John 16:1-4. As they did not premeditate what to say, and as they depended upon the Spirit, He would give them utterance and words to speak.

In Deuteronomy 13:1-11, the Law commanded the rulers to enquire diligently if any prophet or dreamer having signs and wonders accompanying him or if he led Israel to follow after other gods.

All such were to be put to death, after diligent enquiry for the truth.
The religious leaders, out of envy, felt that this Jesus was a false prophet and dreamer, leading the Jews after 'another god' even a 'false god,' and that this 'new sect' was leading away from the truth and the True God.

Such is human nature and religious bigotry, which calls good evil and makes evil good.

If they had cared to study their own Scriptures, and compare all that Jesus said, and did, and was; then they would have found that He was actually bringing men to God, as the Only Begotten Son of God.

e. **The Answer of Peter.** vs. 8-10.

Peter is once again, "filled with the Holy Spirit." Compare Acts 2:4 with Ephesians 5:18.

One Baptism, but continual filling with the Spirit.

Peter declares this healing of the lame man was a good deed. Acts 10:38. Jesus went about doing good, and healing all that were oppressed of the Devil.

When questioned as to what means this miracle had been performed, Peter tells them that it was by the Name of Jesus Christ of Nazareth. He charges them with the act of the crucifixion — "Whom ye crucified."

He witnesses of the resurrection — "Whom God raised."

What stinging conviction would be upon the Sanhedrin, and the High Priests and Rulers. It was evident that the disciples could not have done this of themselves, which they had confessed.
It was evident that it had been done by the power of a Name; and they knew that a Name could have no power unless the Person whose Name it was, was alive!

No one could use a dead person's Name to do a notable miracle like this.

It was irrefutable proof that the Christ they had crucified was alive, and was backing up the use of His Name on earth.

The Priests had paid the guards of the Tomb large sums of money (probably the people's Tithes and Offerings and Temple Tax) to tell lies that they had been asleep.
They paid them to lie concerning the resurrection and the events of that morning. Matthew 28:4, 11-15.

The Sanhedrin also knew that every true prophet of Jehovah in the Old Testament, who prophesied and preached in the Name of JEHOVAH (the LORD); and had signs and wonders following their ministry, had such as evidence of their credentials!

Here this sign and wonder, and the preaching was being done in the Name of the LORD; but in that Name as revealed in the Name of the LORD JESUS CHRIST.

The Old Testament prophets ministered in the Name of the Lord God.
The New Testament ministers preached in the Name of the Lord Jesus.

Acts Chapters 3 and 4 center around "The Name." The Name always meant the Person.

"Where two or three are gathered together in My Name, there I AM in the midst." Matthew 18:20.

Notice the use of The Name in Acts 3:6, 16; 4:7, 10, 11-12, 17-18.

As there was no other Name in the Old Testament by which any could be saved, now Peter says the same concerning the Name of Jesus.

The Sanhedrin commanded them and threatened them not to teach or preach at all in the Name of Jesus, because the Name meant the Person.

The Name of the Lord Jesus Christ was not merely a theory, or a doctrine or a theological argument in the Early Church. The Name was a Power — A PERSON — risen and ascended and glorified, living in the power of an endless life, to stand behind and back up the use of that Name.

The Devil fears the Name of Jesus in operation. It is a living and powerful Name.

f. **The Rejected Stone.** vs. 11.

The Stone set at naught, made as nothing, by the Religious Leaders is Jesus Christ Himself.

The Builders found no place for Him. He was the Stone that they could not 'fit' into their building, their program, their religion, their traditions.

The Sanhedrin knew the Old Testament prophecies concerning "The Stone" or "The Rock."
There were many prophecies concerning the Stone-Rock which were distinctly Messianic.

Note some of the prominent Scriptures:

1. Christ is the Anointed Stone, Bethel. Genesis 28:18-19; Luke 4:18; Acts 10:38.
2. Christ became the Stone of Stumbling and Rock of Offence to unbelieving Jewry. Romans 9:33.
3. Christ was the Smitten Rock, from whence the Living Waters of the Holy Spirit flowed out. Exodus 17:5-7; I Corinthians 10:1-4.
4. Christ is the Foundation Stone, laid in Zion. Isaiah 28:16.
5. Christ is the Rock upon which the Church is to be built. Matthew 16:18.
6. Christ is the Headstone (Capstone) of the Temple, even His Church. Ephesians 2:20; I Peter 2:1-9.
7. Christ is the Stone which will crush all who will not fall upon Him in true brokenness. Matthew 21:42-44.
8. Christ is the only place and Rock of Revelation. Exodus 33:21-33.

The Lord Jesus applied these Scriptures concerning "The Rock" to Himself. The Religious Rulers knew these Messianic prophecies. Here we see Peter applying it to the Lord Jesus, Jesus of Nazareth.

In Christ we see the fulfilment of all that "The Rock-Stone" means in prophecy. In Christ we may hide, as Moses was hidden in the Cleft Rock, and there we behold the Glory of God and hear His Name declared in Him.
(Let the Student refer to the Concordance for other Scriptures pertaining to this great Bible theme.)

g. **None Other Name.** vs. 12.

The only Name of Salvation. "He shall save His people from their sins . . . His Name is JESUS." Matthew 21-23.

Acts 2:21, 36. Whosoever shall call upon the Name of the Lord, in the Name of the LORD Jesus Christ, shall be saved.

h. **The Apostles Threatened.** vs. 13-22.

Consider the important points in these verses.

1. They had been with Jesus, verse 13.
   We become like those we live with, and in whose presence we are the most. Who have we been with?
2. Silencing proof.
   The Sanhedrin admitted that they were faced with undeniable, unchallenging and convincing proof and evidence in the healing of this man.
   They could not deny it, or say it was false, verses 14-16.
3. The disciples were happy to suffer for His Name's sake, verses 17-18.

Compare with Matthew 24:9; Luke 21:12-19.

4. True witnesses, verses 19-20.
   A true witness must be one who has both seen and heard. Must obey God first; and not be hypocritical religiously blind leaders who oppose His Name and go against the Word of God.

5. God was glorified, verses 21-22.
   Not Peter, or John or the Apostles. They were only vessels used. No headlines in the Newspapers, or Local Papers or Religious Magazines glorifying man. They glorified GOD!

   "When the Holy Spirit is come, He will glorify Christ." John 16:14. He will not glorify man, or movements, or organizations or sects. He will glorify the Son of God.

i. **Their Own Company.** vs. 23.

After being further threatened not to speak or preach in this Name, the disciples went to their own Company.

They did not go to the Synagogues, or onto the ground of those who did not believe on the Risen Christ.
They went to the ground of faith. "Their own Company.

j. **Early Church Prayer Meeting.** vs. 24-31.

The prayer in these verses is founded upon Psalms 2.
They prayed the Word!
They prayed for more boldness to preach, asking the Lord to confirm with further signs and wonders, and to teach concerning the Resurrected Jesus, in spite of opposition.
Their prayer was to the Father, through the Son, and by the Holy Spirit. Jude 20; Ephesians 2:18.

Note the "Keys" in these verses to the Book of Acts.

Jesus said "Upon this ROCK (Himself) I will build MY CHURCH, and the Gates of Hades (Hell) shall not prevail against it: and I will give unto thee THE KEYS OF THE KINGDOM of Heaven . . . whatsoever thou shalt bind on earth shall be bound in heaven, and whatsoever thou shalt loose on earth shall be loosed in heaven."

Here in Acts we see the Lord adding to and building His Church. Acts 2:41, 47.

Peter is using "The Keys" of the Kingdom to bind and to loose, and the Gates of Hades are not prevailing against the Church.

The Lord is working from heaven with His Church on earth. Mark 16:18-20. It is a victorious Church.

Without "The Keys" of the Kingdom, the Church stands powerless and bewildered and ineffective before a religious and political world. Only these things in operation make them the Church, HIS Church. Only these Keys make the Church effective in ministry.

**The Keys of the Kingdom in Acts.**

1. The Word vs. 29 ) The Keys of the Kingdom.
2. The Name vs. 30 ) in operation.

3. The Spirit vs. 31 ) Each dependent on the
4. The Prayers vs. 31 ) other.

These 4 Keys are linked in one chain; linked together in operation.

These Keys became lost over the "Dark Ages" of Church History, through sin and unbelief.
The Devil took away THE WORD, and it became a 'closed and forbidden book.'

Sin and Satan and evil powers caused THE SPIRIT to depart from the Church, as the Church depended less and less upon the Holy Spirit for ministry.

Satan substituted lifeless forms and sectarian Names which divide the Body of Christ, denominational Names, instead of THE NAME of Jesus. Compare I Corinthians 1:10-13. His Name alone makes us one.

Then PRAYER became a worship of images, relics, superstitions and rites; a matter of empty words and forms, instead of being a power with God and with men.

God is restoring these "Keys" to His Church today. These will be the marks of the True Church, marching forth conquering and to conquer.

These Keys are linked together in operation.

Old Testament Ministries spoke "The Word" of the Lord.
They moved as "The Spirit" came upon them.
They ministered in "The Name" of the Lord God.
They waited upon the Lord in "Prayer" for the will and mind of God.

The Word must be quickened by the Spirit, who gives power to use the Name effectively, and all this is made possible as the Church seeks the Risen Lord in Prayer.

He who was THE WORD made flesh, needed the Anointing SPIRIT upon Him, as He ministered in His Father's NAME, and His whole life was a life of PRAYER.

What the Rod of God was to Moses, so was the Name of Jesus to the Early Church. Exodus 4:17; Mark 16:17.

As the disciples prayed in one accord (vs. 24. Compare Acts 1:14; 2:1), upholding the Word of God in prayer, then the place was shaken and the Holy Spirit came upon them in power.

k. **Unity of the Early Church.** vs. 32-37.

A summary of the important points in this section are as follows:

1. Unity of believers, verse 32.
   One heart and one soul. Christ's prayer "that they all might be one," as in the unity of the Godhead. John 17; I John 5:7-8.
   Divine unity in the Church. Not a man-made unity, but a unity of the Spirit, a unity of the Faith.
   Many members, yet One Body. Ephesians 4:1-16.
   Many hearts, many souls, yet all made one heart, one soul.
   One of the secrets of the Early Church. One accord, one place, one heart, one soul.
   There the Lord commands the blessing. Psalms 133; Acts 1:14; 2:1, 46; 4:24, 32; 5:12; 2:44-45; Jeremiah 32:28-40.

2. All things in common, verse 32. Compare Acts 2:44-45. Not man-made communism, but the Holy Spirit outpouring subdued inbred selfishness and

possessiveness, which gave way to unselfish liberality.

3. Great power and great grace, verse 33.
The ability of the Spirit upon the ministry. The nature of the Spirit of God also manifest. God is gracious, and the Grace of God is manifested in giving.
God gave His Only Begotten Son. John 3:16.
The Son gave ministries to the Church. Ephesians 4:8-10.
The Holy Spirit gives gifts to the Church. I Corinthians 12:1-9.
That same Spirit of giving is now upon the early believers. John 1:14-17; Romans 3:24; 5:1-2. The grace of giving.

4. Freewill offerings, verses 34-35.
Offerings were laid at the Apostles' feet.
They were not given by compulsion, but voluntarily. No one was obliged to give, nor was it commanded. These were freewill and Voluntary Offerings. It was entirely a personal matter concerning how much to give.
This was in fulfilment of that which happened in the Old Testament.

    a. Freewill offerings at Feast of Pentecost. Deuteronomy 16:9-17.

    b. Freewill offerings for building of the Tabernacle. Exodus 35:4-29.

    c. Freewill offerings for buildings of Temple. I Chronicles 29:1-20.

    In each record, all was voluntary, or freewill. "Every one whose heart stirred him up, and whose spirit was made willing came and gave, and rejoiced."

    The New Testament Chapters concerning the right attitude and spirit of giving are found in II Corinthians, chapters 8 and 9.

    Giving is upon the basis of the Law of Love. Love gives. This is exactly what happened in the Early Church under the operations of the Holy Spirit.

    The offerings were laid at the Apostles' feet. No longer being taken to the Temple Treasury (Mark 12:41) or to the Temple Priests, but to the New Temple and New Ministry which the Lord Jesus was establishing.

    The people had confidence in the Apostles when they laid the money at their feet. The Ministry was not out to enrich themselves on the Freewill Offerings or Tithes of the people.

    What a contrast and example for the Ministry today.

5. Distribution to the needy, verse 35.
Refer to Deuteronomy 15:1-11. Israel was to give freewill offerings to "the brother, the poor, and the needy," etc. Here the needy saints are supplied.

6. An Example of Giving, verses 36-37.
Barnabas, who later on would be working with the Apostle Paul, sells all he has and lays it at the Apostles' feet. "Barnabas" — Name interpreted, "Son of Consolation."
The new name signifies the new nature. Acts 13:1-2.
A Levite sold his land, and brought the money to the Apostles.

(Note — The Lord knew that in AD 70 Jerusalem would be desolated, and Jewry scattered; hence those who sold the land and gave to the Lord could not lose in that time! The land would be useless and desolated!)

## ACTS CHAPTER 5

IN CHAPTER FIVE is seen the first tragedy in the Early Church, and the first mention of Satan, the Enemy of Jesus Christ and the Church.

a. **Satan Against the Church.** vs. 1-11.

BUT . . .
The scene changes! In the midst of that Glory and blessing and grace and power upon the Ministry and the people, SATAN is seen at work, and that which had begun in Divine blessing now closes with Divine judgement.

Up to this time, the opposition had been from without, through the Religious Leaders.

Now Satan works in a more subtle way from within, and that is through some members of the Church.

Satan's tactics have never changed. If he cannot destroy the Church, then he will corrupt it. If he cannot beat them, then he will join them! The enemy within is more deadly than the enemy without.

Ananias and Sapphira were believers — not unregenerate persons.

Let us note that the sin was met with Divine discipline.

b. **The Sin of Money—Love and Deception**

The first sin in the Early Church was over money.

It is important to understand what this sin was, and why the Divine discipline was so drastic.

1. **What the sin was not.** vs. 2, 4, 8.
The sin was not in having land or having possessions.
The sin was not in selling the land for a certain amount of money. It was their property.
The sin was not in refusing to give. No one was under compulsion to give. All was given by freewill.
The sin was not in not giving it all as this was a personal matter also.

2. **What the sin was.**
The sin was in not keeping a vow or promise to give it all.

Note this in the Amplified New Testament.
Refer also to Deuteronomy 23:21-23 and Ecclesiastes 5:1-6.
The sin was in letting the thought of Satan conceive in the heart. James 1:12-15.
The sin was in agreeing, conniving and conspiring together to keep back a part.
It was deliberately planned by them both, to wrongfully appropriate the money.
The sin was in acting a lie, giving a lying impression that they were giving all.
The sin was in attempting to deceive the Holy Spirit, and the ministry; in tempting, or trying, or testing the Holy Spirit to see whether this would be detected.
It was not a sin of ignorance, but a sin of presumption.
Appearing to be and do what was really not so.
A sin of hypocrisy and a sin of covetousness.

Here we have the first mention in Acts of these words:

a. Satan

b. Deceive

c. Liar

d. Money

Four words which are often connected. The very nature and character of Satan is the Liar, the Deceiver, the Adversary. His name is his nature!

The New Testament has numerous warnings against MONEY, and against lying and deception. Revelation 21:8, 27; 22:15; Hebrews 3:13.

Judas let Satan put the thought into his heart to betray Christ for money, and met with death. John 13:2, 27; Acts 1:18.

Here the same thought concerning money is met with death.

SIN when it is conceived bringeth forth DEATH. James 1:13-15.

The process of all sin is as follows:

a. Seed thought implanted by Satan.

b. Conception in the mind.

c. Formation and development.

d. Birth, or sin brought forth.

e. End result — death.

c. **The Word of Knowledge.** vs. 3-4, 7-9.

In these verses we see further 'Acts of the Holy Spirit,' being manifested in the 9 Gifts of the Spirit. I Corinthians 12:8-9.

The Holy Spirit knows all things. He gave Peter a fragment of that 'all-knowledge,' which was a 'Word of Knowledge.' Not the Gift of Knowledge, but simply a 'rhema,' or 'a word.'

The Holy Spirit searches all hearts of all believers and knows our thoughts afar off.

Consider the important truths concerning the Person of the Holy Spirit as recorded here.

1. Reveals the Personality of the Holy Spirit.
   They lied to, tempted and sought to deceive a Person, even the Spirit of God.

2. Reveals the Omniscience of the Spirit. The Spirit sees and knows all things.

3. Reveals the Omnipresence of the Spirit. Everywhere present at the same time. He saw and heard their deception.

4. Reveals also the Omnipotence of the Spirit.
   The Spirit is all-powerful. The Divine discipline of death was administered.

This incident reveals the fact that Satan is the Liar and the Deceiver, and is that Evil spirit working against the Holy Spirit, who is the Spirit of Truth, and who cannot be deceived.

d. **The Divine Judgment.** vs. 5, 9-10.

This is the first record of Divine discipline in the Church. It was not of man, but an act of the Spirit, spoken through man. Peter did not execute the judgement. The penalty for this sin was executed by God the Holy Spirit.

e.

**The Divine Warning.** I Timothy 6:9-10.

"The LOVE of money (not money itself) is the root of all evil."

The first sin in Israel, the Church in the Wilderness (Acts 7:38), after great victory and blessing in entering the Promised Land, was over money. A wedge of gold, and silver, and Babylonish garments!

It brought defeat into the whole Camp of Israel until it was Divinely judged. This was the sin of Achan. Joshua the 7th chapter. Death struck, after the operation of ministry of the Urim and Thummin.

The first sin in the Early Church involves money, and this came after great victory and blessing.
This was Divinely judged in death.

The sin of Ananias and Sapphira, and their death, as two believers, is the antitypical fulfilment of the two sons of Aaron — two priests — who offered "strange fire" before the Lord, and were Divinely judged by death. Leviticus 10:1-3.

The Gospel is life unto life, or death unto death. "That the spirit may be saved in the day of Jesus Christ." Compare I Corinthians 5:5.

"Strange fire" and "strange incense" are not permitted in the Sanctuary of the Lord!

f. **The Spirit of Judgment and Burning.** Isaiah 33:14-17; 4:4.

Either Sin or the Holy Spirit had to go! Had these two believers gone undetected, how much more sin and deception would Satan have brought into the Church?
So great was the power and purity of the Early Church here, that a sin — a lie — could not remain in the Presence of God.

Simon the Sorcerer also had this problem with money, in seeking to buy the power of God. Acts l8:18-25.

Peter was not after money, nor monied members for the Church. This is such a contrast to much of today.

When the Glory of the Former House is seen upon the Latter House, sin and deception will not be able to live in God's Presence, for "judgment is to begin at the House of God." I Peter 4:17.

How much sin goes undetected today? In order to have a glorious Church, without spot or blemish or wrinkle or any such thing, the Holy Spirit will once again be revealed as "The Spirit of Judgment and the Spirit of Burning."

Cleansing, purging, purifying, sanctifying is the power of the Holy Spirit.

"God is Holy, and God is Love." Both are manifested here!

g. **The Result of the Judgment.** vs. 5, 11.

1. **The Fear of God.**

   No division came in the Church, no criticism of Peter, etc.
   A godly fear fell on all. Reverential fear. Fear to grieve the Lord, or to grieve

the Spirit. Fear of falling into the sin of deception, acting a lie, or attempting to deceive one another.
Not the fear of man, nor fear of Satan, but the FEAR OF GOD is to be restored again to the Church through such Divine manifestations.

Fear fell on all inside the Church, upon the believers. Psalms 86:11; 34:9.
Fear fell outside the Church, upon the unbelievers. Revelation 14:7.
No man dare "join up," but the Scripture states that the believers were "added to the Lord," and "added to the Church."

If judgment begins at the House of God, where shall the sinner and the ungodly appear.

2. **The Power of God.** vs. 12-16.

The Fear of God and the Power of God came together. Greater manifestation of the power of God upon a pure Church.
The sick healed, unclean spirits driven out. How could the works of Satan, of sickness, disease and demon spirits resist the power of God, when sin had been dealt with?

SIN, SICKNESS, DEMONS = The Kingdom of Satan.
RIGHTEOUSNESS, HEALTH, THE HOLY SPIRIT = The Kingdom of God.

"They were healed every one," even as under Christ's ministry.

Note the word "overshadow" in verse 15, and compare it with Luke 1:35. The Holy Spirit "overshadowed" the Virgin Mary in the supernatural birth of Jesus Christ, the WORD made flesh.

So the Holy Spirit here is "overshadowing" the Church, The Spiritual Body of Christ, continuing the same ministry and bringing forth the Word.

h. **Religious Opposition increases.** vs. 17-28.

The High Priest, and the Sadducees rise up and are filled with indignation at the increase of the power of the Risen Christ in the Church.

Refer again to notes on Acts 4:1, 5-6. Blind, unrepentant and hardened religious leaders, continue to resist the Spirit of God.

The Ministry of the Spirit, of Angels; and the evident power of God exposed the unbelief of the Sadducees. Acts 23:7-8.

The Apostles are put into the common prison. vs. 17-18.
Fulfilling Luke 21:12; 22:33.

The Apostles were cast into prison a number of times in the Book of Acts. Acts 8:3; 12:4; 16:23-24, etc.

The Angel of the Lord opens the prison doors by night and tells them to go and preach all the words of this LIFE. Verses 19-20.
John 10:10; I John 5:12; Acts 11:18.
"He that hath the Son hath life . . ." Christ was their life. The Law could only minister death.

The motive behind the opposition was envy and jealousy, translated in verse 17 as "indignation."
So the Lord Jesus Himself was delivered by these same High Priests over to death because of envy. Matthew 27:18.

In spite of the miracles, healings, casting out of devils, and manifested power of God in angelic visitation, yet the Religious Leaders persist in blindness, hardness and rejection of the truth that could set them free. John 8:32, 36.

Verse 21. The Disciples teach again in the Temple.
The High Priest and the Sanhedrin, and all the Senate of the Children of Israel came together, and ordered the disciples to be brought out from the prison.

What bewilderment laid hold of them when they came and found the prison truly shut, and the keepers standing without guarding the empty prison. Verses 21-23.

It reveals the miracle that the Angel of the Lord had performed in the bringing out of prison all the Apostles without the guards seeing or knowing of this deliverance.

The Religious Rulers feared where this thing would grow. Verse 24.

They re-arrest the Apostles when they found them preaching again in the Temple, verses 25-26.

Note the use of the word "this."
"This life." vs. 20
"This." vs. 24
"This Name." vs. 28
"This Man's Blood." vs. 28

At Pilate's Judgment Hall they cried "His Blood be upon us and upon our children."
When they did this, they invoked upon themselves and the unborn generations of Jewry the curse of innocent Blood. This curse upon the Jewish Nation (House of Judah) cannot be lifted until they accept this very Blood of Jesus for cleansing. Zechariah 12:10; 13:1; Numbers 35:30-34.
A careful study of the Laws of Moses concerning "innocent Blood" reveals the truth of this statement.

The Name of Jesus became exceedingly hateful to them, as every miracle and witness was a conviction against them for rejecting and crucifying the Christ of God.

The disciples made sure "who" was meant in the preaching of "their doctrine" in verse 28.

i. **The Answer of the Apostles.** vs. 29-33.

The disciples must obey God, verse 29. Acts 4:19; Romans 5:19; Hebrews 5:9.

The death and resurrection of Jesus, verse 30.

The exaltation of Jesus, to be a Prince and Saviour, to give repentance and forgiveness of sins, verse 31.

Repent — "A change of mind, especially in relation to sin, God, and His Son Jesus Christ."

Forgiveness — "A loosing or sending away."

God gives the Holy Spirit to them that obey Him, verse 32. Christ came to restore us back to the obedience from which the First Adam fell. "By one man's disobedience, all were made sinners, and death passed upon all men: by one Man's obedience shall many be made righteous, life being passed upon them."

Conviction — "They were cut to the heart." Verse 33. The Word as a two-edged sword cuts to the heart. Hebrews 4:12-13. Religious and disobedient hypocrites exposed to the truth, yet seek to kill Christ and His Church. John 8:40.
God had a witness for Himself even in the midst of the Council — the Sanhedrin who fears not to speak in defense of the truth.

j. **A Word of Wisdom — Gamaliel.** vs. 34-35, 36-39.

Gamaliel — at whose feet Saul had been trained in the law, as a Pharisee. Acts 22:3.

A Pharisee — A "separationist," speaks a word of warning and wisdom to the Council.

A Doctor of the Law — "had in reputation among the people."

Contrast the two cases Gamaliel quotes in contrast to the situation of the Apostles.

| **Of Men** | | **Of God** |
|---|---|---|
| Theudas, boasts himself to be somebody.<br>About 400 men join unto him. | — | Jesus of Nazareth, born in the days of taxation, rose up and many followed Him. |
| He was slain.<br>All who obeyed him were scattered, and brought to naught. | — | He is slain.<br>God raised Him from the dead.<br>His disciples obey Him.<br>The Church multiplied. |
| Judas of Galilee rose up in the days of taxing, drew away much people after himself.<br>He perished. | — | Many leave the Synagogues<br><br>The Holy Spirit comes to the obedient ones. |
| All as many as obeyed him were dispersed. | — | Believers added daily to the Church. |
| IF this counsel or work be of men, it will come to nought. | — | IF it be of God, ye cannot overthrow it, lest ye be found to fight against God! |

Peter and John have been with Jesus, and are not interested in drawing people unto themselves. The Gospels and the Acts show how the Religious Rulers were certainly found to be fighting against God, as revealed in His Blessed Son, the Lord Jesus Christ.

What a lesson for today. Church History sadly reveals that each "new visitation" of the Spirit of God has been fought by the Religious Leaders because God generally used a man to be His voice.

"Behold, I work a work in your days, a work in which ye shall in no wise believe, though A MAN declare it unto you."
Acts 13:27, 30-41.

So God used Peter, John, Paul and the Apostles; so through the Reformation era God used Luther, Wesley, Calvin, Finney, Booth, Knox, Edwards and many, many others. His voice was heard and fought by ecclesiasticals, even as in the Book of Acts.

Gamaliel's attitude should be that of every believer. This was a "word of wisdom."

Movements of men, maintained and energized by men, collapse in due season. False religious movements maintain existence because they are inspired and energized by a false spirit, and doctrines of Satan and devils.
The True Church of Jesus Christ is maintained and energized by the Spirit of God, and will last for all eternity.

k. **The Apostles beaten.** vs. 40-42.

The disciples are beaten, flogged. For what? For teaching and preaching in the Name of Jesus. vs. 40.
They are further forbidden to preach in this Name. Compare Acts 4:17-18.

They departed rejoicing. vs. 41.
In spite of the flogging, the disciples rejoiced that they were counted worthy to suffer for the Name of Jesus. Acts 4:7. Refer to notes.

The Holy Spirit gave them words in that hour to speak for a testimony against (not merely to) them. Luke 21:12-19; Mark 13:9-13.

The Apostles ceased not to teach and preach, but continued to minister the Word DAILY.

Acts 2:47; Hebrews 3:13.

> "The Lord added to the Church daily."
> "Exhort one another daily."
> "Daily in the Temple, and in every house, they taught."

All this fulfills that which typified in the "daily ministrations" of the Sanctuary or Tabernacle of Moses.

Apostolic preaching and power will bring apostolic results, in signs and wonders, and this will bring apostolic persecution!

## ACTS CHAPTER 6

CHAPTER SIX brings us to the circumstances which brought about the choice of Deacons, and one of these Deacons named Stephen, who would become the First Martyr in the Early Church.

a. **The Sin of Murmuring.** vs. 1.

As the number of the disciples increased, there arose a murmuring amongst the Grecians and Hebrews because the widows were being neglected in the daily ministrations.

The poor, needy, widows and Levites, were blessed under the Laws pertaining to the Feast of Pentecost, by the freewill offerings of the people. Refer to Acts 2:44-46; 4:32-35; Deuteronomy 15:1-11; 16:9-12.

"Murmur" — "to mutter, or grumble, in a low undertone."

The Book of Numbers records what a terrible sin murmuring is in the sight of the Lord, and the Divine discipline it brings.

There were seven murmurings recorded against Israel, and here the same thing begins to creep into the Early Church.

| | | |
|---|---|---|
| 1. | Concerning the way. | Numbers 11:1-3. |
| 2. | Concerning the food. | Numbers 11:4-17. |
| 3. | Concerning the giants. | Numbers 13:32-14:2, 27-36. |
| 4. | Concerning their leaders. | Numbers 16:1-11, 41. |
| 5. | Concerning the Divine judgments. | Numbers 16:41; 17:5-10. |
| 6. | Concerning the desert. | Numbers 20:1-5. |
| 7. | Concerning the manna again. | Numbers 21:4-5. |

Paul says to the saints, "Neither murmur ye." I Corinthians 10:10-11; Philippians 2:14.

b. **How the Deacons were Chosen.** vs. 1-2.

1. **By the suggestion of the Apostles.**

Unity in the ministry was seen over the evident need. Not the result of dictatorship, or lordship (compare Daniel 5:19). The need was made public to the multitude of believers. All the Church was called together.

2. **By the people.** vs. 3, 5.

"Look ye . . . and they chose . . ."
The saying pleased the whole multitude. There was unity of mind in the ministry and the assembly.
The deacons had enough evident qualifications for the people to recognize them.
They were not men seeking position, recognition or promotion in the Church. Psalms 75:5-7.
"A man's gift maketh room for him and bringeth him before great men." Proverbs 18:16.
Joseph, Daniel, Isaiah, Moses, Jeremiah, and others, were brought before great men by the gift God entrusted to them. They did not make room for

their gift, or promote themselves.
The same was true of the 7 men chosen here.
It is God who makes a deacon. The Church must recognize and accept, or reject.

c. **The Ministry of a Deacon.**

Though the word "Deacon" is not specifically used here, it is clearly implied in the use of the Greek words in verses 1 to 2.

Verse 1. The Greek word for "ministration" is "diakonia."
Verse 2. The Greek word for "serve" is "diakonea."
The Greek word for "deacon" is "diakonas."

This Greek word is translated as follows:

| | | |
|---|---|---|
| Deacon | — | 5 times |
| Servant | — | 7 times |
| Minister | — | 20 times |

The word essentially means, "A Servant, one called to serve, to wait, or an attendant."

A Deacon is 1. A Servant to Christ.
2. A Servant to the Church.
3. A Servant to the Ministry.

d. **Qualifications of a Deacon.** vs. 3. I Timothy 3:8-13.

Scripture lists the qualifications of Deacons.

1. A man from among you. Must be a believer, not an outsider.
2. Of honest report. Good character and reputation, both inside and out the Church.
3. Full of the Holy Spirit. Not only in the Baptism of the Spirit but living the Spirit-filled life. Living, walking, and moving in the Spirit.
4. Full of wisdom. Wisdom is the principal thing. Compare Proverbs 8.
5. Must be grave. Reverent, sincere in spirit.
6. Not double-tongued. Not double-minded or two-faced. James 1:8; Psalms 12:2.
7. Not given to much wine. Not a drunkard or given to excesses.
8. Not greedy of filthy lucre. Not covetous, or having a love for money.
9. Holding the mystery of the Faith in a pure conscience. Clear conscience in all.
10. Must be proven first. A time of probation. Not a novice.
11. Must be found blameless, and above reproach.
12. The deacon must have a wife that is grave also.
13. Not a slanderer. "Diabolis," Greek. The Devil is a slanderer. Gossiper, or whisperer.
"Telling the truth in such a way as to give the lying impression." Proverbs 10:18.
14. Sober. Self-controlled. Watchful. Of a disciplined mind.

15. Faithful in all things. Reward is for faithfulness.
16. Household, wife and children must be ruled well. Compare verse 5. If one cannot rule his own house, one cannot rule the house of God.
17. The husband of one wife.
18. The Office of a deacon is purchasing a "good degree."
19. The qualifications of the Deacon are very similar to that of the Elders, as in I Timothy 3:1-7.
    Compare verse 8, "likewise," and verse 10 "also."

e. **The Ordinations of Deacons.** vs. 6.

The 7 men were chosen and these men had proved themselves before the Church and the ministry. They are set before the Apostles, and the Apostles appoint them to their service. Verse 3. This confirmed the choice of the people.

The Apostles were men who gave themselves continually to —

1. Prayer, and
2. The Ministry of the Word. vs. 2, 4.

They had no New Testament as yet. The Holy Spirit gave them the Inspired Word and the revelation to the Written Word from the Living Word, Jesus Christ.

The Deacons were ordained by prayer and consecration to their Office, by the Laying on Of Hands by the Apostles.

"Lay hands suddenly on no man." I Timothy 5:21-22; Hebrews 6:1-2.

Refer to the Doctrine of the Laying on of Hands. These things are spoken of as "The First Principles of the Doctrine of Christ."

f. **Deacons and Deaconesses.**

It is worthy to note the following examples of those who served as Deacons, as servants to the Church and the ministry, and how they served.

There is no mention as yet of Prophets, or Teachers, or Evangelists or Pastors or Elders.
The New Testament is in the progress of development, "line upon line, here a little, there a litt.e"

The first Office pertains to the Deacon — the "servant ministry."

It is the Spirit of Christ to serve one another in love.
The Lord Jesus Himself is the supreme example of the Deacon. The ministry of the Deacon will be Christ re-living His life and ministry in and through him, as the Servant of all.

"The Son of Man came not to be ministered unto (Greek Diakoneo,) but to minister (to serve, to act as a Deacon,) and to give His life a ransom for many." Mark 10:45.

1. The 12 Apostles acted as Deacons also, and learned to be servants of all, in the Spirit of Christ.
   Note Christ's rebuke in these Scriptures for position seeking. Matthew 23:1-12; Mark 9:33-35; 10:35-44, 45; I Corinthians 3:5.
   He that would be great among us shall be a servant (deacon) to all. Compare Jeremiah 45:5.

2. Timothy served as a Deacon to Paul and to the Churches. Acts 16:1-3; I Thessalonians 3:1-2, 6.
3. Tychicus was a Deacon first also. Ephesians 6:21-22. A faithful minister (Deacon.) Colossians 4:7-8, 9.
4. Erastus served with Timothy, as Deacon to Paul in his travels. Acts 19:21-22. Ministered, or acted as Deacon to him.
5. Epaphras served as a Deacon. Colossians 1:7-8; 4:12-13. A faithful minister (Deacon.)
6. Onesiphorus acted as a Deacon to Paul. II Timothy 1:16-18.

It is clear that these men served as Deacons to the Churches and the ministry, as unto the Lord.
These first proved themselves in the Local Church before they came into the particular Ministry-gift Christ had given them.

They travelled at times with the Apostles, and also from Church to Church, taking messages and reports of the welfare of the Churches and the ministry, etc.
They were servants to the Local Churches ministering in the distribution of the freewill offerings to the needy, the widows, the poor, and ministering in temporal things.

The Elders and the Deacons work together in the Local Church. Phil. 1:1-2.

The Scriptures also reveal that certain women worked in the Office of a Deaconess,as servants to the Church.

1. Paul the Apostle commended Phebe as a servant (Greek Diakonas) or Deaconess of the Church at Cenchrea. Paul asks the Church at Rome to accept her in the Lord and to assist her in whatever business she needed of them.
2. In the Gospels we find that "many women ministered (Greek Diakonas) unto Christ of their substance. Luke 8:1-3; Matthew 27:55-56.
3. Martha, Mary, Mary Magdalene and other women followed Christ and ministered to Him as Deaconesses. Luke 10:38-42; John 12;2.

Elders were chosen and ordained by the Apostles.
Deacons were chosen by the people, and ordained by the Apostles.

Elders were chosen to rule.
Deacons were chosen to serve.

Of these 7 men chosen to be Deacons, Stephen, the first named becomes the first martyr of the Early Church.
His witness and testimony is given in Acts 7.

Philip, another Deacon, is the first mentioned Evangelist in Acts, and his ministry as such is recorded in Acts, Chapter 8.

Both proved themselves in the Local Church at Jerusalem. The true Spirit of Christ should be manifest through all believers.

"By love serve one another."

Jesus said "I am among you as one that serveth." Luke 22:27; John 12:1-17.

The choice of Stephen and Philip among the 7 Deacons in Chapter 6 prepares for Chapters 7 and 8 in which Stephen and Philip are prominent.

g. **Increase and multiplication.** vs. 7.

The Word of God increased. The Living Word and the Written Word. John 1:1-3, 14.

The disciples multiplied greatly.

A great company of the Priests became obedient to "The Faith." Great victory came as many of the Priests realized that the Aaronic Priesthood was finished, and the Temple worship and Mosaic economy had ceased in God's mind, as witnessed by the Rent Veil.
No longer was there need of animal blood-sacrifices. All had found their fulfilment in Christ Jesus.
A new Temple, a new Priesthood of all believers, a New Covenant and spiritual sacrifices, a New and Heavenly High Priest at God's Right Hand — all these were now in effect.
It was the Order of Melchisedek. Hebrews 7:1-7; Revelation 1:6; I Peter 2:1-9.

h. **Stephen — Ministry and Witness.** vs. 8-15.

As noted previously, the record of the choice of these 7 Deacons is introductory to the:

Testimony and martyrdom of Stephen in Acts, Chapter 7, and Ministry of Philip the Evangelist in Acts, Chapter 8.

1. Stephen, full of faith and power (dunamis.) The ability of the Holy Spirit. Compare verse 3. Great signs and wonders manifested again. The Gifts of the Spirit in operation. I Corinthians 12:7-11.
2. The Synagogues oppose the truth, disputing with Stephen.
   Foretold by the Lord Jesus. John 16:1-2.
3. They could not resist the Wisdom and Spirit by which he spoke.
   In fulfilment of Luke 21:12-17.
   The Holy Spirit as the Spirit of Wisdom spoke through Stephen even as through the Lord Jesus.
4. False witnesses brought in to testify against him, even as they did to Christ, in Matthew 26:59-68.
   They went contrary to their own Law of Moses, of whom they accused Stephen with blasphemy. Deuteronomy 19:15-21; Exodus 20:16.
   They charge Stephen of blasphemy against:
   The Holy Place, the Temple,
   The Lord God,
   The Customs which Moses delivered.
5. Stephen is brought before the Council, or the Sanhedrin.
6. The Glory of the Christ within shone upon the face of Stephen even as:
   a. Moses' face shone in Mt. Sinai, Exodus 34:29-35, and
   b. Christ's face shone in Mt. Transfiguration, Matthew 17:1-3.

   This is the Glory that will remain, while the Glory of the Law passes away. II Corinthians 3.

   The Temple, the Law, and Moses himself all prophesied and pointed to Christ Himself, but the Rulers became so engrossed in the form and the letter, they missed the One that all these pointed to.

## ACTS CHAPTER 7

THE SEVENTH CHAPTER OF ACTS is a continuation of the events pertaining to Stephen, one of the 7 Deacons chosen in Chapter 6, and who is now brought before the Sanhedrin.

Here we have Stephen's marvellous "Defense" of the Christian Faith. It gives a remarkable panoramic view of the History of the Israel Nation, beginning with Abraham and culminating in the rejection of Jesus Christ, the Just One.

The address of Stephen before the Council is also remarkable in the fact that he carries his hearers through the History of the Nation as found in their own Old Testament Scriptures, and yet he never once mentions the Name of Jesus in verses 1-53.

The only express reference to Jesus of Nazareth is that which is found in his conclusion in verse 52, where he speaks of Him as "The JUST One."

The record of Scripture concerning Stephen may be divided into two sections:

The Man

The Message

1. **THE MAN STEPHEN — LIKE Christ in his life, ministry, testimony and witness.** Acts 6:8-15.

   a. **In His Life and Ministry.**
   Stephen as a Deacon, servant of all. vs. 5.
   Chosen from among the people. vs. 3.
   Of honest report, full of the Spirit and Wisdom. vs. 3.
   Did great miracles and wonders among the people. vs. 8.
   Full of Faith (Grace) and the Holy Spirit. vs. 5, 8.
   Opposed by the Synagogues, who disputed with him. vs. 9.
   Unable to resist the Spirit and Wisdom by which he spoke. vs. 10.
   Charged with blasphemy against Moses, The Law, The Temple and The Customs. vs. 11, 14.
   Stirred up the people, the Elders and Scribes against himself.
   These took him to the Council. vs. 12.
   False witnesses testify against him. vs. 13.
   His face shone as an Angel with the Glory of God. vs. 15. Compare Matthew 17:2; Exodus 34:29-35.
   Thus Stephen's life and ministry remarkably compares with that of the Risen Lord he served. He was "like Jesus."

   b. **In His Trial before the Sanhedrin, and Death.** Acts 7:54-60.

   The hearers were cut to the heart, and gnashed on him. vs. 54.
   He saw heaven opened and the Glory of God and JESUS STANDING at the Right Hand of God. vs. 55.
   (Note — This same verse was foretold by Jesus Himself to these same High Priests at His own trial and death. Matthew 26:64.)
   Compare Mark 16:20; Psalms 110:1-2; Hebrews 10:9-15. Hebrews 10:9-15.
      Jesus ascended on high, then SAT down! Daniel 7:13-14.
      Here Stephen sees Jesus STANDING — to receive the First Martyr of the Early Church Cf. Michael Standing. Daniel 12:1-2.

   This verse was proof of Christ's resurrection, ascension and glorification to the Father's Throne.

JESUS — THE SON OF MAN. The Heavenly High Priest. The glorified humanity of the Son of God. vs. 48.
They cried out with a loud voice, stopping their ears. vs. 57.
They cast him out of the City and stoned him. vs. 58.
According to the Laws of Deuteronomy 17:1-7; John 8:59; Hebrews 13:13.
Stephen cried with a loud voice. Compare Matthew 27, 46, 50.
He committed his spirit to the LORD Jesus. vs. 59. Luke 23:46.
He prayed for his enemies, for forgiveness, verse 60. Compare Luke 23:34.
Then fell asleep in Jesus. vs. 60. Compare I Thessalonians 4:14.
Jesus gave up His life in death.

Thus Stephen was indeed "Like Jesus" in his life and ministry, and in his witness before the Sanhedrin and then his death under false witnesses outside the City of Jerusalem.

Stephen — His Name interpreted is prophetic. "A Crown."
A Deacon becomes the First MARTYR (Witness. Greek Acts 1:8.)
In the New Testament Church. Acts 22:20.

As Abel was the First Martyr of the Old Testament, and received the Martyr's Crown, so was Stephen of the New Testament and receives the Martyr's Crown.

Hated and killed "for His Name's sake," Matthew 24:9. Stephen had drunk deeply of the Spirit of Christ, the Calvary Spirit, and now was drinking the "same Cup and being baptized with the same Baptism" as his Master had experienced.

"To live is Christ, and to die is gain." Philippians 1:21.

"Fear not them that kill the body . . . and after that . . ." Luke 12:4.

"The Blood of the Martyrs is The Seed of The Church."

2. **THE MESSAGE — OF CHRIST in His rejection, humiliation and exaltation.** Acts 7:1-53.

It is significant to note again that Stephen never once mentioned The Name of Jesus in his witness, yet the whole of Stephen's message reveals CHRIST JESUS in His Ministry, Rejection, Humiliation and Exaltation to the Father's Right Hand.

The Holy Spirit brought the application of the message right home to the hearts of the Council in convicting power, making them know WHO was meant in the historical survey of the Chosen Nation!

The Holy Spirit spoke through Stephen as promised by the Lord Jesus in Mark 13:9-13. When brought before the Councils, it was to be given them in "that hour" what they were to speak.

Stephen's address shows how saturated in the Word of God he was.

There is absolute Divine Order and Divine Pattern in the progression of this Chapter. It may be considered Nationally, Prophetically, Typically, as well as Dispensationally and Personally.

In order to appreciate the contents and get to the very "heart" of Stephen's Sermon, it is worthy to note the following basic facts.

The key truths of the whole Chapter may be summarized as follows:

a. Each of the Persons or Places referred to are remarkable types of Christ.

b. Each of these Persons experienced in their lives a very similar pattern that Christ experienced.

1. Each was called and sent of God.
2. Each was rejected by their brethren the first time, and experienced rejection and humiliation at the hands of others.
3. Each were exalted of God in due time, and then accepted by their brethren the second time.

c. All reveal the failure of the Chosen Nation to hear God speak through "A Sent One."

Thus each is prophetical of The Lord Jesus Christ.

He was called and sent of God the Father, unto His own.
His own Nation received Him not, but rejected Him. At the hands of His own brethren He experienced rejection, and humiliation in His Coming.
Then He was exalted to His Father's Right Hand, and will not be accepted until "the second time," in the Days pertaining to His second Advent.

d. The "key verse" or phrase of the whole Chapter is suggested to be in verse 13.

"And at **THE SECOND TIME** . . . was made known to His brethren."

**The FIRST TIME** — Rejection, humiliation, resistance, spiritual deafness, and hardness of heart.

**The SECOND TIME** — Exaltation, glorification, spiritual blindness lifted. This is the History of the Jewish Race!

Study these several Scriptures which speak of "The Second Time." Joshua 5:2; Isaiah 11:11; Jonah 3:1; Jeremiah 1:13; I Chronicles 29:22; Hebrews 9:28; Numbers 9:11; Acts 7:13.

## HISTORICAL SURVEY OF ISRAEL

**1. Abraham.** vs. 2-7.

The God of Glory appeared to Abraham. Genesis 15; Genesis 12:1-3; Romans 4:1-2; Exodus 34:29-35; Nehemiah 9:7.
In the beginning GOD. Genesis 1:1.
Israel was the only Nation who had the visible manifestation of the Shekinah Glory of God. Romans 9:4; Exodus 13:21-22.
Abraham — The Father of all who believe.
God called Abraham the first time, but Abraham did not obey fully until the second time. Compare Genesis 11:31 with Genesis 12:1.
If we are Abraham's Seed, spiritually, then we will believe Jesus Christ.
Abraham obeyed after his father, Terah, died. John 8:37-44.

2. **Abraham, Isaac and Jacob.** vs. 8. Exodus 3:6; Genesis 22:15.
The Three Fathers. The foundation of the Chosen Nation.
These Three Men, typical of the Fulness of the Godhead Bodily. Each manifesting the characteristics typically, of the Father, Son and Holy Spirit.

Abraham — Type of the Father God, the Beginning, Covenant-holder, the Promise, the Foundation, the one who was willing to offer his Only Begotten Son. Hebrews 11:16-17.

Isaac — Type of the Son of God. Typically slain and resurrected after the third day. Genesis 22. Hebrews 11:19.
Isaac is the second person in that tri-unity of men.
God called to Abraham the second time from heaven at this typical sacrifice. Isaac — the central one of the trinity.

Jacob — Type of the Holy Spirit, as the third person of that trinity of men. The Fruitful one, the Multiple one, the Anointer of the Bethel Rock with oil.

3. **The 12 Sons of Jacob.** vs. 8. Genesis, chapters 48-49.
The Founders of the 12 Tribes of Israel, the Chosen Nation.
The Household of Faith.
The Israel of God. All their Names holding prophetical truths.

4. **Joseph.** vs. 9-19. Genesis, chapters 37-50.
One of the richest types of Christ, as the beloved and rejected son of the Father.
Joseph — sent to his brethren by his father. Rejected, sold for silver to the Gentiles, falsely accused, cast into prison, interprets dreams of three days to the prisoners, out of which one lives, and one dies.
Joseph is later exalted to the Throne, given a Name at which every knee bows.
Then he was made known and accepted of his brethren "the second time."
Joseph was born of Rachael, the second wife of Jacob.

5. **Moses.** vs. 20-38. Deuteronomy 18:18; Hebrews 11:24-25.
Another remarkable type of Christ, as the Prophet-deliverer.
Children slain at birth of Moses, yet he escapes in Egypt.
Moses — rejected of his brethren, and suffers a period of humiliation. He is accepted the "second" time when he declares the Name of God, as I AM, in ministry of signs and wonders.
To Moses is given the Law Covenant, the Tabernacle, the Glory of God, and Holy Oracles.
Note in Moses' life span the $3 \times 40 = 120$ years. Verses 23, 30 and 36.

6. **Church in the Wilderness.** vs. 38-39.
"The Called Out Company." Israel, with the Tabernacle and Priesthood and Sacrificial worship system becomes a remarkable type of the New Testament Church Order in its earthly pilgrimage.

7. **Aaron, the High Priest.** vs. 40-43.
Aaron also was a type of Christ as the High Priest of God, Numbers 16.
Aaron was rejected as God's ordained High Priest by rebellious Israelites.
God caused the Rod to bud as being His Seal upon Aaron's Ministry.
Aaron was exalted and accepted the second time.
Israel however, falls into idolatry, and substituted the Tabernacle of Molech for the Tabernacle of Moses, and brings in the Star of Remphan instead of the Star of Messiah.

8. **Tabernacle of Witness.** vs. 44. Exodus, Chapters 25-40; John 1:14.
The Tabernacle is typical of Christ, the True Tabernacle of God.
Christ Jesus is the True Tabernacle of Witness. The Witness of the Father.
In Him is God's Name, Glory, Habitation, and Voice heard. He is all the truth personified as typified in the Tabernacle furnishings.

God's Voice speaks through Him as our Mercy Seat. Numbers 7:89; Romans 3:25. Notice that God rent the second veil in the Temple at Christ's death. Matthew 27:51.

9. **Joshua and Canaan Rest.** vs. 45.
Joshua also typified the Lord Jesus as the Leader into the True Promised Land, and Spiritual Rest. Joshua 5:2; Hebrews 4:8 margin.
Joshua was rejected of his own brethren the first time, after he had brought the message of God's Promised Canaan Rest. The Congregation threatened to stone Joshua along with Caleb. Numbers, chapters 13-14.
After 40 years (compare 40 Jubilees,) Joshua is exalted by God as the Leader into Canaan, with the New Generation.
It is the second generation, who experience the second circumcision. Joshua is accepted the second time.

10. **David, the King.** vs. 45-46.
Typical also of the Son of David, Jesus Christ. The King, and Messiah.
David has two sections in his experience also.
David is first a Shepherd, and is anointed in the midst of his brethren, but experiences a period of rejection, suffering and humiliation at the hand of Saul, and Anointed of the Lord.
Later on, David is exalted to the Throne, and accepted by all Israel the second time.
In his rejection he gathers to him a great army. I Samuel 22:1-2.
David is also the second King to reign over all Israel.
The Man of war, and much bloodshed.

11. **Solomon, The King.** vs. 47-50.
Solomon is typical of Christ as the Builder of the Temple, by the Spirit. Solomon was a man of wisdom, and uses the materials prepared by David before his death, for the Temple of the Lord. Builds by the wisdom of God. The Temple is prophetic of Christ and His Church. John 2:21; Isaiah 66:1-4; I Kings 8:27; I Corinthians 6:19.
The second veil was rent in the rebuilt, or second Temple. Matthew 27:51.

12. **The Holy Spirit.** vs. 51.
The conclusion of Stephen's sermon is the charge of resisting the Holy Spirit, as did their fathers.
Stiffnecked and uncircumcised in heart and ears — spiritual condition. Though under the Covenant of Circumcision (Acts 7:8,) yet spiritually they were Uncircumcised, or, Gentilized!
Deuteronomy 9:6, 13; 10:16; Jeremiah 6:10; 9:26; Romans 2:25-29. A Jew is one inwardly, and circumcision is of the heart, in the spirit, and not in the flesh or of the letter.

13. **The Prophets rejected.** vs. 52.
All Prophets pointed to the Lord Jesus as THE WORD, and all experienced rejection and humiliation at the hands of Israel, their own nation. Matthew 23:31-36; Luke 13:31-35; Matthew 21:46.
It was consummated in the rejected Son of God — THE Word made flesh.

14. **The Law by Angels.** vs. 53.
The 10 Commandments, given by the Lord God, by Angels, to the Mediator Moses, yet the Nation continually violated this Law. Galatians 3:19; Romans 2:3; Hebrews

2:1-4; 12:25.
The First Tables had been broken, by Moses, by the people.
The Second Tables were kept hidden in the Ark of the Covenant.

**SUMMARY** — vs. 52.

The Prophets foretold the coming of **THE JUST ONE**, and now the Nation had rejected and slain Him: they had become the murderers and betrayers of the Christ of God.
The Son of God, the Just One, was the second Person in the Godhead.

Thus, as Joseph, Moses, David, and Aaron were rejected the first time by their own brethren, then exalted and accepted the second time, so the Lord Jesus was rejected the first time by Jewry who will accept Christ by faith and be grafted into the good Olive Tree, in the "second time." Romans 11.

Jesus Christ will return **THE SECOND TIME** without sin unto salvation. Hebrews 9:28.

Verse 54 tells us they were "**cut** to the heart." Literally, they were sawn asunder, or excessively irritated.

## ACTS CHAPTER 8

THIS CHAPTER takes up another of the Deacons chosen, even Philip, and shows his ministry in the spreading of the Gospel to Samaria.

a. **Persecution scatters The Word.** vs. 1-4.

Enter Saul! vs. 1. Saul is introduced here as being a leader in the persecution of the Early Church, and his conversion to the Lord Jesus is dealt with fully in Acts, chapter 9.

Great persecution came against the Church at Jerusalem. The Devil has tried Religious and Political opposition from without; he has tried Spiritual corruption from within, and here we see the enemy seeking to scatter that which he could not destroy or corrupt.

God also has His hand in the matter for one of the dangers of the Church has been the danger of centralization. God meant the Word of the Gospel to go into "all the world, to every creature."

Persecution did not destroy the Word, it simply scattered it. It was scattered to a wider field, even the world.
The Parable of the Sower was being fulfilled. The Sower went forth scattering the Seed of the Word on all types of ground.

Stephen's death, like the corn of wheat which had to die, began to bring forth fruit, to multiply. John 12:24.
A great harvest comes to birth through his death. The word of the Early Church was "Go ye," not merely "Come ye."

The 12 Apostles remained in Jerusalem.

Stephen is taken to burial, and lamentation is made over him.

Saul — later on to become the Apostle Paul — makes a systematic persecution of the believers, going from house to house and brought men and women to prison.

The disciples were scattered as the "good seed of the Kingdom," and they "scattered the Word" everywhere they went. Compare Matthew 13:1-30.

b. **Philip the Evangelist — Public Ministry.** vs. 5-8, 12.

The Lord Jesus is the supreme Evangelist, the Father's Herald, who announced the Good News of salvation and redemption. Luke 4:18.

There are 3 specific references to "Evangelist" in the New Testament.

1. The Ministry of Evangelist is among the 5-fold Ascension Gift Ministries, set in the Body of Christ. Ephesians 4:11.
2. Timothy was to do the "work of an Evangelist."
   Acts 21:8; Acts 6:5; II Timothy 4:5.
   It is worthy to note that Philip "proved himself" in the Local Church at Jerusalem as a Deacon first before his ministry as an Evangelist came into operation.

Evangelist means "One who announces good tidings."
The Greek word for "preaching" is often translated from the Word which involves evangelism.

Two Greek words used are as follows:

1. "Kerusso" — "To proclaim as a Herald," — vs. 5.
2. "Euaggelizo" — "To announce Good News." — vs. 4, 12, 25, 35, 40.
   The word "Evangelist" is derived from this word.

   In Acts 8:4, 12, 25, 35, 40, the word is translated "preach."

To PREACH is "to proclaim as a Herald, to announce the Good News," hence we get Evangelist, Evangelization, Evangelism.

Philip's Ministry was in the Church, and of the Risen Lord, and then he went down to Samaria and "evangelized the City."

Philip was a Bible Evangelist, qualified in Character and Ministry. What he was and what he did measured up to the standard of the Word.

1. He went to Samaria. Acts 1:8. Jerusalem first, then Samaria.
   Note also John 4:9, 1-42. Christ's Ministry in Samaria.
   The 12 Apostles were forbidden to go to Cities of Samaria. Matthew 10:5.
   The Samaritans were looked upon as dogs, Gentile dogs. They were a mixture of race, being placed in the Cities of Israel after the House of Israel was taken into Captivity to Assyria.
   These people became known as Samaritans. II Kings, chapter 17.
   Luke 10:33; John 8:48; Luke 17:16.
   Though the disciples were forbidden to go to the Samaritans before the Cross, now the Gospel is for all the world.
   In Samaria were the firstfruits of Christ's ministry.

2. Philip preached Christ. A Person, not merely a Doctrine. vs. 5.
3. Philip preached the Gospel of the Kingdom and The Name of Jesus Christ. vs. 12.
   Acts 4:12; Matthew 10:7-8.
4. Philip preached the Gospel of the Kingdom with Signs following. Mark 16:15-20.
   The sick were healed, devils were cast out. Demonstrating the power of the Kingdom and the Name of Christ. Great joy came to the City as many received the Word.
5. The Samaritans received the Word, and were born again and then baptized in water in the Name of the Lord Jesus Christ. vs. 12, 16.
   John 1:11-12; 3:1-5; I Peter 1:23; I John 5:1.

These were the signs of a Bible Evangelistic Ministry.

c. **Simon the Sorcerer.** vs. 9-11, 13.

Here in these verses we see the first contact of Christianity with the power of Witchcraft, or Spiritism.

Simon, which means "hearing" was a Sorcerer.
Sorcerer means "A practicer of magic arts, enchanter with drugs, observer of clouds, witchcrafts."

Simon was a magician, and practiced divination, foretelling of future events, revealing secret things by supernatural means, by the power of evil spirits. A user of charms, etc.

The whole City was held in bondage to sin, sickness, disease and demon-power through this Witch-Doctor!

These Sorcerers were always opposers of God's Messengers.

They were condemned under the Law of Moses, and the curse of Divine Judgment. Deuteronomy 18:9-14; Isaiah 47:9-12; 57:3.

Egypt, Babylon, Greece, Rome and all Nations had their Wise Men, Newcromancers, Sorcerers, and Magic Arts, endeavouring to contact the spirit realm. Daniel 2:2; Malachi 3:5; Exodus 7:11; II Timothy 3:8-9.

Satanic Cults and Occultism increasing in these End-Times are simply a renewal of these Ancient Cults. Operations multiplying today.

In Acts 13:6-12, Paul brought Divine Judgment upon a Sorcerer.

In Acts 19:13-20, the believers brought their "Black Magic Books" and burnt them in the fire, as God brought the power of His Word into manifestation.

It is also worthy to note that the Greek word for "Sorceries" as used in the following Scriptures, is "Pharmakeia," from which we get our words, "Pharmacy, or Chemist," and means "Makers of Enchanters with Drugs."
Revelation 9:21; 18:23; 21:8; 22:15; Isaiah 8:19-20.

In Galatians 5:20, the same word is translated "Witchcrafts."

With the increase of Drugs, etc., it is evident that there is a spirit or evil power behind or associated with many of these Drugs!

Philip's Ministry in Christ was greater than the power of Simon the Sorcerer and his evil Ministry in the City.

Contrast Philip's Ministry and Simon's Ministry.

| **Philip** | **Simon** |
|---|---|
| Philip the Evangelist | Simon the Sorcerer |
| Herald of Good News | Enchanter, Black Magic |
| Preaches Christ | Gave out that he himself was some great one |
| Liberated the people | Bewitched the people |
| The Power of the Gospel | The power of Satan |
| The Kingdom of God — Light | The Kingdom of Satan-darkness |
| Philip, full of the Holy Spirit | Simon, full of the evil spirit |

Simon, however, recognized that there was greater power in Philip than that which he operated, and he believes and is baptized under Philip's ministry.

d. **Peter and John — Apostolic Ministry.** vs. 14-25.

Jerusalem hears that Samaria had received THE WORD (not Philip!) but THE WORD through Philip. vs. 14. Compare I Peter 1:23; John 1:11-12.

They send down to Samaria Peter and John who now lay hands on the Samaritans that they might receive the Holy Spirit. Wonderful cooperation and recognition and flowing together of the various ministries in the Church, given by the Ascended Lord.
Peter and John supplied something in Ministry that Philip lacked. There was recognition — not competition!

Another area that Peter helped the Church in Samaria was that which pertained to Simon the Sorcerer. vs. 18-24.

Philip had baptized Simon the Sorcerer upon his confession of faith, but the Holy Spirit allowed the coming of Peter and John and the reception of the Holy Spirit by the Samaritans to cause Simon to expose himself, and that which was hidden in the heart.

It needed the right circumstances to expose this area in his life.

Simon saw that the Holy Spirit was given by the Ministry of the Laying on of Hands, and sought to purchase this 'gift' and 'power'.

There must have been some visible, audible and tangible evidence that he "saw" that made him covet such power. He did not covet the power that Philip had in healing the sick, casting out of devils, etc., but he did desire this 'power.'

This brought to manifestation the secrets of his heart. Simon's experience was external and not of the heart. This is seen in the strong language Peter uses.

1. The evil thought of his heart. vs. 20, 23. Compare Judas. John 13:2.
2. Desired to purchase the Gift of God with money. vs. 20.
   The Holy Spirit Gift cannot be 'bought.'
   Judas had betrayed Christ for money.
   Ananias and Sapphira held back part of the money.
   Simon wants to buy the power of God for money.
3. Simon had no part nor lot in this matter. vs. 21, i.e., Logos/Word.
4. His heart was not right in the sight of God. God sees the heart. Compare I Samuel 16:7.
5. Called to "Repent." Repent of this wickedness. vs. 22.
6. Ask and pray to God for forgiveness of heart. vs. 22.
7. Peter perceives he is in the gall of bitterness. vs. 23.
   Compare Deuteronomy 29:18; Matthew 27:34; Hebrews 12:15.
   Undoubtedly bitter over Philip's power and ministry in the City, as they turned from him unto the Lord Jesus.
8. Simon was in the bond of iniquity. vs. 23.
   A bond forged by iniquity to fetter souls. Amp. N.T. Isaiah 58:6.
9. Simon asks Peter to pray for him that none of these judgments would come upon him. vs. 24.

The whole language above reveals the condition of Simon's heart, even though he had professed faith and was baptized in water.

In verse 25, we see Peter and John (a) Testifying and
(b) Preaching (Greek Evangelizing,) in
the Villages of the Samaritans.

There must always be both. We can only preach truly that which we have testified in our own experience.

This Chapter is a contrast in spirit to that attitude of James and John in Luke 9:51-56, when they desired to "call down fire from heaven" on the Samaritans who would not receive the Lord and themselves.

Here Peter and John call "the fire of the Holy Spirit" in the Baptism of the Spirit upon the Samaritans.

e. **Philip the Evangelist — Personal Ministry.** vs. 26-40.

In the midst of great crowds and blessing, Philip is called to the desert by the Angel of the Lord to minister to one hungry soul. vs. 26.

Christ is concerned with the individual, not just the crowds. This is especially seen in the Godpel of John.

Philip was immediately obedient to the Lord.

The hungry soul was and Ethiopian, a man of great authority under Candace, The Queen of Ethiopia, having charge of all her treasure.

He had come to Jerusalem to worship. Reveals a hunger in his heart after the TRUE God, the God of Israel.

What had he found in Jerusalem? Ritualism, form, ceremony, tradition, unbelief, spiritual deadness, Temple corruption and impersonal theology and religion!

As he reads the Scripture he realizes he lacks understanding. Though he understood not the Word, he still read it! God had an interpreter of the Word there at the right time.

The Spirit of God worked both ends. He worked on Philip, and He was working on the Ethiopian. Evangelist and convert would be brought together by the operation of the Spirit.

The Spirit goes before the Word, and works with and through the Word.

Study in connection with this Section, Psalms 68:18-19, 31 with Ephesians 4:11.

"Ethiopia would stretch out her hands to God," and He who had ascended on high and gave "Gifts to men" would have theat ministry Gift there at the right moment!

There were blind guides at Jerusalem. Matthew 23:16, 24.

Philip ran to him, to get there on time for his 'text,' and he preached unto him JESUS! His life, ministry, death, burial and resurrection, ascension and exaltation. John 1:29.

This Ethiopian Enuch became the first baptized believer of Africa.

"The Spirit said . . ." vs. 29. The Acts of the Holy Spirit.

Philip preaches from Isaiah, chpater 53, the greatest Messianic revelation in all the Old Testament Prophets.

The Ethiopian is baptized in water. vs. 36. Believing with all his heart, there was nothing to hinder his obedience to this ordinance. They went "down into the water." Immersion, not sprinkling.

Philip experiences supernatural transport, as the Spirit of the Lord "caught him away." vs. 39-40.

Elijah had such transport at times. I Kings 18:12; II Kings 2:16.
Philip had this experience also.
The Church will be caught away in the appointed time. I Thessalonians 4:17.
It is significant of the Eagle-wing power of Holy Spirit translation.
Miraculous transport.
There are no 'iron or bamboo curtains' that God cannot get through.

Philip evangelized in the Cities until he came to Caesarea. vs. 40.
Acts 21:8-9. Here he is found in later years.

As has been truly said: "Philip was the right man in the right place at the right time saying the right thing to the right person." And who organized it? The Holy Spirit! Zechariah 4:6.

## ACTS CHAPTER 9

THE NINETH CHAPTER of Acts centers around the conversion of the Apostle Paul, and brings to attention the man whom the Lord had especially chosen to bring the Gospel to the Gentiles, once the Apostle Peter had opened the door of Faith.

a. **Saul — The Destroyer.** vs. 1-2.

Saul was one of the main leaders in the persecution of the Early Church. Under his leadership, men and women were committed to prison. Acts 7:58; 8:1-4; 9:1-2.

"The corn of wheat to multiply,
Must fall into the ground and die." John 12:14.

Consider who Saul was. Philippians 3:1-7.

1. Circumcised the 8th day. The Covenant of Circumcision.
2. Of the stock of Israel. Pure Hebrew origin.
3. Of the Tribe of Benjamin. Of Rachel, not Jacob's handmaid.
4. A Hebrew of the Hebrews. Not half-caste.
5. Touching the Law — A Pharisee. The straitest sect.
   Acts 22:3; 23:6; 26:5.
6. Concerning zeal — persecuting the Church. Acts 22:3-12; Galatians 1:13-14.
7. Touching the righteousness of the Law — blameless. Externally righteous. A morally righteous man.
8. A Tent-maker. Acts 18:3.
9. Also had a Roman Citizenship. Acts 22:28.
   His name reveals his nature. Saul means "Destroyer."

Here we see Saul with letters of authority from the Priests to slaughter and persecute and imprison the Disciples, and bring them to death.
Thus fulfilling Mark 13:9-13; John 16:1-4.

b. **The People of "The WAY."** vs. 2.

It is worthy to notice the use of this expression "The Way," as seen in the Book of Acts.
The Early Church believers were known as people of "The Way." (Greek.) Refer to Acts 9:2; 18:26; 19:9, 23; 22:4; 24:14, 22; 16:17; 18:25; 26:13; 9:17, 27.

1. In Genesis 3:22, 23, "The Way" to the Tree of Life was barred by the Cherubim and Flaming Sword.
2. In Exodus 26:31-33, "The Way" into the Holiest of All was barred by the Cherubim inwrought in the Veil.
3. At Calvary, God rent the Veil from top to bottom, and "The Way" was made manifest by the Eternal Godhead in the Atonement at the Cross. Matthew 27:50-51.
4. Paul tells us that Jesus Christ's 'flesh' is a NEW and LIVING WAY, and now we have access into the Holiest of All, by the Blood of Jesus. Hebrews 9:6-11. Christ is the New Tabernacle, the New Temple, the New Priesthood. He is The Way to God, by His own Body and Blood.

5. He, Himself declared "I AM THE WAY, The Truth, The Life." John 14:1, 6. The Way is a Person. HE is The Way. All other ways of mankind lead to destruction. He is The Truth. Outside of Him is deception. He is The Life. Outside of Him is death!
   He is The New and Living Way. He became this through His death and Resurrection. Hebrews 8:8; 10:20.
   The Resurrection is God's Seal upon His Son.
   The Rent Veil is God's Sign that The Way is now open into His eternal presence, through Blood Atonement of the Lamb of God.

This was the glorious truth involved in calling the Early Disciples "The People of THE WAY."

Judaism carried on the form in the Temple, declaring The Way was still closed. For 1500 years the Veil testified that this was so. None dared enter without Blood.

God's testimony of the Rent Veil signifies that The Way is open, and The Way to God is through Christ.

No wonder they were called "The People of the Way."

c. **Saul apprehended of Christ.** vs. 3-9.

There are three accounts of Saul's conversion to Christ.
Acts 9:3-9; 22:1-21; 26:1-8. The most prominent points are noted.

1. The LIGHT from heaven, at MIDDAY, above the brightness of the sun.
   There is only one bright light that exceeds that of the Sun and that is the GLORY of the Risen Christ.
   Revelation 1:13-17; Matthew 17:1-6; Mark 9:2-7; Luke 9:28-35.
   It is the Glory of the Father upon His Son. John 17:1, 5, 22-24.
   The SON (SUN) Glory!
   The outshining of the Glorified Son of Man. Hebrews 1:2-3; 2:9.

2. Hears a Voice. Revelation 1:17; John 18:1-6.
   As they fell to the ground at the sound of His Voice, 'I AM,' in the Garden, so Saul falls to the ground here.
   The travellers with him heard the voice, saw the light, but did not hear the actual words spoken to Saul.
   Compare John 12:28-29.

3. Saul was persecuting Christ. "Why persecutes thou ME?"
   Christ was suffering affliction, persecution, and prison, etc., in the members of His Body.
   Note Colossians 1:24; I Corinthians 8:11-12; Matthew 25:31-46. "As much as Saul did it to the least of the Brethren, he was doing it to Christ."
   The spiritual and mystical union of Christ and His Church is seen here. Luke 10:16; Ephesians 5:30.

4. Saul acknowledges Christ's LORDship.
   "Who art thou LORD?"
   Saul recognized it was a Divine visitation, supernatural. He believed it was the LORD God of the Old Testament, who had appeared to Moses in the Burning Bush. Exodus 3:1-3, 14-15.
   The Jehovah of the Old Covenant.
   Imagine his amazement when 'the Voice' answered "I am JESUS whom thou persecutest."

The despised, hated and crucified Nazarene; but now, the risen ascended and glorified Son of God. The very One Stephen saw in his death and martyrdom. Acts 7:55-56, 59; 22:19-20.

Jesus of Nazareth was all He claimed to be. He was the incarnate Son of God, Deity made flesh, the Messiah of God. Crucified of men, raised by God, and glorified to the Throne of the Father, from whence He had poured forth the Promised Holy Spirit.
The revelation dawned upon Saul concerning the LORD JESUS! Colossians 3:17.

5. God called twice to Abraham (Genesis 22:11,) twice to Moses (Exodus 3:4,) twice to Samuel (I Samuel 3:10,) and here the Lord Jesus calls twice to Saul. It was the ONE Lord. The Name of Deity. Not just a mere Title, but the Name of God in redemptive power. Deuteronomy 6:4. The moment Saul called Jesus 'LORD' he was born again. I Corinthians 12:1-3.

6. Submission in the body of Christ.
"What wilt Thou have me do, Lord?" Saul now submits to the LORD Jesus, even as unto the LORD God.
As an Apostle he could say he had seen the Lord. I Corinthians 9:1; 15:8. It is evident from Acts 9:17, 27 and 22:14 with 26:16 that Saul both *saw and heard* the Lord Jesus Himself in His glorified state at the Father's Throne.
Saul now obeys, submitting himself to a member of the Body of Christ, Ananias. Submission and obedience to the Risen Head.

7. Confirmation of His will.
The Lord tells Saul to enter the city and there He would confirm His will to him through another member in the Body.
In Acts 26:16-18, the Lord speaks directly to Saul in vision.
In Acts 22:12-16, the Lord confirms through Ananias that same vision.

d. **Blinded Eyes.** vs. 8. Acts 22:11.

The Glory of that Heavenly Light blinded Saul's eyes. It was a supernatural blindness.
His literal blindness was symbolical of that spiritual blindness upon the heart and mind of the Jew, that blindness in Judaism which is on their hearts in the reading of the Old Testmaent. II Corinthians 3:13-16.
"The Veil is done away in Christ."

Verse 18 tells us that there "fell from his eyes as it had been scales."

Supernatural healing of his eyes. Literally and spiritually. The scales fell from his eyes and he saw CHRIST. Saul, or as he was to become, the Apostle Paul, saw Christ in all the Old Testament Scriptures, in the Law, the Psalms and the Prophets. Luke 24:27, 44-46.

What a contrast! The Saul who entered into Damascus a few moments before as a proud, zealous, bigoted and murderous Pharisee is now a silent, blindly-led, submissive Christian!

e. **Three Days and Three Nights.** vs. 9.

Saul fasted 3 days and 3 nights. This identified him with the 3 days and nights of Calvary's Atonement. Matthew 12:39-40.
A total fast, from food and drink.
This was the foundation of Saul's ministry.

Note also these other 3 days in Scripture, all of which point to that which pertains to the foundation of our salvation, even the 3 days of the Atonement. Genesis 22:4; Exodus 3:18; 15:22-27.

f. **The Disciple Ananias.** vs. 10-18.

As the Lord prepared both Philip and the Ethiopian, working at both ends and bringing them together in His way and time, so He does the same here. Saul and Ananias — both prepared by visions by the same Lord.

In verse 13, we have the first use in Acts of the word 'saints' as spoken concerning the Christians.

g. **The Name.** vs. 14-16.

Consider the emphasis on "The Name" on these verses, once Saul had been apprehended of Christ.

1. He called upon the Name. To invoke in prayer or worship, even as Old Testament Saints "called on the Name of the Lord (God.)" I Corinthians 1:2; Acts 9:21. "This Name."
2. Saul was a chosen vessel to bear My Name. II Timothy 2:20-21.
   A Vessel unto honour.
3. Chosen to suffer for His Name's sake. He who had caused others to suffer for that Name would now suffer for that Name himself.
4. Calling upon the Name. In water baptism. Acts 22:16; Romans 6:3-4.
   This Name was also called (invoked) upon him in Baptism.
   The Name of the Godhead. Matthew 28:19.
5. Preached boldly in the Name. 9:27, 29.

   Saul was willing to live and die for the Name of the Lord Jesus.

h. **Apostolic Ministry.** vs. 15.

Ananias confirms Saul's Ministry. Saul would be a witness to:

1. The Gentiles. Apostle to the Gentiles. ) Acts, chapters
2. The Kings. ) 13 to 28 deal with
3. The Children of Israel. ) that fulfilment.

How touching and comforting it must have been to Saul, as in verse 17 he hears Ananias say, "Brother Saul, the LORD . . . Jesus . . ." Confirming the same Name upon which he, himself had called on the Damascus Road.

Thus Saul is converted, healed of blindness, baptized in water and filled with the Holy Spirit, and is ministered to in the laying on of hands relative to ministry for his life.

No wonder he said he was "A pattern to them that should believe." I Timothy 1:6.

i. **Saul at Damascus 'certain days.'** vs. 19, 20-22.

In these verses we find that Saul began preaching that JESUS was indeed the very Christ, proving by comparison of the Old Testament prophecies and types, and by the facts concerning the history of Jesus of Nazareth that He indeed was the exact fulfilment of all these Scriptures, that He was the very Son of God.

Not only the Son of Man, but the Son of God. This title or phrase is especially peculiar to the Apostle John and also to Paul in their writings. It involves His Deity, Virgin Birth and Sinlessness.

j. **Saul in Arabia.** vs. 23.

In connection with this verse and the Epistle to the Galatians, we find evidence that Saul went to Arabia between verses 22 and 23 of Acts 9.

"The many days" cover this time-period.

| | |
|---|---|
| Galatians 1:15-16. | Saul's apprehension of Christ on the Damascus Road. Acts 9:1-18. Then 'certain days' at Damascus preaching Christ. Acts 9:19-22. |
| Galatians 1:17. | Journey to Arabia. The 'many days' of Acts 9:23. |
| Galatians 1:17. | His return again to Damascus. Then came the 'basket' Episode and his escape. Acts 9:23-25; II Corinthians 11:33. |
| Galatians 1:18-19. | His journey after 3 years to Jerusalem, to see Peter, and James only. Abode there 15 days. Acts 9:26-29; 22:17-21. |
| Galatians 1:20-21. | Goes to the regions of Syria and Cilicia. Acts 9:30-31, then back through Caesarea to Tarsus, his own home town. |

It is from Tarsus that Saul is bid to come to Antioch by Barnabas, from whence Saul's great missionary journeys center. Acts 11:25.

| | |
|---|---|
| Galatians 2:1-21. | Then 14 years later, Saul (Paul) goes up to Jerusalem over the dispute concerning circumcision and the Gentiles having to keep the Law of Moses. Acts, chapter 15. |

The information as given above is briefly covered in Acts 9:23-30.
Barnabas, "Son of Consolation" was a real blessing to Saul as he took him and introduced him to the Apostles at Jerusalem in his short visit there. Later on, God would knit the hearts of these two men together and separate them to the Ministry unto the Gentiles.

k. **The Church at Rest.** vs. 31.

Then had the Churches (Literal Church) rest. ONE Church, yet having Local Assemblies in the Cities and Villages.
Note the words in the verse here.

| | | |
|---|---|---|
| **Rest** | — | Matthew 11:28 |
| **Edified** | — | I Corinthians 14:12 |
| **Walking** | — | I John 2:6 |
| **Comfort** | — | John 14:16 |
| **Multiplied** | — | Genesis 1:28 |

**SUMMARY:**

In relation to the Apostle Paul it is seen that he holds a unique place among the Apostles of the New Testament, and it is possible that his name will be in the Twelve Foundations of the Holy City. Revelation 21:14.

Matthias was chosen by lot under the prayer of the 11 Apostles in the Upper Room in Acts, chapter 1.
Saul, or Paul, is chosen by the Lord direct from heaven, in vision and voice as seen in Acts, chapter 9.

Matthias is recognized as of the Twelve (1) Before Pentecost, Acts 1:26.
(2) At Pentecost, Acts 2:14.
(3) After Pentecost, Acts 6:2.
and even by (4) The Apostle Paul, I Corinthians 15:5.

Paul is seen as a remarkable prophetic "Pattern" of the End-times and Apostolic Ministry of the Last Days, which will bring the Church unto perfection and maturity. I Timothy 1:16; I Corinthians 15:8-10.

He says "Am not I an Apostle, have not I seen the Lord?" I Corinthians 9:1-2. He says, "Paul an Apostle, not of man, neither by man, but by Jesus Christ, and God the Father." Galatians 1:1.

Paul said he felt as if he were one born out of due season!

The revelation that Paul was given in relation to the Church is unique to his Apostolic Ministry.

In Arabia, undoubtedly Paul "received of the Lord" that which he delivered unto the churches. I Corinthians 11:23; Galatians 1:11-12.

Compare Moses of the Old Testament and the revelation and pattern that was given to him for "The Church in the Wilderness" (Acts 7:38,) and the Law Covenant, the Aaronic Priesthood, Mt. Sinai in Arabia, and that revelation which was given to the Apostle Paul concerning the New Testament Church, the Body of Christ, the Priesthood of all believers in the New Covenant, in that same desert of Arabia. Galatians 1:17.

Another great comparison is that pertaining to the Old Testament King Saul and the New Testament Apostle Saul (Paul.)
Both came from the same Tribe of Benjamin, both had signs and wonders by the Spirit of God, both began their experience with God in a 3-day foundation, but one ends up losing the crown, while the other one gained the crown.
It seems as if God made up in the Saul of the New Testament what was terribly forfeited in the Old Testament Saul.

Saul, "the destroyer," now becomes Paul, "the worker, or, little." The change of name was indeed a change of nature.
The old name was the old nature. The new name was significant of the new and Divine nature of Jesus Christ manifest.

(For the Student, we suggest the following outline worthwhile searching into, for the Old Testament Type becomes prophetical of the New Testament fulfilment, and it shows forth that Paul who "laid the foundation" will have his name in the Twelve Foundations of the Holy City, the New and Heavenly Jerusalem. I Corinthians 3:10-11. Revelation 21:14; Ephesians 2:20-22.)

This Section is taken from Rev. W. W. Patterson's "General Bible Themes."

**Truth as Revealed in Type and Filfilment**

| **O. T. Type and Prophecy** | | **N. T. Antitype and Fulfilment** |
|---|---|---|
| GOD revealed to *Natural* Israel | — | GOD revealed to *Spiritual* Israel |

| | | |
|---|---|---|
| The Church in the Wilderness | — | The Church in the New Testament, |
| Acts 7:38 | — | Church of the Firstborn. Hebrews 12:23. |
| Exodus 3:15-16 The LORD GOD of | — | Matthew 3:16-17; 28:19. In THE NAME |
| your fathers | — | of |
| (1. Abraham | — | (1. The Father, and of |
| The God of (2. Isaac and | — | Godhead (2. The Son, and of |
| (3. Jacob | — | (3. The Holy Spirit I John 5:7 |
| The *12 Sons* of Jacob. Genesis 48. | — | The *12 Apostles.* Matthew 10:1-4. |
| Then the *70 souls* of Jacob's | — | The *70 sent* forth by Christ. |
| house who went into Egypt. | — | Luke 10:1. |
| Genesis 46:27. | | |
| Then the *innumerable host* of | — | The *inumerable* host of the |
| Natural Israel. Genesis 22:17. | — | Redeemed, Spiritual Israel. Rev. 7:9 |
| "As the sand upon the seashore." | — | "As the stars for multitude." |
| Hebrews 11:12; Romans 9:27. | — | Hebrews 11:12. |
| Rueben, *one of the 12 sons* of | — | Judas, *one of the 12 Apostles* |
| Jacob, sinned, and lost or | — | sinned, and lost his Bishoprick. |
| forfeited his Birthright. | — | John 6:71; Matthew 26:21-25; 47-49; |
| Genesis 35:22; 49:4; I Chronicles 5:1. | — | 27:3-5; Acts 1:16-20. |
| Jacob adopted the two sons of | — | The New Testament 'adopts' two |
| Joseph, | — | Apostles, |
| 1. *Manasseh,* the elder, | — | 1. *Matthias,* chosen by lot, |
| to become a great people. | — | Acts 1:21-26; 2:14; 6:2; |
| Genesis 48:19a. | — | I Corinthians 15:5. |
| 2. *Ephraim,* the younger, to | — | 2. *Paul,* chosen by the Lord, |
| become a multitude of | — | and becomes the Apostle to the |
| Nations. Genesis 48:19b. | — | multitude of Nations, Gentiles. |
| | | Acts 9:1-15; 22:6-21; 26:12-23. |
| Ephraim is *set before* Manasseh, | — | Paul is *set before* Matthias and takes |
| and receives a *Double Portion.* | — | the lead in Acts. |
| Genesis 48:22; Jeremiah 31:9. | — | Receives a *Double Portion* of Spirit. |
| Ephraim now becomes God's | — | Portion of the *Firstborn.* |
| *Firstborn.* | — | II Kings 2:9. |
| Ephraim is listed amongst the | — | Paul's name is thus possibly (??) in |
| Twelve Tribes. Tribal Name. | — | the Foundations of the City. |
| This made 13 Tribes in Israel | — | Matthias and Paul make 13 Apostles. |

(Unquote.) *Selah* — Pause, meditate and reflect!

The Author

**Ministry of Peter at Lydda and Saron.** Acts 9:32-35.

Peter came down to the Saints (Literal "Holy ones, set apart, or separate ones") at Lydda. All believers are called to be Saints.

Here at Lydda, a lame man is healed. The power of the Name of Jesus once again manifested as further proof that the Risen Christ was confirming His Word with signs following in His Church. Mark 16:17-20.

The result? Two Cities "turn to the Lord," that is, turning from the power of Satan and the Kingdom of Darkness unto the power of Christ and the Kingdom of Light.

**Ministry of Peter at Joppa.** Acts 9:36-43.

At Joppa we see the power of resurrection life. Here we have the first record of any Apostle raising the dead. Matthew 10:8.

It is worthy to note that the Disciples here sent for Peter, the Apostle, to come. Why? Because this was distinctly associated in Apostolic Ministry in the Will of God.
Apparently these Disciples did not have the power to raise the dead of themselves, or of their own will.

Resurrection life is manifested against the power of Death.

Dorcas as a Disciple had a ministry of helps, of good works, of alms and mercy. "Which she did."

Peter puts all forth from the room, even as Jesus did (Matthew 9:25,) kneels down and prays concerning the Will of God, and then having obtained it, speaks the Word of Faith.
So did Elijah when he raised the dead. I Kings 17:19.
So did Elisha when he raised the dead. II Kings 4:33.

This was the Gift of Miracles in operation.

"Many believed in the Lord." Not all! Every healing and miracle in the Acts was a powerful demonstration of the reality of the Resurrected Christ, the ascended Son of God, Jesus of Nazareth.

There is no greater power than the power of Satan in death. But He who is the resurrection and the life conquered death! John 11:46-48; 12:9-11. Ephesians 1:18-20.

Jesus said, "Though one were raised from the dead, yet some will not believe." Luke 16:30-31.

Dorcas can also be viewed as being typical of the Church in her experience of "Resurrection Life."

## ACTS CHAPTER 10

ACTS CHAPTER 10 begins the fourth step in the Commission of Christ as given in Acts 1:8.
The Gospel was to be taken to the whole world in the following order:

| | | |
|---|---|---|
| Begin at Jerusalem, | ) | Acts, chapter 2 |
| Judea, | ) | Acts, chapters 7 to 9 |
| Samaria, and then to the | ) | Acts, chapter 8 |
| Uttermost part of the earth. | ) | Acts, chapters 10 to 28 |

Here we see the Church among the Jews, then the transition period from the Jews to the Churches established among the Gentiles.

In these Chapters THE DOOR OF FAITH is opened to the Gentiles.

It is necessary to consider some brief facts concerning God's plan and purpose in the Dispensations of Time as regards to the Gentile Nations, for, Acts, chapters 10 and 11 give a complete departure from all that has been so far, as the Lord by His Spirit brings the Gentiles into the Mystery Body of Christ, composed of both Jew and Gentile. Ephesians 2:11-22; 3:1-6.

1. The first use of the word "Gentiles." Genesis 10:1-5. After the Flood, at the Tower of Babel, we have the Origin of all Nations, both Hebrew and Gentile Nations. Genesis, chapters 10 and 11.
   All the earth is divided according to the 3 Sons of Noah.

| | | | | |
|---|---|---|---|---|
| | ( Shem | The Hebrew or Chosen Israel Nation | ) | |
| Noah | ( Ham | The Servant Races | ) | Gentiles |
| | ( Japheth | The Enlarged Races | ) | |

From the call of Abraham through to the First Coming of Jesus Christ, God dealt specifically with the CHOSEN HEBREW NATION — not with the Gentile Nation.

To this Chosen Nation was entrusted:

1. The Sacred Writings, the Infallible Scriptures.
2. The Covenants, and the Promises therein.
3. The Giving of the Law, and the Shekinah Glory.
4. And mainly, the Seed Race, through whom Christ THE SEED should be born, according to His humanity. Romans 3:1-2; 9:1-5.

It was through this Nation that the Seed, Christ, should come, and through whom ALL NATIONS of the earth would be blessed and find salvation.

The choice of the Hebrew race was distinctly for the purpose of preserving the Sacred Scriptures, holding the Covenants and Promises, and the preservation of a Seed line from which the Messiah would be born to bless the whole world.

In spite of all these God-given advantages and privileges, the Chosen Nation generally proved to be a failure and became more evil and corrupt than the surrounding Gentile Nations.

Jesus Christ "came unto His own (House) and His own received Him not." John 1:11.

In the Ministry of Christ and the Apostles before the Cross, none were to go to the Gentiles, but only to "the lost sheep of the House of Israel." He forbad them to go into any City of the Gentiles. Matthew 10:5-8.

At odd times, Gentiles did reach over into the Dispensation of Grace, and through faith, received blessing from Christ, which shamed the Chosen Race in their unbelief. Matthew 15:21-28; Luke 7:1-10; John 4:1-27.
This is seen in the healing of the Centurion, the Syrophenecian's daughter and the saving of the Samaritan woman and her witness to her own City.

These examples became a shadow of the coming blessing, response and faith of the Gentiles after the rejection of Jewry and after the death, burial and resurrection of Jesus Christ, with the outpouring of the Holy Spirit upon "all flesh."

Even under the Old Testament, odd Gentiles were blessed in relation to the Chosen Nation, which was the Age of the Law. Luke 4:24-28.

This is evidenced in these incidents:

The City of Nineveh under the Ministry of the Prophet Jonah.
Daniel was a witness in Babylon.
Joseph was a testimony in Egypt.
Elijah and Elisha blessed odd Gentiles.
Ruth and Rahab were Gentiles also, yet through Grace and Faith came into Covenant Blessing in Israel.
Other Gentiles became blessed by the Covenant by the rite of Circumcision and keeping of the Law, as proselytes. Genesis 17:12-13; Exodus 12:48.
Cf. Romans 2:14-15.

2. **Old Testament Prophecies of Blessing on the Gentiles.**

The Prophets foretold the day coming in which the Gentiles would be blessed.
Note expressly these important Scriptures:
Genesis 22:18, "In thy Seed (Christ) shall all nations be blessed."
Galatians 3:8, 14-16, 29, This Seed is Christ and His Church.
Isaiah 11:1-5, 10; 42:1-16; 49:6-12, 22; 54:3; 60:1-5, 11, 16; 61:6-9; 66:19; Jeremiah 16:19; Malachi 1:11.

"I will give Thee (Christ) for a Light to the Gentiles."
"My NAME shall be great among the Gentiles."

3. **New Testament Prophecies of Blessing on the Gentiles.**

"A LIGHT to lighten the Gentiles." Luke 2:32. Jesus, The Light of the world.

"And in HIS NAME shall the Gentiles trust." Matthew 12:18-21.
John 12:20-24; Galatians 3:14; Matthew 28:18-19; Mark 16:17-20; Acts 1:8.

Here the Lord tells them to preach the Gospel to every creature; and to go into all the world discipling all nations, even to the uttermost part of the earth.

It is here in Acts, chapters 10 and 11, and onwards, that a direct movement of the Holy Spirit comes to bring these prophecies to pass upon the Gentiles, through Christ.

Peter the Apostle does not, as yet, realize or understand the full plan of God to include the Gentiles. They do not as yet see the revelation of the BODY OF CHRIST. This distinctive revelation was given to the Apostle Paul, who became the Apostle to THE GENTILES, even as Peter was the Apostle to THE JEWS.

Peter is simply preparing for Paul.
Acts the 9th chapter brings to view the Apostle to the Gentiles, while Acts the 10th chapter shows Peter opening the Door of Faith to the Gentiles which ministry he passes on to Paul to continue.

In Acts 2, Peter uses "The Keys of the Kingdom" to open the Door of Faith to the JEWS.

In Acts 10, Peter uses these same "Keys of the Kingdom" to open the Door of Faith to the GENTILES. Matthew 16:18-19.

Once the Door was opened, it remains open for Paul to step into and continue the Apostolic Ministry to the Gentiles.

With these important facts before us, let us consider Peter's ministry here as he is sent to the Gentiles to open the Gospel Door.

a. **Cornelius — The Gentile.** vs. 1-8.

The Lord gives to Cornelius a Vision.
Cornelius is a Centurian of the Italian Band.
Though he is a Gentile, he is a devout man, one that feared God with all his house, a giver of alms, and a man who prayed to God alway.
He is a proselyte of the Jewish Religion and Faith.

God works both ends by His Holy Spirit once again. God works on the Jew (Peter) and upon the Gentile (Cornelius) through the means of two visions.

The Angel in Vision tells Cornelius and the necessary details for his full obedience. He told Cornelius the Apostle's name, the City where he was lodging, the occupation of the host, and the street address.

However, the Angel did not minister to Cornelius the Word of the Gospel, the Words of Salvation. I Peter 1:12; Hebrews 1:14.

Angels are but ministering spirits sent forth to them who are heirs of Salvation. God reserved the Word of Salvation to be spoken through the man Peter to Cornelius. Cornelius was immediately obedient to the Vision.

b. **Peter — the Jew.** vs. 9-20.

The Lord gives to Peter a Vision.
Peter, the Apostle with the Keys of the Kingdom.
In this Vision he sees a sheet let down from heaven, touching the four corners of the earth, having clean and unclean beasts in it.

Four is the number of earth, world-wide, universal number.
This Vision was repeated 3 times. The perfect testimony of God in the number three. Genesis 41:32; Deuteronomy 19:15; 17:6.

The common and unclean were about to be cleansed by God.

The interpretation and revelation was deeper than the Ceremonial Law of Meats, as in Leviticus the 11th chapter. Compare Hebrews 13:9 and Colossians 2:16-17.
Animals, Birds, etc., are symbolic of the various Gentile Nations before God, as also the Hebrew Nation.
Note, Daniel 7:1-10; Revelation 13:1-2; Daniel 8:1-7, etc.
All Nations, Hebrew and Gentile, symbolized today by various Animals or Birds.
God only can cleanse the common and unclean Nations.

Verse 19: "The Spirit said . . . I have sent them." It was the work of the Holy Spirit fulfilling the Word of the Son of God. The Spirit and the Word working together as one. The Holy Spirit is seen at work in the earth building the Church, the Mystical and Spiritual Body of Christ; Locally and Universally!

c. **Peter goes to Caesarea.** vs. 21-33.

The Holy Spirit has been leading Peter beyond the sectarian walls of Judaism into the revelation of the Body of Christ.

The Spirit brought in the Jews.
The Spirit brought in the Ethiopian.
The Spirit brought in the Samaritans.
Now the Spirit is bringing in the Gentiles, baptizing them all into THE ONE BODY. I Corinthians 12:13.

The Gentiles are being grafted into "The Good Olive Tree" (Romans 11) by faith in Christ.

Here Peter the Jew (of the 'Clean Nation') came under the same roof with a Tanner and the Gentiles ('the Unclean Nations'.)

Peter refuses the worship of Cornelius. Both were but men! The Romans worshipped Caesar as God. This was deification of a man. But Peter would not accept worship of any man.

Here the Acts of the Holy Spirit are in operation as He works on both ends, bringing Peter and Cornelius together.

Verse 30. Cornelius tells Peter and his company that he was fasting four days ago, and at the 9th hour he received the Vision giving him the heavenly information required.

The "4 Days" is typical of the 4 Days of the Lord, or, 4000 years, from Adam to Christ, at the end of which the Word and the Spirit comes to the Gentiles to take out of them a people for His Name. Acts 15:14.
"A Day unto the Lord as a Thousand Years."
Note these several illustrations of the "Four Days." Exodus 12:3-6; Genesis 2:17; II Peter 3:8; Psalms 90:4; John 11:39.

It was at the 9th hour, or 3 p.m. The time of the Evening Sacrifice. God always works in connection with the Atonement and the Sacrifice of His Only Son.

Verse 32. Connect with Acts 11:14. "Words by which we can be saved." God uses "words" to bring us Salvation.

d. **Peter's Sermon to the Gentiles.** vs. 34-43.

Peter perceives (has spiritual insight into) that God is above all Nations, and looks upon the heart.
Racial, Religious and Social prejudices are all dissolved in this fact. God is no respector of persons, or faces, whether Jew or Gentile.

Pride of Race )
Price of Face )
Pride of Place ) All cease to exist in the Body of Christ.
Pride of Grace )

The Ministry of the Word covered the main points in the Life of Jesus. It covers Messiah's Water Baptism in Jordan, His Ministry, His Death, Burial and Resurrection.
He is spoken of as being the fulfilment of the Prophet's utterances.

"God (The Father) anointed Jesus of Nazareth (The Son) with the Holy Spirit (The Spirit.)" Acts 10:38. The Godhead involved in the whole plan of Redemption. I John 2:20, 27; Luke 4:18-21.

| i.e. | The Father | — | The Anointer. Luke 4:18-21 |
|---|---|---|---|
| | The Son | — | The Anointed. Acts 10:38. |
| | The Holy Spirit | — | The Anointing. I John 2:20-27. |

There was utter dependence upon the Holy Spirit to make Christ real to the heart. Remission of sins comes through believing in and upon His Name.

e. **The Sovereign Outpouring of the Holy Spirit on the Gentiles.** vs. 44-48.

God promised to pour out His Spirit "upon all flesh." Joel 2:28.

The Holy Spirit had only been poured out upon the select in the Hebrew Nation in Old Testament Times; Prophets, Priests and Kings!

In the Book of Acts, we have two Sovereign Outpourings of the Spirit.

The first was upon the Jews in Acts 2:1-4.
The next is upon the Gentiles in Acts 10:44.

All other 'outpourings' were through Ministries in the Church, and by the Laying on of Hands.
Man baptizes with water. Acts 1:5.
Jesus Christ is the Baptizer with the Holy Spirit.

When Peter was interrupted by the Outpouring of the Spirit upon the Gentiles, he realized that he could not refuse them Water Baptism, for one was the pointer to, or completion of the other. Matthew 3:11.

If it was good enough of the Lord Jesus to baptize the Gentiles in the Holy Spirit, then it was good enough for Peter to baptize them in Water!

How did they know the Gentiles had received the Spirit? "They heard them speak with tongues and magnify God."

Peter commanded them to be baptized in water. Water Baptism was not "an optional" in the Early Church. It was necessary to full obedience!

**SUMMARY:**

Acts, chapter 10 is the New Testament revelation and antitypical fulfilment of that which is typified in Genesis, Chapters 6 and 7.
The following is a remarkable comparison between these two occasions:

| O. T. Type and Prophecy | | N. T. Antitype and Fulfilment |
|---|---|---|
| Noah — Preacher of Righteousness | — | Peter, Preacher of Righteousness |
| The 3-storied Ark of Salvation | — | The Triune God – The One God |
| or Triune Ark | — | of Salvation |
| The 7 of each clean animals taken out | — | The House of Israel and Judah |
| The 2 of each unclean animal taken out | — | The Gentiles taken out |
| The Word of Preaching | — | The Word of the Gospel |
| The Holy Spirit striving and moving | — | The Holy Spirit moving and falling |
| Animals enter by the Door into the Ark | — | Jew and Gentile enter by the Door of Faith in Christ. |
| Animals all one in the Ark | — | Jew and Gentile — one in Christ |
| Subdued natures, food for all | — | Divine nature — Spiritual food |
| The end of Ungodly Flesh | — | The End of the Flesh-life of sin |
| The Flood Waters of Baptism | — | The Waters of Baptism for all |

## ACTS CHAPTER 11

THIS CHAPTER IS a continuation of the events of the previous Chapter.

a. **Peter's Testimony at Jerusalem concerning the Gentile Visitation.** vs. 1-18.

The full revelation and distinction between LAW AND GRACE has not yet been given to the Early Church.

There was still much contention over the two great Ceremonial Laws, Circumcision and Clean and Unclean Meats.
This is dealt with particularly in Acts 15.

When Peter arrives back in Jerusalem they who were of the Circumcision contended with him for going to the Gentiles.

Peter testifies to the fact that it was not him but THE HOLY SPIRIT Himself who had led him to go to the Gentiles, and settled for him the whole matter of the Gentiles coming into blessing in the Gospel.

It was the Spirit who gave the Vision to Peter. vs. 4-10.
It was the Spirit who sent the Angel to Cornelius. vs. 11.
It was the Spirit who told Peter that He had sent the men.
The Spirit told Peter to go with the men, doubting nothing.
The Spirit Himself fell on the Gentiles as they heard Peter preach the Word. vs. 12-13.
The Holy Spirit had manifested Himself in other tongues, exactly as He had on the Day of Pentecost in the Upper Room Disciples. vs. 15-16.

It was the Spirit Himself who had overruled Peter's racial, religious, social pride, prejudice and distinctions. The Spirit made no distinction; therefore why should Peter make distinction?

The Gentiles received "words" whereby they could be saved. vs. 14.
Romans 10:17. Faith cometh by hearing the Word of God.

"The Spirit fell on them as on us at the beginning." vs. 15.
God's Pattern and Standard.

The Gentiles received "the like gift." Verse 17. Compare Acts 2:38-39.

God granted the Gentiles repentance unto life. Verse 18. John 3:16. Life out of death.

Peter was to find out the truth that "IN CHRIST there was neither Jew nor Gentile." Galatians 3:28; Romans 10:12; 15:9, 16; Acts 17:26; I Corinthians 12:13, 27; Romans 9:24.
The middle wall of partition had been broken down at Calvary, and God was making of both Jew and Gentile ONE NEW MAN! Ephesians 2:12-20.

Racial and National barriers cease to exist in Christ, and in those who truly discern the Body of Christ.
Jew and Gentile are washed in

The One Blood, of

The One Saviour, and baptized together into

The One Name of the Lord Jesus Christ, and baptized

By One Spirit into

The One Body of Christ. All are one in Him!

"Whether we be Jews or Gentiles, all are baptized in ONE Body." I Corinthians 12:13.

b. **Persecution scatters.** vs. 19-21.

The disciples who had been scattered abroad preached the Word everywhere they went.
To scatter the saints was to scatter the Seed of the Word. Matthew 13:38; Luke 8:11.

Note the progression in these Chapters.
In Acts 9, the Apostle to the Gentiles is apprehended of Christ.
In Acts 10, the Door of Faith is opened to the Gentiles under Peter's Ministry. Here in Acts 11:22, we are brought to Antioch, from which the great Missionary work to the Gentiles spreads. It is here that Paul comes into Ministry and the founding of the Gentile Churches, beginning from the City of Antioch.

The Word increases, and many Grecians are brought to Christ as foretold in John 12:20-24; Luke 2:32; John 7:35.

The Church at Antioch was planted there by unnamed and unknown disciples who were scattered in the persecution.

As the first Chapters in Acts center around the Apostle Peter and the Church in Jerusalem and its activities, so the remainder of Acts centers around the Apostle Paul and the Church at Antioch and its activities in reaching the Gentiles.

c. **Barnabas sent to Antioch.** vs. 22-26.

Note — Acts 4:36-47; 9:27. The Church at Jerusalem sends forth Barnabas to go to Antioch.

At Antioch Barnabas recognizes the Grace of God, and exhorts the believers to cleave to the Lord.
Under his ministry much people were added to the Lord.

1. Acts 2:41 Added
2. Acts 2:47 Added to the Church
3. Acts 5:14; 11:24 Added to the Lord

One cannot be added to the Church unless added to the Lord. The Church is the Fulness (completeness) of Him who filleth all in all. In this way the Body of Christ grew and increased as members were added to the Lord and baptized into the One Body, and thus Head and Body were one, each being the complement and completeness of the other. Ephesians 1:22-23.

Verse 23. The believers had purpose of heart.

The character of Barnabas is described in verses 23 and 24. What he was and what he did.

He was a good man, full of the Holy Spirit and faith.
Under his ministry the believers were added to the Lord.

It is from Antioch that Barnabas goes to Tarsus, Saul's home town, to seek him out and bring him to Antioch. Barnabas, undoubtedly by the Spirit, realizes Paul's Ministry to the Gentiles was needed here and goes to seek him out. Acts 9:30.

It shows a wonderful cooperation and recognition of Ministries in the Church, the Body of Christ.

It was Barnabas, "Son of Consolation," who introduced Paul (Saul) to the Apostles at Jerusalem, and it is Barnabas who brings Saul to the Church at Antioch here. Together they teach the Word, and the hand of the Lord was with them. Matthew 28:18-20.
The believers needed to be taught the Word of the Lord.

d. **Disciples called "Christians at Antioch".** vs. 26.

In the New Testament the believers are known by various designations.

They were called "Disciples." About 250 times.
They were called People of "The Way." Acts 9:2, etc.
They were called "The Sect of the Nazarene." Acts 24:5.
Here they are called "Christians." Acts 11:26; 15:17; 26:28; Isaiah 65:15; I Peter 4:16.

The NEW NAME for the believers.

The COMPANION BIBLE comments on this verse saying: "Though the Name may have been given first by the Gentiles in mockery, the usage of the word by the Holy Spirit indicates that *its real origin was Divine.*
The Jews could not have given the Name. "Christos" was to them a sacred word." Unquote. (Emphasis — The Author).

This Name was given at Antioch, not at Jerusalem.

It was The Presence and Anointing of the Holy Spirit upon Jesus of Nazareth that made him The CHRIST. The Anointed One! The Risen Head of the Church. And it is that same Presence and Anointing of the Holy Spirit in and upon the Disciples that made them CHRIST–ians, or Anointed Ones.
The Body of Christ. The Body of the Anointed One.
Hence the Church is called the Body of CHRIST. I Corinthians 12:12, 27.

The very Name "Christ" involves the Eternal Godhead in the Anointing upon the Church.
(Refer to Notes on "The Name of God in Water Baptism.")

e. **The Prophet Agabus at Antioch.** vs. 27-30.

This is the first mention of Prophets in the Book of Acts.
The Ministry of the Prophets (plural); not just one Prophet. I Corinthians 14:29-30.

There was a distinctive Ministry of the Prophets in the Early Church.

Here Agabus, one of the Prophets, signified (spoke by a sign from the Spirit) that there would be a famine in the whole earth. The Holy Spirit spoke through the Prophet in some specific and definite manner.
The Prophet foretold! Not just forthtelling. The Spirit caused it to be recorded that "It came to pass."

The test of a true Prophet is found in Deuteronomy 18:21-22; Jeremiah 28:9.

The Ministry of the Prophet is dealt with more specifically under comments on Acts 13:1, where the difference between Old Testament and New Testament Prophets is noted.

The practical effect and result of the prophecy was relief for the needs of the Church in Judea.

In verse 30, we have the first mention of the word "Elders" in the Acts. The Ministry of Elders is dealt with in Acts 14:23. It is worthy to note that the word and ministry of Elders is always in the plural. It is never used in the singular as regarding the Church or Local Churches.

The Ministry of the Elder is as old as the human race, and particularly involved the main duties of ruling and teaching.

The words "Bishop, Presbyter, or Elder" all refer to the same Office in the Church, as also the word "Overseer." These words include the Person, the Ministry, the Office and the Function, each word bringing out a facet of the same Office which the Lord set in the Church. I Timothy 5:17.

Refer to notes on Acts 14:23 on the Ministry and Qualifications of Elders.

## ACTS CHAPTER 12

ACTS CHAPTER TWELVE brings us to the close of the scene of the Ministry of Peter, the Apostle to the Circumcision, and upon the main activities of the Church at Jerusalem.

Only once again is Peter mentioned in the Book of Acts, in Acts 15:7-14, which is the Council gathering of the Church at Jerusalem over the matters of Circumcision and the keeping of the Law of Moses in relation to the coming in of the Gentiles.

The Church at Jerusalem only comes in view twice more, and this is over the Gentiles and Circumcision as noted above, and then in Paul's final visit and rejected Testimony there in Acts 22.

Chapters 1 to 12 have particularly concerned Peter's Ministry, and Jerusalem as being the center from which the Gospel goes forth to Judea and Samaria. Acts 1:8.

Now Acts, chapters 13 to 28 cover the Ministry of Paul from Antioch, which becomes the center from which all Gentile Churches are founded and the Gospel goes to the Uttermost parts of the Earth. Acts 1:8.

The Church at Jerusalem degenerates over the years from the early Glory into Legalistic, Pharisaical Religionism, becoming more and more Sectarian minded and bigoted, until God smashes the whole of that system in A. D. 70.

The Church at Antioch enters into the Glory of Christ and blessing unto the Uttermost parts of the then known world.

a. **Political Opposition against the Church.** vs. 1-2.

Satan has used Religious opposition against the Church so far. Now it turns to Political opposition. James, the brother of John, is slain by the sword. James is the First Martyr (Acts 1:8. Greek word for "Witness" is "Martyr") among the Twelve Apostles.

It fulfilled Christ's prophetic word to him, given in Matthew 20:20-23.
James indeed "drank of the Cup that Christ did, and was baptized with the Baptism that He was to be baptized with."

b. **Miraculous deliverance of Peter.** vs. 3-19.

Peter is kept in prison in the midst of 16 soldiers. Undoubtedly they had heard of the previous 'escapades' of the Apostles being delivered from prisons by Angels; hence they would take no more 'risks' of such things happening!

The word 'Easter' in verse 4, should properly be "after the Passover". cf. Mark 14:1, 2. This was mistranslated from the Latin. Easter was a Pagan Festival unto the Queen of Heaven. It was Idolatry.

The Feast of Passover and Unleavened Bread was closely linked. Verses 3-4. with Exodus, the 12th chapter.

However, in spite of soldiers and guards, the Angel of the Lord rescues Peter out of prison, causing his chains to fall off, taking him right past the guards outside of the City, where the iron gate opened to them of its own accord.

There are no chains that cannot fall, and there are no iron gates that will not yield to the Lord, when He wills it to be so.

Peter thought it was a vision but realized the reality of this miraculous deliverance when he was past the City gate.

Questions immediately arise here.

Why should Stephen be stoned to death, yet Paul is stoned to death and then miraculously raised up?

Why should Philip be supernaturally transported to witness to one soul, and yet Paul is left in many weary travels for Christ and the Church?

Why should Peter and the Apostles be delivered by Angels out of prison, yet Paul is left to die in prison writing Letters to the Churches which he founded?

Why should God raise Dorcas, a woman, from the dead, and not Stephen?

Why should God let James be beheaded, yet the same night Peter is to be beheaded sends an Angel to deliver him out of that same prison?

The Only answer is that God rules in the heavens and in the earth, and it is His Sovereign will that is being done, in all and above all and through all, and in spite of men and devils.
"All things work together for good, to them that love God and do His will." Romans 8:28; Ephesians 1:5, 9, 11; 6:12; Colossians 1:9; 4:12; Daniel 4:25.

The Early Church surrendered to His Will. We must learn to recognize that God is above all, and to submit to His Sovereign Will.

Surely Peter must have remembered his own boastful words in Luke 22:33, as he went to prison. He was asleep, in peace, when the Angel awoke him and delivered him.

c. **The Believers' Prayer Meeting.** vs. 5, 11-19.

Though unceasing and earnest prayer was made for Peter's deliverance, it is evident that faith was not fully manifest. Why? Because faith is dependent upon the knowledge of God's Will. They did not know whether God willed to deliver Peter or not, or whether God would permit him also to be slain, as was James.

It is impossible to have faith apart from The Word or A Word from God. Romans 10:17.

It was not unbelief, but uncertainty! When Peter came to the Door they thought it was his ghost, and kept on praying for him. Hence when they opened the door and saw him, they were astonished.

All believers manifested faith, whether they were delivered or not. It takes faith to be delivered, and it takes faith when one is not delivered. Hebrews 11:29-31.

The Hebrew children declared this, when they said "Our God is able to deliver, and He will deliver . . . but if not . . . we will not bow." Daniel 3:15-18.

God's Word is His Will and this creates faith. We must submit wholly and unconditionally to God's Sovereign will.

"The Blood of the Martyrs is the Seed of the Church."

The guards were put to death when they found that Peter had disappeared from the prison.

In verse 17, we are told that "Peter departed to another place." This is the last mention of Peter (except for the Jerusalem Council in Acts 15,) and the close of history concerning him, in Acts.

d. **Divine Judgment upon Herod.** vs. 20-25.

Herod, hardened in heart, in spite of the miraculous deliverance of Peter, enthrones himself and receives worship due only to God.

As he sat on his Royal Throne, arrayed in his Royal apparel making a speech, the people acclaim him as 'a god' and not a man. The Angel of the Lord immediately smote him because he did not give God the glory.

Roman Emporers were acknowledged as 'Lord,' ascribing Deity to man. Deification of man. People gave worship to Deified man which belonged only to God.

The same Angel which brought deliverance to Peter smites Herod in wrath. Hebrews 1:14. Life to one, death to the other.

Herod forgot that there was One King in Royal apparel on the Heavenly Throne ruling over all earthly Thrones. Daniel 5:23; I Kings 22:10, 19.

Satan fell because he desired to be "like God." Isaiah 14:12-15.
Man fell because he thought he would be "like God" also Genesis 3:5.

Scripture says that Herod was "eaten of worms." Verse 23.
This is symbolic of "the worm that dieth not." Isaiah 66:24; Mark 9:44-46. It points to that Lake of Fire.

Verse 24. Herod may be eaten of warms, but THE WORD GREW and MULTIPLIED.
The Word of God is Eternal, Incorruptible and liveth and abideth forever. I Peter 1:23.
Such a glorious contrast to oration and words of Herod.

Verse 25. Refer to notes on Acts 13:5.

## ACTS CHAPTER 13 And 14

FROM THESE CHAPTERS on to the close of the Book, Antioch takes the center place, and the Apostle Paul comes into prominence of ministry.

a. **Ministries in the Church at Antioch.** vs. 1-4.

"There were in the Church at Antioch certain Prophets and Teachers."

It is noteworthy to see the development and progression in the revelation of the Ministries which God has set in the Church, according to Ephesians 4:9-13.

| | | | |
|---|---|---|---|
| The Twelve Apostles. | Acts 1. | ) | |
| The Seven Deacons. | Acts 6. | ) | I Corinthians 12 |
| The Evangelist | Acts 8. | ) | The Ministries |
| The Prophets | Acts 11:27; 13:1-2. | ) | in the |
| The Elders | Acts 11:30. | ) | Body of Christ. |
| Prophets and Teachers | Acts 13:1. | ) | |
| Apostles | Acts 14:14. | ) | |

All the Fulness of Ministry, Grace and the Spirit; all the Fulness of the Godhead dwells bodily in the Son of God, the Head of the Church. Colossians 1:19; 2:9. All that Fulness is to be manifested in the many-membered Body of Christ in the earth. These Ministries are simply the expression of Christ flowing down into the members of the Church, which is His Body.

b. **The Ministry of the Prophet.**

It is essential to understand the particular difference between the function of the Old Testament and New Testament Prophets, for a proper recognition of this Ministry of Christ in the Church.

1. The Office of the Prophet is an Ascension-Gift Ministry set by the Lord in the Church. Ephesians 4:11.
2. God has set in the Church, Apostles first, secondarily Prophets. I Corinthians 12:28-29.
3. There is no record that Jesus Christ ever chose one Prophet before His Crucifixion and His Ascension.
   He chose Twelve Apostles only, which became the foundation ministry of the Church. These came at the close of the Old Testament period and the ushering in of the New Testament age.
4. The Ministry of the Prophet is to the whole Body of Christ, and given until the Church comes to a 'perfect man.' Ephesians 4:9-16.
5. The Church is built upon the foundation laid by the Apostles and Prophets. These two Ministries work together. Ephesians 2:20-22; 3:1-5; 4:11-12. The Mystery of the Church was expressly revealed to the holy Apostles and Prophets by the Spirit. Luke 11:49.
6. Christ is THE Prophet — THE WORD made flesh. Deuteronomy 18:18. All other Prophets are pointers to Him, and are the expression of Christ in the Body.
7. There are various expressions of this same Ministry even as is evidenced in the Old Testament Prophets, so also in the New Testament Ministries.

**The Old Testament Prophet.**

Old Testament Prophets fall into two main categories, which helps in distinguishing New Testament Prophets' Ministry from that of the Old Testament Prophets.

1. **Prophets of Guidance.**

   Moses, Samuel, Elijah and Elisha, Aaron, and others, were Prophets particularly used in the Ministry of guidance. The Word of Wisdom, Word of Knowledge, Forthtelling and Foretelling, and Miracles — all confirmed that they were the Prophets of Jehovah. These revealed and declared the Mind of God, and many times His personal Will to the people. They were God's spokesmen.

2. **Prophets of Vison and Scripture.**

   a. Daniel and Zechariah especially are Prophets of Vision, or, Seers, in which God gave Visions which they recorded under Divine inspiration as infallible prophecy.
   They foretold the future and destiny of the Nations of earth. Daniel did not utter these things forth as in the Office of a spokesman, or Prophet to the people.

   b. **Prophets of Scripture.**

   Ezekiel, Isaiah, Jeremiah, Joel, Hosea, Amos, and all of the Prophets spoken of as 'Major and Minor' Prophets moved especially in the realm of Prophecy — the Prophetic Scriptures. They moved in the fullest sense of Foretelling and Forthtelling the destiny of the Nations, both Hebrew and Gentile.
   Through these Prophets came infallible Scripture. God overruled the imperfections and infirmities of these men, and brought forth infallible revelation through fallible men, using their personalities under the Spirit's control. However, most of these were not used in the area of miracles, as were the Prophets of guidance.

These Prophets of Scripture became God's voice for the then present generations and also for all future generations.

The essential function of the Old Testament Prophets were as follows:

1. Old Testament Prophets used in guidance.
2. Old Testament Prophets used to utter and write infallible Scripture.

Guidance was given to the Prophet or the Priest by the Spirit, or by means of Vision, Voice, Visitation, Word or Dream, or by Urim and Thummin, because the Holy Spirit was not yet available for "all flesh" under the Old Covenant Dispensation.

Infallible Prophecy is spoken of in II Peter 1:20, 21.

There will be variations of the Prophetic Ministry in the New Testament Church, as there was in the Old Testament, as God willed to use them, but these essential differences will always remain.

**The New Testament Prophet.**

It is important to remember these facts.

1. No New Testament Prophet was ever used in controlling or guiding and governing the believer in the will of God, but often used in confirmation of the already known and revealed will of God.

2. No New Testament Prophet was ever used in the utterance or writing of infallible Scripture. All prophetic utterances were judged by the Word of Scripture. I Corinthians 14:29-30, 32. Most of the New Testament was written by Apostles. The reason is evident! God was making complete break between the operations of the Old Testament Prophet in this New Testament Dispensation of the Spirit when the Spirit was available for all.
   To go back to seeking guidance through Prophets is to resort back to Old Testament methods. The Scripture teaches "As many as are led by the Spirit, they are the sons of God." Romans 8:14.

Definition and distinction must be recognized between:

1. Prophecy of Scripture. II Peter 1:20. Inspired infallible Prophecy.
2. The Spirit of Prophecy. Revelation 19:10.
3. The Gift of Prophecy. I Corinthians 14:3, 31. A fragmentary word.
4. The Office of a Prophet. I Corinthians 14:29-32.

   All may prophesy, but not all are Prophets.

Guidance in the New Testament for the Believer is by:

The infallible Word of God — the complete revelation of His will as in Scripture.

The Indwelling Spirit of God, always leading to and never contrary to the Word He inspired.

God often may and does confirm through Ministries set in the Church His already known and revealed will.
This is seen in the Ministry of Laying on of Hands. Hebrews 6:1-2.

c. **The revealed New Testament Ministry of Prophets.**

   1. Agabus foretold (predicted) by the Spirit the coming famine in Acts 11:27-28. He did not give guidance as to what to do, but the disciples responded to send relief. Acts 11:29-30.
   2. The Prophets without doubt were the ones through whom "the Spirit said" in Acts 13:2.
      This was confirmation of God's will, already known and revealed to Saul by the Lord Jesus on the Damascus Road, and confirmed by word of mouth through Ananias, and now re-confirmed through the Prophet here. Not guidance, but confirmation!
   3. The Prophets ministered the Word of God to the Church, in exhortation and confirmation. Acts 15:32.
      A Prophet also means, "A public expounder of God's Word." Ministry of foretelling — telling forth the Word.
   4. According to I Corinthians 14:29-30, 32, the Prophets had a distinct ministry Gift of utterance in prophecy, which was part of the prophetic Office.
      It means "to flow forth, to speak, to bubble forth and over like a fountain."

      It involved
      a. Exhortion, "to stir up"
      b. Edification, "to build up"
      c. Comfort, "to bind up"
      d. Conviction,

e. Confirmation,

f. Revelation, reaching into the hearts of men. These were not counted infallible, but were judged by the Word and by the Spirit in the midst.

5. Acts 21:8-14 gives a remarkable distinction between the Gift of Prophecy and the Office of a Prophet.
   Though Philip the Evangelist had four daughters who did prophesy, they were not prophetesses, for God sent the Prophet Agabus down to foretell what would happen to Paul at Jerusalem, again confirming what Paul already knew.
   Refer to Notes on Acts 21:8-14

6. The New Testament warns us to beware of False Prophets. Acts 13:6; II Peter 2:1; I John 4:1.
   By their fruits ye shall know them. Matthew 7:15; 24:11, 24; Revelation 16:13.
   The final test is the Law and the Testimony. Isaiah 8:20; Deuteronomy 18:22; Jeremiah 28:9.
   The Ministries are given for the edifying and perfecting of the Saints. Ephesians 4:11-13.

(N.B. The Comments on the Ministry of Prophets are rather full because of the necessity of understanding and appreciating this Ministry as God is restoring such to the Church today, as part of the full five-fold Ministry of Christ. Also it helps to keep things in Divine and Scriptural balance.)

d. **The Ministry of Teachers.**
   "There were in the Church at Antioch Prophets and Teachers."

1. God has set Teachers in the Church. Acts 13:1-2.
2. Christ is THE Teacher sent from God. John 3:2.
3. Firstly, Apostles; secondarily, Prophets; thirdly, Teachers. I Corinthians 12:28-29; Ephesians 4:11.
   It is one of the Ascension-gift Ministries given to the Body of Christ, along with other Ministries, to bring the Church unto maturity.
4. There is great warning and admonition to Teachers in James 3:1-2.
5. The Teacher needs the Anointing of the Spirit, who alone is THE True Teacher. I John 2:20, 27-28.
   The Comforter is the Teacher who leads and guides us into all Truth. John 14:26; I Corinthians 2:13. The Truth is in Jesus.
6. "Thine eyes shall see thy Teachers." Isaiah 30:20.
   God is restoring Teachers to the Church in these days as in the early Church. The Teacher works through the Word, not speaking as the Scribes and Pharisees, but having that Divine ability to impart knowledge and understanding to the people, teaching the revelation given to the Apostles and Prophets. Mark 1:22; Matthew 7:28-29.

   Wisdom, knowledge, and understanding, the anointing of the Spirit in illumination, and the ability of the Spirit — these are the things that enable the Teacher to speak as the very "Oracle of God," I Peter 4:10-11.

   Israrel suffered much because there was no "Teaching Priest." II Chronicles 15:3-4.

   The Lord Jesus Christ is The Teacher, and it is His Ministry manifested and operating in the Body.

The Great Commission included, "Go and teach all Nations." Matthew 28:16-20.

e. **The Holy Spirit said** . . . vs. 2-4.
The setting in the Church at Antioch made room for the Spirit to speak.

1. They ministered to the Lord. Compare I Samuel 3:1; II Chronicles 29:11; Ezekiel 44:17-27. As ministering Priests.
2. They fasted. Compare Matthew 9:14-15. Flesh subdued.
3. The Spirit said. Not merely man, not the Church, but the ministry of the Spirit in and through vessels.
The Personality and Deity of the Spirit revealed again.
"Separate unto Me . . . to the work that I have called them."
The Spirit, as executive in the Church, called, chose, elected and equipped the Ministries.
Headquarters operating from Heaven, by the Risen Head.
4. They fasted and prayed.
5. They laid hands on them. Identification, confirmation, and edification.
The Ministry of Laying on of Hands. First Principles. Hebrews 6:1-2; I Timothy 5:22. Both proven Ministries — not novices!
6. They sent them forth. The Ministries and the Church.
The human side. Human responsibility.
7. Being sent forth by the Holy Spirit. The Divine side.
Divine Sovereignty. The Spirit must send.
Barnabas and Paul are called 'Apostles' for the first time in Acts 14:14. i.e., "Sent ones." Luke 10:1.
He sent the 12 Apostles in Matthew 10:1-7.
He sent other 70 in Luke 10:1.

IN THE REMAINDER OF CHAPTER 13, we consider Paul's "First Missionary Journey."

This First Missionary Journey is covered in Acts 13:4-52; 14:1-28.

## PAUL'S FIRST MISSIONARY JOURNEY

Acts 13:4-52 — 14:1-28

a. **Ministry in Cyprus.** 13:4-28.

1. Verse 4. Departure from Antioch.
Paul's pattern in the Gentile Cities was to go to the Jew first. To the Synagogues.
2. John Mark is taken as their 'minister' (Deacon, servant.)
Acts 12:25. Assistant to the Apostles. Acts 15:37-38.
3. At Paphos the Apostles have to deal with a Sorcerer, even as Philip and Peter and John had a Sorcerer to deal with in Acts 8. Elymas, the Sorcerer was Divinely judged through Paul, who was filled with the Spirit as this judgment was pronounced. Note the reason for this judgment.

a. **His sin.**
He was a Jew. He knew the Scriptures which demanded judgment on Sorcerers. He became a False Prophet (Ezekiel 34,) which was condemned also in the Old Testament Scriptures. Then he became a Sorcerer — a dealer with evil spirits, charms, etc. Compare Acts 8:9-24, with Deuteronomy 18:10-12.
He willfully resisted the Truth of God's Word, and the Spirit of God.

b. **His character.**
He sought to turn others from the Lord. He was a son of the Devil, an enemy of all righteousness, and a perverter of the ways of the Lord.
Compare Matthew 13:38; John 8:44; I John 3:8.
Full of all subtilty and mischief. Like the serpent. Genesis 3:1.

c. **His judgment.**
The same power of God which struck Paul blind on the Damascus Road now strikes Elymas blind for a season.
This also was an "Act of the Holy Spirit."
The Lord heals blind eyes, or makes eyes blind. Acts 9:7-18.
His physical blindness was the symbol of his spiritual blindness and state of darkness.
No wonder "The Deputy believed, being astonished at the Doctrine of the Lord!"
The mist upon Elymas, and not seeing the Sun (The Son?) for a season. The Light of the world not seen!
This is typical of the power of God which will be manifest in the Last Days in Divine judgment on willful opposers of the Gospel.

4. Saul (The Destroyer) is first named Paul (Little, The Worker) here.
The New Name significant of the New Nature.
From here on it is "Paul and Barnabas" and not vice versa.

b. **Ministry at Perga.** vs. 13.

1. Perga in Pamphilia. John Mark departs from them and returns, not to Antioch, but to Jerusalem, where his home and mother were. Acts 12:12, 25.
Literally, "withdrew away." Acts 15:36-40.
Later on he went back to Antioch, and Barnabas desired to have him go with them again on the second Missionary Journey, but Paul did not want him.
Contention and separation resulted. Both Barnabas and Paul were partly right.
However, later on, Barnabas was able to help John Mark, and he turned out to be "profitable to Paul in the ministry."
Colossians 4:10; II Timothy 4:11.

2. Paul's confidence is restored in John Mark in due time. Compare Proverbs 25:19.

c. **Ministry at Antioch in Pisidia.** vs. 14-52.

1. Here we have Paul's first recorded Sermon. It follows a very similar pattern to that of Stephen's preaching in Acts 7, and also to that of Peter's in Acts 2.

2. To the Jew first. To the Synagogues. Paul appeals to the very Scriptures they professed to believe and trust in.
He declares the historical facts concerning Jesus of Nazareth, as being the exact fulfilment of that spoken of in the Law and the Prophets.

3. Note again verse 27. Religious blindness and spiritual deafness is seen in regard to the very things they profess to "see and hear."
   Compare Isaiah 6:9-10; Luke 24:27, 44-46; 23:34.

4. Verses 38-41. "I work a work in your days, a work which ye will in no wise believe though a man declare it unto you."
   The MAN Christ Jesus, declared by a Man, and by the Ministries in the Church.
   Quoted from Habakkuk 1:5; Isaiah 29:14.
   Church History has proved the truth of this verse over and over again.
   People despise and wonder and perish!
   God works a work in each generation. He uses a person or movement of the Spirit to declare it, but some will not believe.
   "Through THIS MAN is preached forgiveness of sins." Only in Christ Jesus.

5. The Gentiles respond to the Word of God. Verses 42-43, 46-48.
   The Jews are filled with envy and jealousy. They contradict and blaspheme.
   Religious, bigoted and blinded Jewry.
   Further opposition and persecution manifests itself against the Apostles, even as against Christ in Jerusalem.
   The motive was envy. Matthew 27:18. It is the same today.

6. Consider the emphasis on "The Word" in 13:5, 15, 26, 42, 44, 48, 49. The Jews judged themselves unworthy of Eternal Life, by rejecting the Word. They put it away from them.
   So do men judge themselves today in like manner.

7. Devout and honourable women and Chief men were deceived into being stirred up against the Apostles.
   They should have known better instead of becoming tools in the hands of a bigoted and unbelieving people.

8. The Apostles did as Jesus told them and shook off the dust of their feet. Luke 9:5.
   In spite of the rejection and expulsion, they were filled with joy and the Holy Spirit.
   Supernatural joy. The fruit of the Spirit. Not natural joy which is dependent upon good circumstances and conditions.

d. **Ministry at Iconium.** 13:51-52; 14:1-6.

God continues to bless the Gentiles. Compare Isaiah 42:6; 49:6; Luke 2:32; Isaiah 55:6; Romans 1:16; 10:19.
Acts 13:46-47. Gentiles ordained to Eternal Life. God was giving a LIGHT to the Gentiles.

1. Paul goes again to the Jew first. 14:1.
   Great multitudes believe, both Jews and Gentiles.

2. Unbelieving Jews oppose the Apostles again. Their minds were infected with evil. The evil of unbelief always works this way, even as the Serpent beguiled Eve through her mind. II Corinthians 11:3.

3. The Lord confirmed the Word and "gave testimony" to the Word of His Grace. Hebrews 2:3-4.
   Signs and wonders were done by the Apostles. Mark 16:15-20.
   Romans 15:19. The signs of Apostolic Ministry.

4. The result? Division! Two parties. Some stood with and for the Apostles in the Gospel, others stood against.
   The Gospel demands no neutrality. We are either for or against the Christ of God. Luke 11:23; 9:50.
   It is either decision or division!

e. **Ministry at Lystra.** 14:6-20.

1. At Lystra they preached the GOOD News. The Law Age was not good News.
2. Here we have the first recorded miracle of healing under Paul's ministry. It is similar to the miracle of healing under Peter's ministry in Acts 3.
   It is also typical of the healing of mankind. Mankind became impotent in his walk from birth, a cripple from birth. He had never walked until the Gospel of Christ came to him.
   Paul perceived that he had faith, which comes through hearing the Word. Romans 10:17.
   He gave the command of the Word of faith. He spoke the Word and it was done. The Gift of Miracles and Faith in operation.
3. The reaction was that they sought to make the Apostles "as gods come down in the likeness of man."
   God — The Son — was made in the likeness of men in the incarnation, in order that men may be made in the likeness of God.
   John 1:1-3, 14; Philippians 2:5-11; Daniel 2:11.
4. Verse 12. The men at Lystra worshipped the Planets.
   Roman Emporers accepted the worship of men. Paul and Barnabas refused such worship. Worship was due to God alone.
5. The heathen and idolatrous Priests seek to make a sacrifice to these "gods as men."
   Rejecting the supreme sacrifice made by the God-Man at Calvary for all sin, they seek to sacrifice to men.
   Human nature is to deify and sacrifice to men!
6. Paul and Barnabas declare they were men of like passions; of the same human nature as they were. Compare James 5:17.
7. Note the whole of Paul's Sermon here to the Gentiles. Verses 15-18. Compare this with Romans, chapter 1.
   He points them to the *God of Creation.* Psalms 19:1-4. The gods they were worshipping were created by their own hands, and were inferior to them, having eyes and seeing not, having ears and hearing not. Dumb idols with eyes, ears, nose and mouth, yet unable to see, hear, smell or speak. Psalms 115:1-8.
   How could the True and Living God be like unto these dumb idols, inferior to the ones who worshipped them?
8. Paul is stoned, even as was Stephen. II Corinthians 11:25; II Timothy 3:11-12. God in grace miraculously delivers Paul out of death into life by resurrection, to fulfill his ministry.

f. **Ministry at Derbe and return to Antioch.** 14:20-26.

1. They preached the Gospel and taught many at Derbe. Verses 20-21.
2. Then they returned back through the Cities previously visited. Then back to

Lystra, the place of the stoning. John 10:31; 8:59; 11:8. Even as Jesus went back to places, they sought to stone Him. Paul cared more for the disciples than he did about the stones.

3. Ministry. Confirming. Exhorting. "Through much tribulation we enter the Kingdom of God."
   Ordaining and commending to God and His grace. Verses 22-24.
4. Return to Antioch from whence they had left. Verse 26.
   There they declared what GOD had done with them. Verses 26-28. God had opened the Door of Faith to the Gentiles. The same Door which let the believing Gentiles in, shut the unbelieving Jews out.
   So also in the "Days of Noah." John 10:7-9. Christ is THE DOOR presented to Jew and Gentile alike. All may enter through faith. Two sides to every Door. Inside (Faith,) and Outside (Unbelief.)
5. Thus, several Churches are established in the First Missionary Journey over several years of preaching the Gospel.

g. **Ministry of Elders Ordained.** vs. 23.
The Apostles ordained Elders in Every Church.

1. Elders ordained in every Local Church ("Called out company" — The Ecclesia.")
2. Ordained by the Apostles, Paul and Barnabas.
3. Ordained with Prayer and Fasting.
4. Ordained with the Laying on of Hands. Hebrews 6:1-2.
5. **Qualifications of Elders** are given in I Timothy 3:1-7, and Titus 1:4-9 by the Apostle Paul.

   The Elder must be: —

   a. Blameless. No accusations against him.
   b. The husband of one wife.
   c. Vigilant. Wide awake. Watchful.
   d. Sober. Of a sound and disciplined mind.
   e. Temperate in all things. Self-control.
   f. Of good behaviour.
   g. Modest. Chaste. Not conceited.
   h. Given to hospitality. Generous. Not a miser, or selfish. Liberal.
   i. Apt to teach. To tend, rule guide and lead the Flock of God into the green pastures of the Word.
   j. Not given to wine. Margin, "Not quarrel as drunks do."
   k. Not a striker. Not one who hits back, strikes the sheep, or whips with the Word. Not a quitter.
   l Not after money. Not a hireling.
   m. Patient. Patience with God, and with the sheep necessary. Impatience breeds disasters in the Church.

n. Not a brawler. Not a fighter for himself, or for his position.

o. Not covetous. Unlawful lusts.

p. Must be able to rule his own house and family well. His home-order is a type of the Church-order. God's House.

q. Rules well. Not a novice, or one newly come to The Faith.

r. Must be proven.

s. Must have a good report of outsiders. In business life. In work. Must be conscientious.
Thus the Elder must not be a beginner, or filled with pride, but the Gift will make room for him as he is proven in the Local Church first.

6. **Ministry of Elders.** Acts 20:27-35; I Peter 5:1-4.

a. Ministry of the Word.

b. Ruling, tending and shepherding the Flock of God. Hebrews 13:7, 17; I Timothy 5:17.

c. Elders together constitute the Presbytery. "Praise Him in the Assembly of the Elders." Psalms 107:32.
The 5-fold Ministries constitute Eldership.

d. Prayer and ministry to the sick. James 5:14.

e. Local Churches ruled by the Elders. Elders is always used in the plural in relation to the Local New Testament Churches. Not a dictatorship, or lordship or popedom, or one-man rule, but the Eldership, the Oversight ordained of God.

f. Elders and Deacons together minister in the Local Church. Philippians 1:1.
Elders were never voted in or out by the people. They were ordained by the Laying on of Hands by the Presbytery, or by Apostles and Prophets, before the Church.
There was recognition, and cooperation in the New Testament order. I Peter 5:1-7.

## ACTS CHAPTER 15

ACTS CHAPTER 15 is one of the most important Chapters in the History of the Church, for the principles established there maintain all through the Church Age, and are applicable to the Church world-wide.

The contention as set forth in this Chapter threatened to divide the New Testament Church into two great factions consisting of Jew and Gentile.

However, the truth of the Body of Christ is that there is ONE BODY, in which there is neither Jew nor Gentile — all are one "in Christ."
Galatians 3:28; I Corinthians 12:13; 11:29; Ephesians 2:11-22.

a. **The Conflict between Law and Grace.** vs. 1.

Here we see certain men coming down from Judea teaching that the Gentiles had to be circumcised and keep the Law of Moses in order to be saved.
It was a conflict between Jew and Gentile, Circumcised and Uncircumcised; between the Ritual Law and the Spiritual Law; between Flesh and Spirit.
It was a conflict between Salvation with Circumcision, or Salvation without or apart from Circumcision.

b. **Dissension and Disputation.** vs. 2.

Paul and Barnabas, Circumcised Hebrews, dispute with the Judaizing teachers, who are legalists, mixing Law with Grace, having Christ in one hand and Moses in the other.
The Apostles stood up against this 'leaven of legality' which was being planted in the Churches of the Gentiles.
There was strong dissension, or, 'standing up against,' and much disputation, or 'joint seeking,' as the matter was debated.

c. **The Conference at Jerusalem.** vs. 3-4.

Seeing the 'problem' had come from Judea and from the Church at Jerusalem, the Apostles agreed to go back to the 'home Church' from whence these legalistic teachers had come and have the matter dealt with there.

Paul and Barnabas went up to Jerusalem, and declared what God had done amongst the Gentiles (The Uncircumcised.) They declared how God had manifested His saving Grace without the rite of Circumcision.

d. **The Question and Case at hand.** vs. 4-6.

In connection with Acts Chapter 15, it is also profitable to read Galatians 2:1-14.

At Jerusalem, the Apostles and the Elders and the whole Church are gathered together.
This was but a temporary Council convened at Jerusalem for the settling of a Doctrinal matter. It was not 'Headquarters of the Church,' but the matter had to be dealt with there because these Teachers came from the Jerusalem Church.
The principle of truth is that all problems should be dealt with in the Local Church where they originated.

Verse 5. The Sect of the Pharisees, who were believers in Messiah, stated that the Gentiles must be 1. Circumcised, and
2. Keep the Law of Moses, in order to be saved. Verses 1 and 5.

These Pharisees were ritualistic, and legalistic. Missing the spirit of the Law, they contended for the Letter and the Flesh. Compare Romans 2:25-29.

In Verse 6, the Apostles and Elders gathered together to consider the matter.

Please note. The whole Church is gathered together to consider the question in hand, but the discussion and decision was reached by the Ministry, by the Apostles and Elders. Verses 12 and 22.

e. **The Case concerning Circumcision.**

1. **The Case FOR Circumcision.**
Further disputation took place. Verses 2 and 7. For and against Circumcision. Here the contention is stated out and discussed.

The points in favor of Circumcision would be as follows:

a. Circumcision was given before the Law to Abraham, as the Seal of the Abrahamic Covenant. Genesis 17; Romans 4:11. Anyone refusing this rite was 'cut off.' It was only as they were Circumcised that they were counted as being in Covenant-relationship with God, and counted as the Covenant Seed, entitling them to the Promises and Privileges in the Covenant.

b. It was called "The Covenant of Circumcision." Acts 7:8.

c. So serious was this rite in the eyes of Jehovah that He sought to kill Moses who had not brought his own children into Covenant-relationship with God, yet was going down to Egypt to bring deliverance to the Nation of Israel on the basis of that Covenant. Exodus 4:24-26.

d. Circumcision was also confirmed under the Law of Moses. Exodus 12:43-50; Joshua 5:1-10.
So important was this rite that none dare partake of the Passover Feast without Circumcision, whether Hebrew or Foreigner.

Thus the Sect of the Pharisees and the Judaizers had such arguments for Circumcision.
They debated that it was the Sign and Seal of the Abrahamic Covenant, and then confirmed under the Mosaic Covenant. The whole of mankind was divided into two classes, the Circumcision and the Uncircumcision, or, the under-Covenant-people, or the without-Covenant-people — Jews and Gentiles. Ephesians 2:11-13; Jeremiah 9:25-26.

Therefore they contended that the only way into Covenant blessing for the Gentiles was by the Rite of Circumcision, which involved the Abrahamic Covenant; and again, by keeping the Law of Moses, which involved the Mosaic Covenant.

The 'wedge' was Covenant-relationship, by virtue of the rite of Circumcision. All of this looked good in the case for this rite.

2. **The Case AGAINST Circumcision.**
The case against Circumcision is dealt with in verses 7 to 18, and it is given by several of the Apostolic band.

a. **Peter's Testimony.** Verses 7-11.
Note also Galatians 2:1-9. Peter is the Apostle to the Circumcision. Peter declares the Lord's dealings with him in the sending forth of the Holy

Spirit upon the Gentiles, as noted in Acts, chapters 10 and 11. The Gentiles heard the Word of the Gospel and believed. Romans 10:17. God knows the hearts of all whether they be Jews or Gentiles.
God gave them witness by giving them the same Holy Spirit as unto the Jews.
God made no difference. God made no distinction.
God purified their hearts by faith. Verses 8-9.

Peter continues to say that the rite of Circumcision and the Law was "A yoke of bondage" that none were able to bear. Verse 10.

Jesus said: "Take My yoke upon you . . . My yoke is easy." Matthew 11:28-30.

Paul said to the Galatians who were troubled by these same legalistic Teachers, "Be not entangled again with the yoke of bondage." Galatians 5:1.

The Law and Circumcision was a yoke of bondage to the flesh. In Christ we exchange the yoke of bondage for the yoke of His grace.

"Thy freedom is my grand control."

Peter summarizes his comments in verse 11, by saying that the Gentiles through GRACE (undeserved, unmerited and unearned favor of God bestowed upon man,) would be saved, as also the Jew. Ephesians 2:5-22, 8-9.

Peter's Testimony is that the work of God, by the Spirit upon the Gentiles, was without the rite of Circumcision, and without the Law, and they were saved by grace, through faith, God giving them the Sign and Seal of the NEW Covenant in the Baptism of the Holy Spirit.

The Gentiles are brought into Covenant relationship with God through the grace of Christ by faith, and it is the Spirit who bears witness to their salvation.

Neither Jew nor Gentile are saved by the Law, or by Circumcision!

b. **Barnabas and Paul testify.** vs. 12.
Note also Galatians 2:1-9. Paul is the Apostle to the Uncircumcision.

Both Barnabas and Paul testify what God had wrought in miracles and wonders amongst the Gentiles. This was manifest proof that God was visiting the Gentiles in Grace, even though they were Uncircumcised and were without the Law, being Strangers from the Covenants of Promise.

Miracles and wonders of Grace in previous Dispensations, or before the Cross, had been mainly done in the midst of the chosen Hebrew Nation, by which God attested that they were His people and He was their God.

God now testifies the same thing that the Gentiles are His through redeeming Grace. Romans 2:1-11, 12-22; 3:29-30; Romans the 4th chapter.

The revelation given to Paul is that all the world — Jew or Gentile — is guilty before God, and all are under death, with or without Law, with or without Circumcision.

Only by God acting in Grace towards mankind could anyone be justified at all. The Circumcision, with the Law, failed to keep that Law, thus becoming as Uncircumcision, or 'Gentile-ized,' and under death.

The Uncircumcision, without the Law, failed to keep and obey the Law of Conscience, and thus they were under death.

God moves in His Grace, by His Spirit, through Christ in order to redeem both Jew and Gentile out of death.

Paul's argument in Romans chapter 4 is to witness to this fact.

The truth was foreshadowed and typified in Abraham, the Father of all who believe, whether they be Jews or Gentiles.

God gives him the Covenant Promises of Grace in:

a. Uncircumcision, or when he was as a 'Gentile,' and then later on

b. In Circumcision, or, as a Hebrew.
Romans 4:9-11 especially to be read in connection with the above remarks.

Thus before and after Circumcision Abraham receives the same Covenant Promises of Salvation through Grace, which became prophetic of Salvation becoming available for Jew and Gentile, or, Circumcision and Uncircumcision, through Faith in Christ.
Jew and Gentile are included together in the NEW Covenant of the Grace of God. Galatians 3:14.
The Holy Spirit is given to both through Grace and Faith, and not through Works or Rites of the Law.

(NOTE: Though Paul had Timothy circumcised later on, as in Acts 16:3, yet he refused to have Titus circumcised in Galatians 2:3 at this Jerusalem Conference.
His reason? "To the Jews I became as a Jew, that I might gain the Jews: to them that are under the Law, as under the Law; to them that are without Law as being without Law (being not without Law to God but under the Law to Christ) that I might gain them that are without Law." I Corinthians 9:20-21.

3. **The Testimony of James through Scripture.** vs. 13-18.

It is worthy to note that the final court of appeal was to the infallible Scriptures.
"What saith the Scriptures?"

Though the Testimony and Experiences of Peter may be accepted, and the Ministry of Paul and Barnabas be received to confirm the truth, it was the WORD OF GOD which was the final court of appeal for all.

James quotes an Old Testament prophecy from Amos 9:11-12. This was a real 'Word of Wisdom' from the Scriptures, and settled the whole issue.

As Peter had quoted from the prophecy of Joel on the Day of Pentecost when the Jews came in under the initial outpouring of the Holy Spirit, now James quotes from Amos which involved the coming in of the Gentiles into the New Covenant.

Amos prophecied that God would build again *"The TABERNACLE OF DAVID"* that was fallen down, that God would raise up its ruins — what for? In order that the Gentiles, upon whom God's Name is called, might come in.

It has been noted especially in Acts 10 about the Gentiles coming into blessing,

and here is further confirmation of this fact. Isaiah 11:10; 54:1-5.
Refer to these comments and consider the Old Testament prophecies again concerning Gentile blessing through faith in Christ, who is the Seed of Abraham. Matthew 1:1.

This was the crux of the whole dispute here. The Gentiles were to come into *"The Tabernacle of DAVID," NOT "The Tabernacle of MOSES."*

If the Gentiles were to keep the Law of Moses and be Circumcised, then they would be coming in under the Law, or, antitypically be coming into "The Tabernacle of Moses," with its rites and ceremonies, its animal sacrifices, Aaronic Priesthood, Sabbaths, etc.

But the Gentiles were coming into the NEW Covenant, by faith in the Son of David, Jesus Christ, and into the Spiritual House, and Priesthood after the Order of Melchisedek.

That is, antitypically they were coming into "The Tabernacle of David."

A complete study of this wonderful subject as set out in the Old Testament, in I Chronicles, the 15th, 16th and 17th chapters, etc., shows the following condensed points.

David, in the will of God, established a complete new order of worship in the Tabernacle which he set up in Mt. Zion.

There were two Tabernacles in existence at the same time. The Tabernacle of Moses was in Mt. Gibeon, and the Tabernacle of David was set up in Mt. Zion. I Chronicles 16:37-43; II Chronicles 1:1-13.

There were two companies of Priests in function in these two different Tabernacles.

The Ark of the Covenant, once it was taken out of the Tabernacle of Moses (which at that time had been at Shiloh) never ever returned to the Tabernacle of Moses, but was taken and set in the Tabernacle of David! Typically 'The Glory' departed from Moses' Tabernacle!

In the Tabernacle of David there was a new order of worship in singing and singers, praise and worship, instruments of music, and continual joy and thanksgiving unto the Lord.

David actually transferred "The Holiest of All" into his Tabernacle, while the Tabernacle of Moses at Gibeon had an empty Most Holy Place, having the Holy Place and Outer Court functions only.

Once David offered the dedicatory sacrifices at the Tabernacle of David, there was only "Sacrifices of Praise and Joy" offered in his Tabernacle after that.

ALL THIS IS PROPHETICAL of what was to take place under Christ and the New Covenant.

At Calvary the dedicatory sacrifice was offered once and for all. The Veil of the Temple was rent in twain from top to bottom (Matthew 27:51) signifying the transference of the "Presence of God" to a NEW Temple, a NEW Habitation, even THE CHURCH.

In this "Tabernacle of David," which is the New Testament Church, there would only be offered "Sacrifices of Praise and Thanksgiving" unto the Lord.

In this "Tabernacle" Jew and Gentile would come, through faith in the grace of Jesus Christ.

Hence we are not come to "Mt. Sinai" (Tabernacle of Moses, and the Law Covenant, etc.,) but we are come to "Mt. Zion" (Tabernacle of David and the New Covenant.) Hebrews 12:18-24.

This is the whole revelation of the Epistle to the Hebrews.

(Let the Student refer to "The Tabernacle of David," as set forth in the Word of God.)

f. **The Final Sentence of the Church.** vs. 19-29.

The final sentence is given in these verses.
"Moses hath them in every City which preach him." Compare Matthew 17:1-5. Paul determines to preach Christ in every City. Compare I Corinthians 1:23-24; Acts 9:20.

We either preach Moses or preach Jesus! Acts centers around the conflict over preaching Moses or Christ.

The Father God said, "This is My Beloved Son, HEAR HIM." Matthew 11:13.

Moses (The Law,) and Elijah (The Prophets,) prophesied and pointed to him.

Verses 22 and 25. There was unity of the Ministry and the whole Church over the decision reached.
There the Lord commanded the blessing. Psalms 133.

Verses 23 to 27. They wrote Letters of confirmation and sent them by the hand of the brethren to confirm the spoken decision.

"Brethren of the Gentiles" — One in Christ. Verse 23. Galatians 6:15; 3:27-29; I Corinthians 7:18-20.

"It seemed good to the Holy Spirit (first,) and to us (second.)" Verses 25 and 28. The legalizers were 'troublers and subverters.' Verse 24.

Notice the fourfold admonition of the Letter. Verses 20 and 29.

1. Abstain from meats offered to idols.
   Compare I Corinthians 8:1-13. This was particularly for those of weaker conscience, and the danger of becoming a stumbling block to those who did not believe and know the truth concerning this matter. The idol is nothing, but it is the spirit behind it.
2. Abstain from blood. Compare Genesis 9:4; Leviticus 17:10-14.
   This was given under the Noahic Covenant, and confirmed under the Mosaic Covenant.
3. Abstain from things strangled. Compare Leviticus 22:8.
4. Abstain from fornication. Compare I Corinthians 5:1-13; 6:13-20; 7:2. Immorality and uncleanness forbidden by all the Covenants of God.

g. **The Ministry of Apostles and Prophets in Anitoch.** vs. 30-35.

The Epistle is read to the whole Church at Antioch.
There was great rejoicing.
The two Prophets, Judas and Silas, exhort and confirm the Saints.

"To exhort" — "to call near," to console and encourage;
"To confirm" — "to give support," or strengthen.

It seems that Peter's visit to Antioch, as mentioned in Galatians 2:11-21 took place between verses 35 and 36 of Acts 15.
Here Paul had to withstand Peter to his face because of his fear and compromise with the brethren from Judea over eating with the Gentiles, and then backing out on his own testimony later on. Peter dissimulated, or "backed out" on his own work, testimony and experience of Acts 10 and 11, and what he had spoken at the Conference at Jerusalem.
This was being hypocritical!

**SUMMARY —**

The New Testament teaches the truth concerning that true Circumcision.

1. The True Circumcision is of the heart, and not of the flesh.
   Deuteronomy 10:16; Galatians 5:11; 6:12-14; 5:2-6; Romans 2:25-29; Jeremiah 9:25-26; Romans 3:30.
2. Even under the Law Covenant, though Israel was circumcised in the flesh, yet they were uncircumcised in the heart.
   Deuteronomy 30:6; Jeremiah 4:4.
   Thus their Circumcision became Uncircumcision. They became as Gentiles, 'Gentile-ized' in God's sight!
3. The True Circumcision are those who have no confidence in the flesh, but rejoice in Christ Jesus, and worship in the Spirit. Philippians 3:3; Colossians 2:11-12.
4. The Covenant of Circumcision (Acts 7:8,) involved three things which are fulfilled in the New Covenant, in the heart and in the spirit, and not in the flesh and of the letter.
   1. Shedding of Blood, and the 'cutting off' of the flesh. Significant of the **Death** of Jesus Christ at Calvary, where He was 'cut off' (Isaiah 53:8) for our sins, shedding His Blood.
   2. The Invocation of The Name. Significant of Water Baptism into The Name of the Godhead Bodily, in the Lord Jesus Christ.
      Matthew 28:19-20; Acts 2:34-36.
      Involves **Burial.**
   3. The Rite was performed on the 8th day. It was a Sign and Seal that the person was in Covenant relationship with God.
      Significant of **Resurrection**.

It is the NEW CREATURE, and that Circumcision of the heart, in the spirit, that God only accepts or recognizes. II Corinthians 5:17.
The spiritual fulfilment of Circumcision is found in Water Baptism and Holy Spirit Baptism.
It is the Holy Spirit who is THE SIGN AND SEAL of the NEW Covenant and He is the one who performs that Spiritual Circumcision, through identification in the Death, Burial and Resurrection of the Lord Jesus Christ. Colossians 2:11-12.

The remainder of Acts, Chapter 15, begins Paul's Second Missionary Journey.

## PAUL'S SECOND MISSIONARY JOURNEY

Acts 15:36-41. — Acts 16-17-18:1-23.

THESE CHAPTERS listed above cover Paul's Second Missionary Journey, and will be commented on in this Section.

1. **Departure from Antioch.** Acts 15:35-41.

   a. Paul expresses his concern to visit the Local Churches which had been previously established on his First Journey to see how they were doing. Verse 36.
   II Corinthians 11:28 "The care of all the Churches."
   Paul had the heart of an Apostle, a real 'father' in the Lord.

   b. Contention over John Mark. Verses 37 and 38.
   Refer back to Acts 13:13. Barnabas desired to take John Mark with them again on this Missionary Journey, but Paul refused to have him with them because he had 'withdrawn' on the previous occasion and returned to his mother at Jerusalem.
   Paul realized the dangers of the journey, and fears that John Mark may withdraw again.
   Acts 12:12, 25; 13:5.

   The contention was so great and sharp that Barnabas and Paul separated over the matter. Verse 39.

   Undoubtedly both were partly right. Paul, realizing the young man as yet being unstable and a weakness in his life which had to be dealt with, and Barnabas, "Son of Consolation," also having faith in the young man that he would eventually become a good soldier of Jesus Christ.

   By reading these Scriptures, we find that John Mark, under the hand and ministry of Barnabas became 'profitable to Paul' in due season, so that reconciliation took place.
   Colossians 4:10; II Timothy 4:11; Philemon 24.

   c. Barnabas takes John Mark with him.
   Paul takes the Prophet Silas along with him. Verses 39-40.
   God Himself would work on all in the areas that needed His touch.

   d. They are all recommended by the Church to the Grace of God. John 1:17. His Grace would be inwrought in all.

   e. Paul and Silas go through Syria and Cilicia confirming the Churches. Verse 41.
   Confirming them in the Word of God, and the Gospel of Jesus Christ, and the things they have believed.
   Acts 2:42. The Local Churches established in the faith.

2. **Ministry at Derbe and Lystra.** Acts 16:1-5.

   a. Paul and Silas came to Derbe and Lystra where they find a young man by the name of Timothy.
   Possibly Timothy was converted as a result of Paul's ministry on the first Journey.
   As Paul was the 'fruit' from Stephen's stoning at Jerusalem, so it is possible that Timothy was the 'fruit' of Paul's stoning previously at Derbe and Lystra.

Hence he calls him his "son begotten in the faith." II Timothy 1:1-2; 2:1; 3:10-12.

b. Timothy was (1) A Disciple,
(2) Son of a Jewess, his father a Greek,
(3) Well reported of by the brethren.

Thus Timothy had first proven himself in a Local Church before he was taken with Paul in the Apostolic band.

It is well to note in connection with these verses, Paul's Epistles to Timothy, and the personal references and touches that they have in them, because they cast light on the character of this young man before he came into the Ministry which the Lord had called him to.

Timothy is a sample believer who proves himself in the Local Church first before moving into areas of responsibility and authority in the Church.

c. Timothy is brought before the Presbytery and received the Ministry of the Laying on of Hands and Prophecy.
Paul's desire was to have this young man with him, to develop him into a mature Ministry according to the prophetic Word of the Lord.
Timothy is ordained.

A careful study of these Scriptures show that Timothy was ordained by the Laying on of Hands of the Presbytery, that there was prophetic utterances over him, and also impartation of spiritual gifts.
I Timothy 1:18; 4:13-16; II Timothy 1:6; Hebrews 6:1-2.

None of this was done in haste, but in the mind, will and time of the Lord.

It is a principle of Scripture that future ministries were trained and developed under previous and mature ministries, in the Lord.

Joshua was trained under Moses.
Elisha was prepared under Elijah.
David was involved under King Saul.
The Apostles were trained under Jesus.
Timothy is developed under Paul.

d. Paul takes Timothy and has him circumcised because of the Jews in those quarters. NOT because Paul believed there was value in the rite.
His reason is found in I Corinthians 9:20-21. "That he might win the Jews." If Timothy became as a 'Jew-Gentile,' then he could minister to either Jews or Gentiles.

Refer back to Acts, chapter 15, and the summary, for the decision concerning the rite of Circumcision.

"IN CHRIST neither Circumcision, nor Uncircumcision matters, but A NEW CREATURE." Galatians 6:15.

e. The Apostolic band go through the Churches giving them the Decrees that were ordained at the settlement of the Conference in Jerusalem, even as they had delivered them to Antioch. Verse 4.

f. The result? The Churches were established and increased daily. Divine order.
Establishment in the faith. Compare Jude 3. Strengthened.
Increase in the Church. Compare Acts 2:41, 47.

3. **Ministry forbidden in Asia.** Acts 16:6-8.

   a. Paul and his team go over the regions of Galatia and then were forbidden of the Holy Spirit to preach the Word in Asia.

   Notice the strong language in verses 6 and 7.

   1. Forbidden of the Spirit to preach the Word in Asia.
   2. They assayed to go into Bithynia, but the Spirit suffered them not.

   Important lessons lay here. The Lord knows what Cities are ready to receive the Gospel.
   There is a time for the Word and Will of God. Paul and his band assayed, or attempted to go to these places, but the Holy Spirit, who knows all things and all hearts, forbad them and did not permit them to go.

   Paul could have 'forced the issue' and missed the mind and will of God, and brought unnecessary hardships upon himself and the team, had he not an "ear to hear what the Spirit was saying." Revelation 2:7, 11.

   The Lord Jesus had commanded His Disciples to go into all the world and preach the Gospel to every creature, and to disciple all nations. Matthew 28:18-20; Mark 16:15-20.

   But here the Holy Spirit restrains the Apostles from preaching the Word. There is no contradiction and no disharmony in the Godhead. The principle truth here is that the Spirit goes before the Word and prepares the way for the Word.
   First the Spirit, then the Word! Genesis 1:1-5. This also is an act of the Holy Spirit.
   The Lord Jesus is working by the Spirit who sees and knows all hearts. He knows which Cities are ready to receive the Gospel or not, hence the Spirit moves first always.
   Compare Acts 1:8; 2:4, 14; 8:29, 35; 13:1-3, 5; 19:2-4. In these Scriptures we see first the Spirit, then the Word.

   The Spirit and The Word work together. I John 5:8; Acts 10:19, 36.

   The Spirit and The Word agree. The Spirit will never violate or contradict the Word He wrote. The Church needs both the Spirit and the Word for Divine balance.

   It has been well said: "If we have the Word without the Spirit we will 'dry up;' but if we have the Spirit without the Word we will 'blow up,' but when we have the Spirit and the Word, then we will 'grow up.' "

   The Word without the Spirit is the Letter which kills.
   It is the Spirit who gives the Word life. II Corinthians 3:6.

   God has a Time, and Will and Word and Way for all Cities!

   The Conquest of the Cities of Canaan was according to the counsel of the Lord. Each City was taken in a different manner according to the Word of the Lord to Joshua through the High Priest.

   Spiritually this is so in Acts!

4. **Ministry at Macedonia — Philippi.** Acts 16:8-40.

   a. While waiting upon the Lord at Troas, the Lord gives Paul a Vision. Vs. 8-10.

The Spirit of Jesus (Margin, verse 7) has forbidden them to preach the Word In Asia, and hindered them from going to Bithynia, and the Vision Paul receives here is the Lord's answer to all.

God has a time for each City, and here the Lord desires Paul and his band to go over to Macedonia.

The Apostolic team immediately recognizes that the Vision was the Lord's call to them to go in this direction.

b. They came to Philippi. Verses 11 to 12.

c. At Philippi, Paul and his company find themselves at a 'Prayer Meeting' down by the River side on the Sabbath day. Possibly because there was no Synagogue in this city. Verse 13.
Compare Psalms 137:1. As they had sat by the Rivers of Babylon before.

d. Note verse 14. "A woman which worshipped God, whose heart the Lord opened."
This was a woman of Thyatira. Read in connection with this the Letter of Christ to the Church at Thyatira in Revelation 2:18-29.

She was a worshipper of God.
The Lord opened her heart, that she gave heed to the Word.

In verse 15 she is baptized, and her household, after which she invites Paul and his company to stay with her.

First it is the 'open heart,'
 and then 'open house.'

It takes the Spirit of the Lord Jesus Christ to open such, for all are closed by nature. The heart-maker is the heart-opener!

e. The Damsel possessed with a spirit of divination (fortune-telling,) verse 16. Margin, Spirit of Python.
A Fortune-telling devil in her. Commercialized by her Masters. Under the power and ability of this spirit she was in contact with evil spirits, who caused her to tell fortunes, foretelling future events, giving guidance to those who consulted her.

Note how many Cities had some form of Sorcery or Witchcraft and contact with the spirit realm, in worship, superstition, idolatry and other Satanically-inspired cults.

This woman was not a willing slave, as was Simon and Elymas who were Sorcerers. This woman was a victim of Satan and in need of deliverance.

Python — A large snake which kills its victims by the power of its crushing ability.
Typical of that "Old Serpent the Devil." Revelation 12:9.

Verses 17 and 18. The evil spirit in this woman gave testimony concerning the Apostles. Compare Mark 3:11-12.

After many days, Paul, by the Spirit, discerned this spirit and by the Gift of the Word of Faith cast it out, exorcising it in the power of the Name of the Lord Jesus Christ. Mark 16:17; Luke 10:17-18.
God does not need the testimony of devils to witness for Him. The devils believe and tremble, when men refuse to believe. James 2:19.

From verses 19 to 40 we have the account of Paul and Silas being cast into prison for casting out this spirit of soothsaying from this woman.

The Masters of the fortune-telling woman saw that the hope of their gains was gone, and have the Apostles cast into prison.

Business reasons! Like the people of Gadara, who thought more of their pigs (money) than the need of the demon-possessed victim. Mark 5:16-17.

The Apostles are beaten with many stripes. Compare II Corinthians 11:23-24.

What happens in prison?

1. They are bound fast in the stocks. A set of wooden frames with holes through which the legs were fastened.
   A most uncomfortable position!
2. Their backs are sore with many stripes.
3. Their crime? Preaching the Gospel, and casting out of devils. Preachers in prison.
4. The midnight hour. Verse 25. Blackest hour of the night, but the hour when God would work for them.
   Compare Matthew 25:6; Job 34:20; Judges 16:3; Mark 13:35; Exodus 11:4-6; Luke 11:5.
   The Midnight Hour is also prophetic of this End of the Age.
   Satan opposes as his spirits are cast out.
5. Paul and Silas prayed and sang praises.
   Job 35:10. Psalms 126. The Lord gave them 'Songs in the night.' Not dependent on feelings, or circumstances.
6. The prisoners heard them. Psalms 146:7; Isaiah 49:9; Ephesians 4:1; Isaiah 61:1.
   Hour of deliverance for the prisoners.
   Prison — "The House of restraint, the House of bondage.
7. God sends a great earthquake.
   It was an intellient earthquake. Compare Matthew 27:51-53.
8. All the doors were opened, and all bands were loosed.
   What a testimony and witness to the prisoners. The testimony of an 'Open Door.'
   Note how God faces every generation with 'The Door.'
   Genesis 6:16; Exodus 12:22-23; 38:30; Acts 14:27; Revelation 3:8; Matthew 25:10; John 10:7-9.
   Jesus Christ is THE DOOR!
9. Conviction and conversion of the Jailor.
   The Jailor calls for a light and sprang in asking the question of the Ages, "What must I do to be saved?"
   Not to be saved from the earthquake!
   Verse 30. The Jailor called them 'Sirs' (or, Lords.) Paul said, "Believe on the LORD Jesus Christ."
   Caesar was called 'lord' by the Romans.
   To believe on the Lord means "to commit thyself wholly over to Him."
10. Household salvation. The Jailor and his household were all baptized. God

used the prison experience to bring salvation. The Jailor believed on GOD, through the LORD Jesus Christ. Compare John 14:1, 6.

In verses 35 to 39, Paul exercises his legal rights as a Roman Citizen.

When Paul was beaten and striped by the Jews, he accepted it all in the will of God, but when he could exercise his legal privileges as a Roman Citizen, he did!

"The powers that be are ordained of God. Romans 13:1-3.

After being brought out of prison, they return to Lydia's house, bringing comfort to the new Local Church established there in her house. I Thessalonians 1:2; 2:7.

In connection with the Ministry at Philippi and the Church there, read the beautiful Epistle to the Philippians.

6. **Ministry at Thessalonica.** Acts 17:1-9.

In regards to the Ministry at Thessalonica, it is worthwhile to read the Epistle to the Thessalonian Church.
Here Paul tells of his entrance into the City, after leaving Philippi.
I Thessalonians 2:1-19 particularly.

a. Paul goes to the Synagogue, as his custom was, "To the Jew first." Verses 1 and 2. Compare Romans 1:16; 2:9.

He reasons with them out of their own Scriptures. Compare Acts 13:27.

Paul 'opens and alleges' that Jesus of Nazareth is the Christ of God. He does this for 3 Sabbaths.
The Old Testament Scriptures are a 'sealed Book' unless the Lord 'opens' them to us. Luke 24:27, 44-46; Revelation 5:1-5.

Many Jews believed that there were Two Messiahs to come. One, a Suffering Messiah, and Two, a Reigning Messiah.

Paul proves, opens, and shows Scripture with Scripture, along with the historical facts of Jesus of Nazareth that He was indeed the Christ, the fulfilment of all.

He combined and aligned the Scriptural and Historical proofs of Jesus Christ as the One to whom the Law, Psalms and Prophets pointed.

b. The Jews were divided. Jesus said: "I came to cause division," and all are either for Him or against Him. There is no ground of neutrality concerning His Person. Luke 12:51; John 7:43; 9:16; 10:19.

Some believed and consorted with Paul and Silas; Greeks and quite a number of the chief women. Compare Acts 13:50; Philippians 4:3.

Others believed not and were moved with envy. These gathered the lewd and baser sort of fellows and set the City in an uproar. They charged that these 'have turned the world upside down."

Rather they were endeavouring to have the world right side up! Verses 5 and 6.

The coming of Christ into the life of men brings things right side up and turns wrong things upside down.

Verse 7. It is either King Jesus, or King Caesar. Luke 23:2; John 19:12.

The Apostles are let go while Jason and other brethren are retained.

Wherever the Apostles went, it was either a riot or revival.

Read in connection with this, I Thessalonians 1:7-10; 2:1-10, 14-20.

7. **Ministry at Berea.** Acts 17:10-14.

a. The brethren sent Paul and Silas away by night unto Berea.
Paul once again, as his custom was, goes "to the Jew first," entering in to the Synagogue of the Jews.

Many of the Synagogues actually ended up becoming "The Synagogue of Satan," as Jesus said in Revelation 2:9 and 3:9.

b. It is beautiful to note that the Bereans were more noble than those of Thessalonica.

These received THE WORD with all readiness of mind. Not being hard-hearted, closed, or prejudiced. Nor were they gullible either. It is good to have the attitude of the Bereans.

They searched the Word. They searched the Scriptures daily to see whether these things were so. Even the Apostle Paul must be checked out by the Word of God.

Ministry and people have the infallible Word of God as the test and final authority for all teaching and preaching. Luke 16:29.

c. Many believed, Greeks and men and honourable women. Verse 12.
God always has some who will respond to His Word.

d. The Jews from Thessalonica came to Berea and stirred up trouble and opposition here also.
Note — I Thessalonians 2:1-20, particularly verses 13-16.

Paul is sent away by the brethren, while Silas and Timothy remain behind with the believers.

8. **Ministry at Athens.** Acts 17:15-34.

a. Paul is conducted to Athens, the City of Greece, noted for its 'wisdom.'

Again Paul ministers "to the Jew first," going to the Synagogue, and also to the Market Place, disputing with them daily in the Word of God. Verse 17.

b. He was 'stirred in the spirit' (by the Holy Spirit) as he saw the whole City given over to idolatry, and the worship of idols.

Paul was not there as a 'Tourist Missionary,' nor was he there to see and admire the glory of Greek Athens. Paul seemed totally unimpressed by Greek Art, Culture and Wisdom, etc.

Paul was grieved and roused to anger at the DEIFICATION of everything. The Greeks made gods out of anything and everything, even as the Canaanites.

In verse 18, he was encountered by various Philosophers.

1. **The Epicurians.**
The Epicurians were a Sect of Philosophers that derived its name from Epicurus (B.C. 342-271,) a Philosopher of Attic descent, whose garden at Athens rivalled the "Porch" and the Academy."

His aim was to discover a practical guide to happiness; his search was for pleasure, not absolute truth; and he relied on experience as the test, not on reason.
(Quote — Young's Concordance.)

They were Atheistic, Materialistic, and Worshipped the God of Pleasure.

2. **The Stoics.**
A Sect of Greek Philosophers who received their name from 'Stoa,' a Porch of Athens where Zeno taught. They were severe and lofty Pantheists, and affected indifference in all circumstances.
Zeno was born at Citium, a small town in the Island of Cyprus, about B.C. 357, taught at Athens, B.C. 299, and died B.C. 263.
(Quote — Young's Concordance.)

They were Pantheists, and worshipped God in Nature.
Romans 1:19-26 speaks of this worship of God in Nature, and all in Nature is part of God.
The same spirit prevails today.

They called Paul a 'Babbler,' or, 'blabber with his scrap-picked learning.' Amplified New Testament. *A Seed-Pecker!*

He did have 'The Seed' of the Word, if they cared to listen. I Peter 1:23; Luke 8:11.

They charged Paul with setting forth some new and strange gods (deities,) because he preached (1) Jesus and (2) The Resurrection!

Such is the wisdom of Athens, and the wisdom of this world before the Gospel of God in Christ.

The Athenians were like so many of today. All they desired was to hear "some new thing," some "new doctrine," but they were not hungry for the truth of God that would set them free.

Intellectual curiosity seekers! God was doing 'a new thing' in Christ Jesus. Isaiah 43:19. The True God was revealing Himself in and through His Son, the express image of His Person.

c. **Paul's Sermon on Mar's Hill.** vs. 22-31.

Paul goes to Mar's Hill (The Areopagus) and declares to them the folly of their wisdom and idolatry.

It was the Highest Court in Athens, overlooking Athens with all its idolatries and philosophies and the wisdom of men.

Note Paul's Sermon outline and his approach to the Athenians in contrast to his approach to the Jews.

With the Jew, Paul always reasoned out of the Scriptures, the Written revelation of God. The Written Word.

With the Gentile, Paul always reasoned from Creation, the Created revelation of God. The Creative Word. Genesis 1:1; Romans 3:2; Psalms 19:1-5; Romans 1:19-20.

Creation reveals there is a Creator-God. Creation reveals His power.

Redemption reveals there is a Redeemer-God, and this revelation is in Christ Jesus.

Inspiration, as in the Scriptures, reveals the Nature of God. It reveals His Person.

God cannot be known in His Nature, Character and Being in Creation. This comes by Inspiration and Revelation, in His Word, and finally in the God-Man, the Lord Jesus Christ.

Consider the important outline in Paul's address.

1. Verse 22. The Atheians were 'too superstitious.' Literally, 'too religious,' or 'deeply religious.' Very reverent to demons. Amplified New Testament.

   All men are religious by nature. Man was created to worship God and will worship a god of his own mind or making, or else fall to worshipping Satan as the god of this world, or demon spirits, or self-god!

2. Verse 23. **The Altar to THE UNKNOWN GOD!**
   Athens — filled with idols, and gods, yet this idol-altar expressed the ultimate wisdom of the Greeks. Their final confession was that God cannot be known. He is unknowable.

   This would be true — but for Jesus Christ who revealed the True God and 'declared Him.' John 1:14-18, Amplified New Testament. Matthew 11:27.

   Such is the 'wisdom of Athens.'

3. Verse 24. **The God of Creation.** He is greater than creation, and cannot be confined to human Altars or Temples.
   Even Solomon recognized this when he built the Temple as commanded. Acts 7:48.

4. Verse 25. **The God who is the Source and Sustainer of all life.**
   God needs not that man give to Him for He gave all first to man. Psalms 50:7-13.

5. Verse 26. **The God of all mankind.** Deuteronomy 32:8. When God created Adam, the father of all mankind, He set the bounds and lands for the various Nations to dwell therein.
   Man was created in the image of God. All of 'one blood.'

6. Verse 27. **The God Omnipresent.**
   God is not far from every one of us. Everywhere present.

7. Verse 27. **The God Omnipotent.** All live and move and have their being in God. He is our very life-source.
   Man is 'His offspring,' His creation.

8. Verse 28. Verse 29. **The God who is a Spirit.** John 4:24. Note the word, "Godhead," i.e., The Father, Son and Holy Spirit. Romans 1:20.

   God, as a Spirit being, cannot be represented in material things or belikened to gold, silver, stones, etc., or lifeless and inanimate things.
   The very gods man makes are inferior to the one who makes and worships such.
   How can intelligent man worship idols which have ears, eyes,

nose, mouth, arms and legs, yet have NO LIFE! Psalms 115:1-8; Romans 1:19-23.
Man worships something less than himself, calling it a God! Such is the religious nature of man. Genesis 1:26, 27.

9. Verse 30. **The God who enlightens our ignorance.**
"Times of ignorance" now past. God winked at, or overpassed them previously.
Ignorance is spiritual darkness. The Light of Christ has now come to enlighten man's ignorance. John 8:12; 1:1-3, 4-12. Light through the Gospel.

10. Verse 30. **The God who demands repentance.**
Ignorance enlightened, God now calls all mankind to repentance. "Change of mind," in relationship to Himself, and concerning sin and self.
Refer to Acts 2:38; Hebrews 6:1-2, on the Doctrine of Repentance.

11. Verse 31. **The God who is the Judge of all.**
Paul's emphasis is upon GOD first, before he finally brings in THE SON.
Only as men believe in the True God (Hebrews 11:6,) will they be able to come to God through His appointed Son. John 14:1, 6.

"That Man" — i.e., The Lord Jesus Christ. It is worthy to note that Paul never once uses or names the Name of Jesus in this Sermon.
He declares the briefest facts of "that Man" but does not magnify His Name, as he does in his reasonings with the Jews.

There is (a) The Appointed Judge, ordained of God.
(b) The Appointed Day. The Judgment Day. Hebrews 9:26-27.
(c) The Appointed standard. In righteousness. The Divine standard of righteousness.
(d) The Appointed proof. That Man who has been raised from the dead.
The Resurrected Christ of God.

12. Verse 32 to 34 The Spiritual fruit in Athens.
(a) Some mocked. )
(b) Some procrastinated. ) So today!
(c) Some believed. )

Such was Paul's impression on Athens and Athens' impression on Paul.

In the Epistle to the Corinthian Church, Chapters 1 and 2, Paul well expresses that pertaining to his Ministry at Athens.
"The world with all its wisdom knew not God."
"The wisdom of this world is foolishness of God."
"The Jews require a sign; the Greeks seek after wisdom; but to those who believe, Christ is the Power of God and the Wisdom of God."
I Corinthians 1:18-25.

9. **Ministry at Corinth.** Acts 18:1-17.

a. Paul leaves Athens and goes up to Corinth. It is interesting to see Paul's feelings and his approach when he goes to Corinth, after his apparent fiasco in Athens.

"When I came to you, brethren, I came not with excellency of speech or of wisdom . . . I determined to know nothing among you save Jesus Christ and Him crucified and I was with you in fear, and weakness and in much trembling. . ."

I Corinthians 2:1-5.

Undoubtedly his "excellent speech" in Athens did not win the Greeks or Athenians to Christ; hence he comes to Corinth to simply preach "Christ crucified," and he is in weakness and fear and much trembling after his experience at Athens.

b. Here at Corinth, Paul meets Aquilla and Priscilla, who are Tent-makers by trade, and so Paul labors in his trade with them. I Corinthians 4:12; I Thessalonians 2:9.

Every Jew had to have a trade.
This natural trade was also significant of Paul's spiritual ministry relative to the Church.

Paul was "The Tent Maker," and is building the House or Tabernacle of the Lord, as seen in the revelation of the Church which was given to him.

c. Once again he ministers the Word "To the Jew first" in the Synagogue every Sabbath, persuading Jews and Greeks. Verse 4.

d. Silas and Timothy rejoin Paul at Corinth. Paul is pressed in the spirit. He was completely engrossed with preaching earnestly and arguing and testifying to the Jews that Jesus is the Christ. Amplified New Testament.

The Divine pressure of the Holy Spirit in his spirit.

e. Verse 6. The Jews manifest opposition and blaspheme the things Paul preaches.
Paul shakes his raiment, as did the Prophets of old, and says, "Your blood be upon your own heads: I am clean; from henceforth I go to the Gentiles."

Paul quotes from Ezekiel 33:3-7. As the Watchman was clear from the blood of all he warned, and their blood would be on their own head if they take not warning, so Paul as a faithful Watchman had gone through the Synagogues, warning and testifying to them of the Christ, and now, after persistent rejection and opposition from them he turns to the Gentiles.

This is the first express declaration of Paul that he is going to turn to the Gentiles, even though he had ministered among the Gentiles previously.

Jewry cried: "His Blood be upon us and our children." Acts 5:28; Matthew 27:25.

Paul cried: "Your blood be upon your own heads." Thus they brought the judgment and curse of Christ's innocent Blood on themselves and unborn generations, and now their own blood is also charged upon themselves for continual rejection of the Grace of God in the Gospel of Christ.

f. Paul and his band move into the House of Crispus and his whole Household

are saved and baptized. Verses 7 to 8.
Crispus' House joined hard next door to the Synagogue.
They were not baptized into the Name of Paul, but into the Name of the Lord Jesus Christ. Compare I Corinthians 1:10, 14-17.

g. The Lord gives Paul a vision telling him that "He has much people in this City." Verses 9-10.
Paul is re-assured of the Lord that no danger would come to his life there. His ministry extended over 18 months in Corinth. Teaching the Word of God.

h. The Jews stir up strife and Paul is brought before "The Judgment Seat" (The Bema Seat) and charged before Gallio over "words, names and laws" of the Jews.
Gallio cared for none of these things and the religious differences between the Jews. If it had been wicked villany then it would call for Judgment.

Human nature is to argue over "words, and names and laws" and miss the truth of God.

Sosthenes, the Chief Ruler of the Synagogue was beaten by the Greeks before the Judgment Seat. Gallio cared for none of these things.

God had a work for Paul to do and there were many souls in this City to be brought to Christ.

In connection with the establishment of the Local Church in Corinth, it is helpful to read the Epistles of Paul written to the Church here.
Though the Church at Corinth had many problems, these problems gave to the Church Universal, Epistles and principles of truth that are not found in any other of the Pauline Epistles.

Paul wrote to the Church at Rome from Corinth. Romans 1:7-15; 16:1-2.

10. **Brief Ministry at Ephesus and return to Antioch.** Acts 18:18-22.

a. Pricilla and Aquilla travel with Paul as he moves back to Ephesus.
He had shaven his head in fulfilment of a vow. Compare Numbers 6:18.

b. Once more he goes "To the Jew first" to the Synagogue and reasoned with the Jews out of the Old Testament Scriptures. Compare Acts 17:2-3.

He promises to return to them in due time, as they pressed for him to stay. He desired to be at Jerusalem for The Feast of Pentecost, in order to be a witness to his own Nation at such important Festival Seasons.

c. Paul salutes the Church at Caesarea.

d. Then he returns to Antioch spending some time there with the Local Church, his 'home Church,' from whence he had been sent forth, recommended to the Grace of God.
There he would report all that God had done in this Second Missionary Journey.

This Chapter closes off Paul's Second Missionary Journey.

New Testament Local Churches established were Philippi, Thessalonica, Berea, Athens, and Corinth.

To these Churches we have several of Paul's Epistles, giving to the Church of all time the riches of the glories of truths of Christ.

## PAUL'S THIRD MISSIONARY JOURNEY

Acts 18:23-28 Acts 19-20 Acts 21:1-14.

IN THIS SECTION we cover Paul's Third Missionary Journey. It is evident that the Apostle Paul had several other journeys in his missionary work which are alluded to in his Epistles, but the Book of Acts covers three main Missionary enterprises.

1. **Ministry in Galatia and Phrygia.** Acts 18:23.
   a. Paul spent some time at his 'home Church' at Antioch.
   b. Then we are told that he departed and went over the country of Galatia and Phrygia in order establishing the disciples and strengthening and imparting help to them.
   Compare I Thessalonians 3:2, 13.
   The Churches need the strength of the Ministry in the Word of the Lord.
   This covers another Missionary Journey.

2. **Ministry at Ephesus.** Acts 18:24-28.
   a. A certain Jew named Apollos, came to Ephesus. God had a purpose in leading this Alexandrian Jew to this City.
   Note the character of the man, for he would be used by the Lord in the ministry of the Church.
      1. He was an eloquent man. Cultured.
      2. He was mighty in the Scriptures. Saturated with the Word.
      Well versed in the Scriptures. Colossians 3:16.
      3. He had been instructed in "The Way of the Lord."
      Actually taught by word of mouth, or hearsay! He had not been taught by revelation.
      The New Testament Scriptures not as yet written.
      The word 'instructed' in Greek is 'katecheo,' and is used in Luke 1:4 and Romans 2:18.

      It means "Orally instructed," or, "to instruct by asking questions and correcting answers."

      From this word is derived "Catechism."
      4. He was fervent in spirit. Burning with spiritual zeal. Hot for the things of the Lord. Not lukewarm or coldness.
      5. He taught diligently the things of the Lord Jesus as they had been handed on to him, concerning the Messianic prophecies pointing to Him.
      6. However it says that he spake "knowing only the Baptism of John." This was insufficient in the light of all that had happened since John the Baptist passed from the scene.
      (Note — This is introductory material to that which happens in Ephesus under Paul's Ministry relative to those disciples who had only experienced John's Baptism. Refer to comments on Acts 19:1-6.
      7. He spake freely and boldly in the Synagogues to the Jews.
      8. Aquilla and Priscilla (Compare 18:1-3, 18) who were still at Ephesus, took Apollos aside and expounded unto him "The Way of God more perfectly."

This reveals that this mighty and eloquent man was humble enough to allow another brother and his wife, Aquilla and Pricilla, to teach him the things of "The Way" more clearly and accurately.

The man was teachable! One cannot teach others if he becomes unteachable himself.

Aquilla and Priscilla had received further light than that which came under John's Ministry. The light that came with John was limited, and simply pointed to a much more needed and fuller light as found in the Ministry and Person of Jesus Christ.

Apollos had incomplete and insufficient knowledge, but the Teacher was teachable.

God moves in His own mysterious ways upon the open heart.

Apollos is such an example to all believers today! It is good to appreciate and receive light and truth from the Lord, but it is an absolute necessity to keep open to the Lord when God has His Ministries there to expound "The Way of God more fully" to us.

God only truly gives Light and Truth to those who are willing to walk therein. Psalms 43:3.

Apollos was willing.

b. Apollos was moved by the Will of the Lord to go to Corinth.
The brethren wrote Letters of recommendation to the believers to receive him.

c. Ministry of Apollos was blessed much in Corinth, and he was able to refute and convince many of the Jews publicly by showing and proving that Jesus Christ was the promised Messiah of the Old Testament Scriptures.

Comparing the Scriptural prophecies and the Historical facts concerning Jesus of Nazareth, that He fulfilled all the details foretold and which were necessary as Divine proof that He was the Christ.

So great was Apollos' Ministry at Corinth that 'party factions' came into being over the personalities of Paul, Peter and Apollos.

All this 'carnality' and 'personality worship,' which is simply idolatry in God's sight, was rebuked by Paul in his Epistle to this Church.
I Corinthians 3:1-7, 21-23.

Paul exhorts that we must not glory in men. We must appreciate the various and different Ministries set in the glory, but we must not deify them.

All Ministries are ours, whether a Paul, a Peter or an Apollos. All are needed for the maturing and establishing of the saints. All are needed for Divine balance in the Church, the Body of Christ, and all bring forth the "portion of truth" which God has deposited in them. One sows, another waters, but God gives the increase!

3. **Ministry at Ephesus under Paul.** Acts 19:1-41.

a. Paul had passed through Ephesus previously and had promised to return in the Lord's will and time. Compare Acts 18:18-21.
In the meantime, God had Aquilla and Priscilla there, and then Apollos had come and received further light, and now Paul returns again.

b. Paul finds certain Disciples there, and asks them the question: "Have ye received the Holy Ghost since (or when) ye believe?"

It is evident that Paul must have 'sensed in the spirit,' that something — or Someone — was absent in the experience of the Ephesians.

They answer that they did not know that the Holy Spirit had been 'poured out.' Literally.

The emphasis in Acts is upon "believing" and "receiving" — not "tarrying."

There was only and ever one "tarrying meeting," but all occasions were "receiving meetings" in the Acts of the Apostles!

This does not do away with the necessity of believers waiting upon the Lord and seeking His face.

c. Paul immediately asks them concerning their Water Baptism. "Unto what (or, unto whom) then were ye baptized?"

If they had been baptized only according to Matthew 28:19, "Into THE NAME of The Father, and of The Son and of The Holy Ghost," then they would have at least 'heard' of The Holy Ghost.

John's message had foretold the coming "Baptism with the Holy Spirit" under the Christ. Matthew 3:1-11.

Nearly all records in Acts show that believers were saved, water-baptized and filled with the Holy Spirit, at or about the same period of time.

Several records show Water Baptism and Holy Spirit Baptism taking place at the same time.

The Ephesian believers had not heard that the Holy Spirit had been poured out. Their experience was very similar to the experience of Apollos, "knowing only the Baptism of John."

d. Paul baptized these Disciples again in (Greek, eis, or 'into') The Name of the Lord Jesus (Christ.) Verse 5.

(Various Translations have Baptism in Acts into the Name of the Lord, or Lord Jesus, or Jesus Christ, and others have the full Triune Name, The Lord—Jesus—Christ, which alone completely fulfills the demand and command of Matthew 28:19, which requires the invocation of the TRIUNE Name of the Eternal Godhead, Father, Son and Holy Spirit.)

e. God sealed this act of Paul by imparting the Holy Spirit Baptism to these Disciples by the Laying on of Hands. Verse 6.

The evidence? "They spake with tongues and prophesied."

(N.B. It is questioned, "Why did he baptize these Disciples again?"
What was lacking in John's Baptism?
Wherein was the difference?
Why was it insufficient to know only the Baptism of John?

If it was a matter of "words and Names" which were so unimportant to Paul, then Paul need not have followed the procedure which he did.

If words of a 'formula' were unnecessary to Paul, and it was the act of Baptism and heart-obedience that was the essential thing, then Paul had no need to do what he did.

What was the lesson here?

The answer to this is by a comparison of John's Baptism and Christian Baptism.

| John's Baptism | | Christian Baptism |
|---|---|---|
| Involved Repentance, | — | Involves the Repentant, |
| And Remission of sins, | — | And Remission of sins, |
| Involved Faith in the coming Messiah, | — | Involves Faith in Christ Jesus, |
| Involved Confession of being a | — | Confession of Faith, |
| Sinner | — | Burial of old self-life, |
| Was by plunging, dipping, or | — | Is by plunging, dipping, or |
| Immersion beneath the water. | — | Immersion beneath the water. |

In all these respects above, both John's Baptism and Christian Baptism are identified.

Wherein lies the difference?
The following gives the answers.

| | | |
|---|---|---|
| John's Baptism was before The Death, Burial and the Resurrection of the Lord. | — | Christian Baptism is after The Death, Burial and the Resurrection of the Lord. |
| John's Baptism was Nameless. | — | Christian Baptism invokes the Name of Christ. |
| John's Baptism was ordained of God temporarily. | — | Christian Baptism is permanent, in the Church. |
| John's Baptism was incomplete, insufficient and inadequate for the New Testament Church. | — | Christian Baptism completes that which was lacking in John's Baptism. |
| John's Baptism was superceded by the Command of Jesus in Baptism in Matthew 28:19-20. | — | Christian Baptism replaces John's Baptism. |
| | | Christian Baptism into The Name Of The Father, Son, and Holy Spirit, into The Name of the Lord Jesus Christ. |

Summarizing the two main points of difference in these Baptisms, we have the following.

1. Christian Baptism is into the Death, Burial and Resurrection of the Lord. It is identification with Calvary's work, the Atonement.

2. Christian Baptism is into the Name of the Eternal Godhead: Father, Son and Holy Spirit, into the Name of the Lord Jesus Christ.

It was not a matter of mere words of a formula to Paul; but it was identification with and into the work of Calvary, and the invocation of the Godhead Name upon these Disciples.

There is power in the proper use of 'The Name' whether in salvation, healing, exorcism, prayer, or water Baptism.

The words of Jesus, of Peter, of Paul, are the infallible words of Scripture.

f. Paul ministers again to the Jew in the Synagogue, for the space of 3 months. Verse 8.
Disputing and persuading the things concerning the Kingdom of God. Compare Acts 1:3, 6; 8:12. The Early Church preached and demonstrated the Gospel of the Kingdom. Matthew 24:14.

g. Results? Verses 9-10.
Division and separation. Divers were hardened and believed not, but spoke evil of "The Way." Compare Acts 9:2 — notes.

Paul departed, separating the Disciples from the ground and area of unbelief.

For 2 years he ministers the Word at Ephesus. Ephesus became a great Church, from which the Gospel sounded out in all Asia. Previously the Spirit had forbidden him to preach in Asia, and suffered him not to go to this area. Acts 16:6-7.

Now it was God's will and timing. It is evident that a number of Churches were established in Asia Minor, and it seems that Ephesus was the center from which many Local Churches were established.
Refer to Revelation 1:10-12. "The Seven Churches which are in Asia."

Here at Ephesus "A great Door and effectual" was opened to Paul. I Corinthians 16:8-9.

h. God wrought special (not the ordinary!?) miracles. Verses 11-12.
Diseases and demon spirits leave the bodies of the afflicted as these clothes were laid upon them.

God often worked and used various things as means of Grace and channels of His appointments.

He used a Brazen Serpent, The Passover Lamb, The Hem of Christ's garment, Clay Spittle, Waters of Jordan, Anointing Oil, Laying on of Hands, etc., in manifesting His healing power.

He is still the same. Hebrews 13:8.

If the power of God is absent, and the Presence of the Holy Spirit, then all these things degenerate into mere 'witchcrafts.'

Hence Hezekiah destroyed the Brazen Serpent, which God had once used for healing Israel, when it became an 'idol' or 'witchcraft.' II Kings 18:4.

Such things can become superstitious nonsense, religious gimmicks, witchcraft and fetishes.

Under the Presence and Anointing of the Holy Spirit they become means of Grace, and channels of impartation of blessing.

i. Presumption at Ephesus. vs. 13-20.

Seven sons of Sceva, vagabond and apostate Jews, who should have known better, took upon themselves to presume to exorcise evil spirits "In the Name of Jesus whom Paul preacheth."

Living in sin and iniquity and presumption, having no legal right to use the Name of Jesus Christ, the evil spirits in the man leaped upon them, stripping them naked, and they fled out of the house wounded.

The evil spirits knew who had spiritual authority over them, and whose

command they would obey.
They knew who had the legal right to use 'The Name.'

The evil spirit spoke through human lips, saying, "Jesus I know, Paul I know, but who are you?" Better translated: "Jesus I acknowledge (ginosko) and Paul I am acquainted with (epistamai,) — you belong to neither and have the authority of neither!"

NOTE: These evil spirits did not even know their own kind — Satan's house, divided against itself is destined to fall!

The Holy Spirit also speaks through human lips.

Jesus said to the 70 Disciples, who returned with joy at the casting out of devils, to "rejoice that their names were published abroad in the heavenlies."

Names written in heaven, or the heavenlies, by the Lord Jesus, and only then is there power to use the Name of the Lord in our legal rights.

What was the result? Verses 17, 18-19, 20.

1. The Name of the Lord Jesus was magnified, made great.
2. Believers who had practiced curious magical arts, and had Black Magic Books with their incantations, brought them and burned them.
   Things used to contact evil spirits were burned.
   Such Books were the words of Satan, and of the activity of Demons.
   Compare Ephesians 6:12-18.
   Great cleansing and confession.
3. The Word grew and multiplied. It grew mightily and prevailed. Compare Psalms 138:2.

j. Opposition at Ephesus. vs. 21-41.

Great stir came about "The Way" at this time. Verse 23. Compare Acts 9:2.

Note the order of opposition Paul suffers:

1. Opposition from the Jew first.
2. Oposition from the Gentiles.
3. Opposition from Evil Spirits.
4. Now it is opposition from the Commercial World.
   The Business Men of the City. Money — the God of Mammon.

Demetrius, the silversmith, who made much money through the little silver Shrines of the "Great Goddess Diana," arouses the business men of the City against Paul.

The Goddess Diana was one of the 7 Wonders of the ancient World. She was one of the principal goddesses of the Greeks and Romans. Her Greek name was Artemis.

Idolatry abounded in these Cities, with all immorality and vile orgies. This was the Deification of a Woman — A Goddess. Behind the worship of idols was a Spirit.
Worshipped by the world.

This Goddess was reputed to have fallen from heaven. The Greeks had numerous gods and goddesses, demi-gods, semi-gods, half-god-half-men.

Confusion breaks out in the City under the spirit of mob rule. Verses 28-29.

The brethren restrained Paul from endangering his life in the midst of such a mob spirit, (verses 30-32) by going into the Theater.

Alexander becomes a real enemy of Paul. Compare verse 33 with I Timothy 1:20 and II Timothy 4:14.

Eventually the Townclerk appeased the howling mob and brought order back into the City, telling Demetrius and the business men that there are proper channels through the Court if they have any real charge against Paul and his party. Verses 35-41.

(Note— The word 'Robbers of Churches,' in verse 37, is properly 'Robbers of Temples.'
The Church is the Called Out Company the believers, and not a material building made with hands.)

After the uproar, Paul embraces the Disciples. Acts 20:1.

Such was the founding of the Church at Ephesus. In connection with this glorious establishment of the Local Church here, it is profitable to remember the Epistles written to this Church.

1. The Church at Ephesus founded. Acts 19.
2. The Epistle to the Ephesians. Written by Paul.
3. The Epistle of Christ to Ephesus, written by John. Revelation 2:1-7.

   Refer also to Paul's final Charge to the Elders of the Church at Ephesus, in Acts 20:17-35.

4. **Ministry in Macedonia.** Acts 19:21-22; 20:1-2.

   a. Paul purposed in the spirit (by the Holy Spirit also) to go into Macedonia and Achaia, and then on to Jerusalem.

   b. He sends two of his assistants (Deacons, Servants,) Timothy and Erastus ahead of him.

   c. He, himself, stays in Asia for awhile. Waiting on the Lord. Seeking His will and mind for that which lay ahead of him.

   d. Paul then goes into Macedonia and ministers in all those areas, giving them much exhortation.

   To exhort means "to stir up." Keeping the believers stirred up over the things of the Lord.

   The saints would be glad to see him in Macedonia, remembering the 'Macedonian call' and response in Acts 16:9-40.

5. **Ministry in Greece and Corinth.** Acts 20:2-3.

   a. Paul came into Greece and ministers at Corinth for about 3 months. Refer to comments, Acts 18:1-23.
   No mention of ministry particularly at the City of Athens!

   b. His life is threatened by the Jews.

   c. Note the Apostolic company in verse 4. All the fruit of Paul's labors. These all precede Paul to Troas.

6. **Ministry at Troas.** Acts 20:5-6, 7-12.

   a. Paul sails from Philippi to Troas and stays there 7 days.
   This was in the time of Feast of Passover, or Unleavened Bread.

   b. He ministers the Word of God as the Disciples "came together to break bread on the first day of the week."

   It is helpful to remember that the Early Church is in the transition period, emerging from the Old Covenant into the full blessing of the New Covenant.

   This is seen in relation to the Sabbath Day and the First Day of the week.

   1. Paul reasoned with the Jews in the Synagogues on the Sabbath concerning Christ Jesus and the Gospel.
   This was how he kept the Sabbath.

   2. Then Paul and the Early Church observed the First Day of the week, as the full light and revelation of the Gospel came through to them by the Ministry of the Holy Spirit.

   This change from the Jewish (Hebrew) Sabbath Day to observing the First Day of the week was in fulfilment of prophetic types and also Scriptures of the Old Testament.

   **Prophetic types.**

   1. The Sheaf of the First Fruits was to be waved before the Lord on "the morrow after the Sabbath."
   Leviticus 23:9-14.

   Paul interprets the Sheaf as the Resurrected Christ before God, who was raised — not on the Sabbath — but "on the morrow after the Sabbath."
   That is, on the First Day of the week. I Corinthians 15:20-23; Matthew 28:1; John 20:1; Mark 16:1-2; Luke 24:1.
   The First Day of the new week was the Day of the Resurrection. The Jews had a 'Christless Sabbath' on the 7th Day.

   2. The Feast of Pentecost and the Presentation of the Two Wave Loaves took place 50 days after the waving of the Sheaf of the First Fruits.
   This was 7 Sabbaths (or, 7 × 7 = 49) and then the 50th Day was "the morrow after the 7th Sabbath."

   This found its fulfilment in Acts 2:1-4. The Feast Day of Pentecost was the 50th Day after the Resurrection of Jesus Christ.
   The Holy Spirit came on the First Day of the week. Not on a Sabbath Day, but "the morrow after the Sabbath."
   The Jews again kept a 'Sabbath without the Spirit.' The Letter and Form of the Law, but not having the Spirit, or the Life. II Corinthians 3:6.

   Hence the two most important foundation events in the Early Church took place, not on the Hebrew 7th or Sabbath Day, but on "the morrow after the Sabbath." In other words, on the First Day of the week.

   1. The Resurrection of the Son of God, Jesus Christ, and

   2. The Outpouring of the Holy Spirit of God in the formation of the Church.

   If the Son of God, and the Holy Spirit by-passed the Weekly Sabbath, it showed that the Shadow was at an end; and this was being fulfilled in the

TRUE Sabbath Rest in the Godhead.

When two Persons in the Eternal Godhead set their seal that the Sabbath Day was ended, and established the foundations of the Church on the First Day of the week, then all believers ought to follow likewise, and accept the Divine Testimony.

**Prophetic Scriptures.**

1. Hosea prophesied, "I will cause her New Moons, Feasts and her Sabbaths to cease," etc. Hosea 2:11.
2. Paul states that we are not to let anyone judge us in respect of New Moons, Holy or Feast Days, or meats, or of keeping of Sabbath Days, which were all a Shadow of things to come.
   Colossians 2:14-16.
3. He says that one man esteems one Day better than another, and others esteem every Day alike. Every one must be fully persuaded in his own mind.
   Romans 14:5-7.
4. The TRUE Sabbath Rest is found "in Christ" and "in the Baptism of the Holy Spirit."
   Matthew 12:28-30; Hebrews 4:9; Isaiah 28:10-12.

   The First Day of the week is not the Sabbath. The 7th Day was and is the Hebrew Sabbath, a Sign for the Nation of Israel. Exodus 31:16-17; Ezekiel 20:12.

   The Early Church moved from the keeping of the Sabbath Day into the privilege of the First Day of the week, because:— Christ rose from the dead that day, and the Holy Spirit was poured out on the Early Church on that same day.

   The believer is under the NEW Covenant and the SIGN of Rest is the Baptism in the Spirit.
   Jeremiah 31:31-34.

   The Nation of Israel was under the OLD Covenant and the SIGN of Rest was in the keeping of the 7th Day.

   The Early Church —

   a. Broke Bread on the First Day of the week.
      Acts 20:7; I Corinthians 11:33.
   b. Laid aside the collections on the First Day of the week. I Corinthians 16:2.
   c. The Lord Jesus rose the First Day of the week.
   d. The Holy Spirit was outpoured at Pentecost on the First Day of the week.
      All this is sufficient Scriptural ground for the Church today!

c. Paul preached through until midnight. Verse 7.

d. A young man, by the name of Eutychus, fell asleep and fell out of the window and died. The Apostle preached him to sleep! The natural!

   Paul raised him from the dead. Apostolic ministry.

The supernatural! Resurrection life.

Peter raised Dorcas from the dead.
Paul raised this young man from the dead. Matthew 10:7-8; Job 19:25; I Corinthians 15:52.

7. **Journey to and Ministry at Miletus.** Acts 20:13-38.

   a. Journey to Miletus. Verses 13 to 16.
   Paul was anxious to be at Jerusalem for the celebration of the Day of Pentecost.

   b. From Miletus Paul sends to Ephesus and calls for the Elders of the Church to come to him. Verse 17.
   Note — "Elders," in the plural. Always plurality of the Ministry in the Early Church.
   The Eldership constituted the Oversight of the Flock.

   c. Consider Paul's final message and address to the Elders at Ephesus.

   Refer also to notes on Qualifications of Elders as in Acts 14:23, in connection with Paul's charge to the Elders here.

   1. Paul reminds them of his own message and ministry, of his own sufferings and temptations. Verses 18-19.
   Humility of mind.
   Though having great revelation from the Lord, yet there was a humility inwrought by the Spirit of God.
   Tears and temptations.
   The Lord saw and knew them all.

   2. His ministry publicly and from house to house.

   3. The First Principles of the Doctrine of Christ. Verse 21.
   Compare Hebrews 6:1-2; Mark 1:15.
   Repentance towards God.
   Faith towards the Lord Jesus Christ.

   4. Paul knows in the spirit (his own spirit, and by the Holy Spirit) that afflictions await him at Jerusalem. Verses 22-24.
   Compare Acts 20:22 with Acts 21:4.
   He is willing to lay down his life for the Gospel of the Grace of God. "None of these things move me." Note, Amplified New Testament on Verses 21-24.

   5. Paul preached the Kingdom of God. Verse 25. Compare Acts 1:3.
   Preached and demonstrated the Gospel of the Kingdom, in the Grace of God. Matthew 24:14.

   6. He declares his purity from shunned responsibiity. Verse 26.
   Pure from the blood of all men.
   As a "Watchman" he has warned within and without. Ezekiel 33:7.

   7. He had declared to them the whole counsel of God as committed to him. Verse 27.
   "Fully preached the Gospel." No part or half-Gospel with Paul.
   No measure or part-counsel of God.
   His Epistles bear record to this statement.

   8. His warning and exhortation to the Elders. Verses 28-31.

a. Take heed to yourselves.
'Self' — the biggest enemy.

b. Take heed to the Flock of God.

c. The Holy Spirit had made them Overseers.
Bishops, Elders, Overseers — all involve the same person.
Though ordained by the Apostles, yet it was the Spirit who had appointed them as Elders.

d. Called to 'feed' (poimen, pastor, shepherdize, tend as a shepherd does his sheep,) the Flock of God.

e. The Church — God's Flock — was purchased with the Blood of God.
Compare Hebrews 13:20; John 1:14; Matthew 1:20-25; Hebrews 9:25.
The Incorruptible Seed of the Father God, having in it the Blood, was planted in the Virgin Mary by the Overshadowing of the Holy Spirit. Jesus Christ is the God-Man. The Godhead was involved in that Incorruptible Blood of Jesus, in the Incarnation.

f. Watch for the grievous wolves. The enemy without. In sheep's clothing. Matthew 7:15; II Peter 2:1.
Feed the Flock — not slay them!

g. Watch among yourselves. Elders arising within. The enemy within. Drawing to 'self.'
Speaking perverse (distorted and corrupt) things.
Party spirit. Personality spirit. Schism. Division.

9. Paul himself was the example Minister and Elder. Verse 31.

10. He commends them to God and His Word. Verse 32.
The Word of His Grace. It is able to build up (edify,) and to give the saints of light their inheritance.
The sanctified, or, "set apart ones."

11. Paul touched not the silver or gold or apparel.
Paul was a worker, and giver. Not covetous. I Corinthians 9:12; II Corinthians 12:17; Acts 20:33, 34-35. Worked with own hands at times.
Paul ministered even to the poor, and weak. Luke 14:12.
Paul used his trade in Tent-making even to support those with him at times when the Churches did not help him.

12. Paul's farewell prayer. Verses 36-38.
This must have been a very touching scene as Paul and the Elders prayed together, weeping and kissing him as they realized they would see his face no more, and then accompanying him to the ship.

This Charge to the Elders is one of the richest 'Charges' in the New Testament, and a challenge to all Elders today.

Read once again the Epistle to the Ephesians as Paul defines some of the richest revelation given to him concerning the Church, to be presented to Christ.
Then read the Lord's Epistle through the Apostle John in Revelation 2:1-7. The Church maintained pure Doctrine but sadly fell from "first love," and was threatened with removal of its Candlestick unless it

responded to genuine repentance.

The Second Epistle of Timothy was written from Rome by Paul to Timothy who was Bishop of Ephesus. II Timothy 4:22, postscript.

8. **Ministry at Tyre.** Acts 21:1-6.

a. The Apostolic team journey to Tyre, where the ship was to unload. Verses 1-3.

b. They find Disciples there and tarried with them for 7 days. Verse 4. Compare Matthew 11:21.

c. Paul is warned once again by the Holy Spirit that trouble waited him at Jerusalem. Verse 4.
Compare Acts 20:22-24.
Though the Spirit foretold what would happen to Paul, he would not be moved from the will of God.

d. The believers accompany the band to the ship, and after prayer together, they embark.

e. The ship sails through to Ptolemais where they stay one day with the brethren there. Verse 7.

9. **Arrival at Caesarea.** Acts 21:8-14.

a. This really closes off Paul's third great Missionary Journey.
At Caesarea they enter into Philip the Evangelist's house. Verse 8.
Philip was last seen in Acts chapter 8 and his great Ministry of Evangelism there.

b. Philip had four daughters which did prophesy. They were not Prophetesses however. They had a gift of prophecy. Verse 9.
How refreshing must have been the fellowship at Philip's house.

c. While at Philip's house, God sends the proven Prophet Agabus down from Judea to Caesarea. Verses 10-11. Compare Acts 11:27-30.

d. Agabus, by the Spirit signified what would happen to Paul when he got to Jerusalem.
Taking Paul's girdle, he bound his own hands and feet saying that this is what would happen to Paul by the Jews there.
"Thus saith the Holy Spirit."

The Jews would then deliver him over to the Gentiles.

Note — Though Philip had four daughters which had the Gift of prophecy, yet God sent Agabus with the Office of a Prophet to speak to Paul.

Once again, this was not guidance to Paul, but confirmation of the already known will of God.

e. Consider these facts. It has been suggested that Paul was out of the will of God going to Jerusalem, and that had he heeded these warnings of the Spirit through the various channels in the Local Churches, then he would not have been arrested.

However, a study of the following Scriptures reveals that Paul was in the will of God.

1. Ananias had foretold to Paul that he was called to suffer for the Name of the Lord Jesus. Acts 9:15-16.

2. Paul himself knew in the spirit, by the Spirit, that bonds and imprisonment awaited him in every City. Acts 20:22-24.
   In Corinth, the Lord assured him no harm would come to his life. This was his first trip there.
   The next time at Corinth, the Jews laid wait to catch him. Acts 18:10; 20:3.
3. Paul knew by the spirit also that he would go to Jerusalem, and then to Rome. Acts 19:21-22.
4. The brethren at Tyre said he should not go up to Jerusalem, through the Spirit. Acts 21.4.
5. Then Agabus the Prophet confirms to Paul what will happen to him when he goes to Jerusalem. Acts 21:13.
   The brethren endeavour to persuade Paul not to go. They interpret the prophecies as a warning for him not to go. However, Paul — though he did not know exactly what would befall him at Jerusalem — knew that bonds and imprisonments and afflictions awaited him in every City.
6. Paul personally knew the will of God for him to go to Jerusalem, even though his witness would not be accepted. Acts 22:17-18; 23:11.

f. When the brethren could not persuade Paul against going to Jerusalem, they said "The will of the Lord be done." Verse 14.

   God's will was being done! God's will was confirmed. It is human nature to try and interpret the prophetic word contrary to the will of God. It is human nature to misunderstand what God is saying.
   Paul knew His Master's will.
   Paul was willing to die for His Master at Jerusalem, if need be. After all, he had been responsible for the death of many early believers!

g. What fellowship there must have been at Caesarea.
   Philip, the Evangelist.
   Paul, the Apostle.
   Agabus, the Prophet.
   Philip's four daughters which prophesied.

h. The Apostolic team leaves with other believers, for Jerusalem. Verses 15-17.

## PAUL'S WITNESS AT JERUSALEM

Acts 21:15-40 — Acts 22 — Acts 23.

AS NOTED PREVIOUSLY, it was the will of the Lord for Paul to go to Jerusalem and be a witness and testimony there, even though the Lord knew the Jews would not accept his Testimony.

These Chapters under consideration cover this witness of Paul in the "Holy City," which in a few years' time would be laid desolate, and the Temple would be destroyed totally, and Jewry would be scattered to the four corners of the earth, "Until the Times of the Gentiles be fulfilled."

Luke 19:41-44; 21:20-24.

1. **Paul at Jerusalem.** Acts 21:15-40.

   a. Paul and his company arrive in Jerusalem from Caesarea, and they are received of James and the Elders of the Church there. Verses 17-18.

b. Paul declares what God had wrought amongst the Gentiles by his ministry. The Jerusalem brethren received the news with joy. Verses 19-20a.

c. The Law-Grace believers. Verses 20b-24.
The brethren at Jerusalem encourage Paul to take on the Nazarite Vow to protect himself and the Church at Jerusalem for receiving him.

Their excitement is that there were thousands of Jews which were believers in Christ, and yet were still zealous for the Laws of Moses.

"All of them were enthusiastic upholders of the Mosaic Law." Amplified N.T.

These were Law-Grace believers. Compare Romans 10:1-2.
Moses in one hand, and Christ in the other hand. Typical of that seen in the Galatian Church.
The compromise of both which produced mixture, Law mingled with Grace. Moses mixed with Jesus!

They tell Paul that the Jewish believers have been informed that Paul does not follow circumcision any longer, or the customs of the Jews, or the Law of Moses. In order to save the situation, when the Jews hear Paul is in the City, they exhort him to go through the Mosaic Rituals as 'proof' that these reports were not so. Verses 21-22.

So Paul according to his principle seen in I Corinthians 9:19-23, follows suit.

He (1) Takes a vow with four men, possibly according to the Nazarite Vow. Numbers 6:1-7. Shaves his head.

(2) Spends charges of purification with these men also.

(3) Goes into the Temple with them for signifying the days of purification were upon him.

(4) Then waits for an Offering to be offered for them. Paul pays Temple expenses.

This vow was for 7 days.

It is important to note that this was not a compromise on Paul's part.
It has been said that if Paul had not stooped to fulfill these Laws of the Mosaic Ritual, then he would not have been arrested in the Temple, while performing these things he did not believe in.
God was in and above all, using these things for His ultimate purposes for Paul's Ministry.

Though Paul obliged in these things, he did not believe they counted to God.

He knew, as the Epistle to the Hebrews clearly shows, that the Mosaic Rituals, with Aaronic Priesthood, Animal Sacrifices and Oblations, Rituals of Purification, etc., all were fulfilled and abolished in the perfect once-for-all Sacrifice of Jesus Christ. Paul found all this in Christ. Hebrews 10th chapter.

He also knew that God had finished with the Temple, demonstrated in the Rent Veil, and though Jewry was carrying on the abominable system, God was soon to have the whole thing smashed to the ground, under Roman Prince Titus, in A.D. 70.

Paul knew that this was the 'transition era' from the Old Covenant to the New Covenant, but he was well aware of the truth and the truth had set him free.

Here he followed his principle of "becoming as a Jew to the Jews that he might win the Jew."

He knew that circumcision availed nothing, nor did any of the other rites of the Mosaic Law. Paul also knew that the Church at Jerusalem was a mixture of "Moses-Jesus-believers," and it was from Jerusalem and Judea he had suffered the most, from brethren that persistently dogged his footsteps, bringing trouble and discord into all the Churches of the Gentiles which he established.

But Paul became all things to all men that he might win some!

d. The Elders tell Paul that they have maintained the Decree established at the Conference concerning the Gentile believers. Verse 25. Compare Acts 15:19-27.
So they have Gentile-believers, who serve Christ, and Jewish-believers, who serve Moses AND Christ.!

e. In Verses 27-32, Paul is arrested.
The 7 days of the Vow and Purification are almost at an end when some of the Jews from Asia, there for the Feast of Pentecost, (Acts 20:16) recognize Paul.

They suppose that he has with him in the Temple an Ephesian called Trophimus, a Gentile, and that their Temple is being defiled by a Gentile. Verses 27-29.

They still call it "this Holy Place." Verse 28.

It is evident that they did not accept that God was finished with the Temple economy, and that the prophecies of Christ concerning the destruction of the Temple and every stone being upturned upon another, were either forgotten or cast aside. Compare Matthew 23:38; 24:1-4; Luke 19:41-44; 21:20-24.

The whole City was moved and shut the Doors of the Temple and took Paul to kill him. Verses 30-31.

The Chief Captain came on the scene as the City was in an uproar, taking with him Soldiers and Centurions, who just came in time to save Paul from being beaten to death. Verse 32. Acts 23:27, 24:7; II Corinthians 11:23-37.

f. The Roman authority gives Paul permission to speak. Verses 33-40.

Paul is bound with chains.
The people are in tumult and violent against him.

Note their cry "Away with him." The same cry given against the Lord Jesus. Luke 23:18; John 19:15; Acts 22:22.

The servant shall be as his Master.

Paul asks for permission to speak to the people and receives it. He speaks in the Hebrew tongue.

In these Chapters we see how the prophetic word of the Lord to Paul, through Ananias, is particularly fulfilled.

Acts 9:15. "Go thy way, for he is a Chosen Vessel unto Me, to bear My Name . . . to suffer for My Name's sake . . ."

1. **Before the Gentiles.**
   Acts Chapters 13 to 20 covers Ministry amongst the Gentiles.

2. **Before Kings** (Rulers.)
   The present Chapters, Acts 24, 25, and 26 show fulfilment of this.

3. **Before the Children of Israel.**
   The Chapters immediately under consideration show the fulfilment of this.
   Acts chapters 22 and 23.

This is Paul's final visit to Jerusalem. Paul had never been fully accepted here. They were rather pleased that his Ministry was to the Gentile Cities, as he was too strong in the revelation of the Grace of God, without the Law of Moses.

What a contrast to the first scenes in the Church at Jerusalem. This Church which experienced the initial Pentecostal Outpouring, the Ministry of the Word in signs and wonders, and the thousands of Jews which had turned to Christ — now it has degenerated into a Legalistic Church, a "Law-Grace-Church."

2. **Paul's Testimony at Jerusalem to Israel.** Acts 22:1-21.
   Paul's Defense, Witness and Testimony before the Jews here is clearly defined and set in order. It is clear cut!

   a. He appeals to his countrymen, for which he had continual sorrow and great heaviness in his heart.
      Verses 1-2. Compare Romans 9:1-3.
      He was willing to be accursed for his brethren after the flesh, so great was his love for them.

   b. The order of his Testimony and Witness.

      1. Declares the fact he is a Jew, born in Tarsus. Verse 3.
      2. That he was brought up in the City of Jerusalem, and sat at the feet of Gamaliel, who taught him according to the perfect manner of the fathers. Compare Acts 5:34. Gamaliel had given a word of wisdom previously not to fight against what God was doing. Paul was a Law-abiding Jew.
      3. His zealousness towards God. Verse 3.
      4. His persecution of "The Way," by delivering believers to prison and death. Verse 4.
      5. His Letters of authority from the High Priest and the Elders to bring believers from Damascus to Jerusalem to be punished. Verse 5.
      6. His miraculous arrest on the Damascus Road, and his conversion to Christ Jesus. Verses 6 to 8.
         The Jewish hearers should have been able to recognize all these things were Old Testament manifestations of Jehovah God to His Ministers. Paul's account of his conversion is very similar to the experience of Moses at the Burning Bush. Exodus 3.
         Refer back to Acts Chapter 9, and comments.
      7. The travellers with Paul saw the light and heard the voice, but did not hear the words spoken directly to Paul. Verse 9.
      8. Paul is directed by the Lord into the City where Ananias by revelation came to him confirming that which the Lord had spoken on the Damascus Road. Verse 10 to 13.
         He called on the Name of the Lord, in the Lord Jesus Christ.
      9. Ananias was well-known and of good report among the Jews. Under him Paul is healed of blindness, water Baptized and receives the Holy Spirit in

the Laying on of Hands. Verses 13 to 16.
His prophetic word to Paul was this:—

a. The God of our fathers has chosen thee.

b. To know His will.

c. To see the Just One.

d. To hear the Voice of His mouth.

e. To be His witness of all he has seen and heard.

10. The Lord tells Paul when he was in Jerusalem previously, (Possibly on his first visit to Jerusalem after his conversion,) as he was in a trance in the Temple, that he was to get quickly out of Jerusalem for the Jews would not be willing to accept his Testimony concerning Christ. Verses 17 and 18.

11. Paul reminds the Lord how he imprisoned and beat people in the Synagogues, and how he sensed the blood of Stephen upon his shoulders, as he stood by consenting to his death and holding his garment. Verses 19 and 20.

    It is clear in all Paul's witness that the blood of Stephen and the saints continually weighed upon his mind and heart, and he was willing to lay down his life as a living sacrifice for his brethren whom he had slain.

    He tells Timothy that he was "a blasphemer, a persecutor, and injurious, but he obtained mercy because he did it ignorantly in unbelief." I Timothy 1:12-13; Acts 7:58; 8:1.

12. The Lord tells him that he will send him to the Gentiles. Verse 21. The word "Gentiles" was Paul's final word. Legalistic bigotry prevailed.
    They were Jews, under Mosaic Law, with Christ in the other hand. They cared not about the salvation of the Gentiles. They rejoiced not that the Lord was visiting the Gentiles to take out of them a people for His Name.

    They cared not that the Prophets foretold the Gentiles would come into blessing through Messiah.

    Such was their Nationalistic attitude and spiritual blindness and bigotry. Compare Acts 13:27 again.

c. Note their cry in verse 22, and compare with 21:36.
"Away with such a fellow from the earth, for it is not fit that he should live."
The rage of the Jews.
Compare I Thessalonians 2:16; Luke 22:18. So said they of Paul's Master.

d. The Jews allow mob-spirit to prevail. Crying out, casting dust into the air, and waving their clothes about. Verse 23.

e. The Chief Captain takes Paul into the Castle to have him scourged.
Paul exercises his legal rights and privileges as having Roman Citizenship to save himself from another scourging. Verses 25 to 29.

Please note: II Corinthians 11:23-28. Paul had received scourgings and floggings and beatings from the Jews, his own countrymen, and accepted it as part of the sufferings foretold to him.
In Corinthians he lists his sufferings in the Ministry of Christ.

However, when it came to Roman scourging and punishment, Paul exercises his rights as a Roman Citizen.

He did this in Acts 16:37, after he had the flogging; here he does it before the flogging.

Paul bore in his body the marks (stigma) of the Lord Jesus. Galatians 6:17.
Paul recognized that the powers that were ordained of God. Romans 13:1-7.

Believers are privileged to avail themselves of these rights of Citizenship so long as they do not conflict against the Word and will of God.

"Scourging" was a terrible form of punishment and chastisement.
According to the Law of Moses, they were to receive 40 stripes save one, or 39 stripes in the flogging.
Many a person would die under such a flogging. Paul suffered this of the Jews 5 times. He had stripes above measure. Deuteronomy 25:3; II Corinthians 11:24.

One has only to read carefully the sufferings of Paul in II Corinthians the 11th chapter to appreciate the love and passion in his heart for Christ and the Church.

He "rejoiced in his sufferings and filled up that which was lacking of the afflictions of Christ in his flesh, for His Body's sake, which is the Church!" Colossians 1:24.

Angels delivered Peter from prison and chains in answer to the prayer of the saints at Jerusalem.

But no Angel delivers Paul from this state in Jerusalem, and how many saints prayed for him?

But God was over all, working all things after the counsel of His own will.

f. The Chief Priests and the Sanhedrin are commanded to appear to bring their charges against Paul. Verse 30.

3. **Paul's Final Testimony before the Sanhedrin.** Acts 23:1-35.

A number of years before, the Lord Jesus Himself stood before the Sanhedrin in trial and was falsely accused and condemned.

Then years later, Stephen stands before the Sanhedrin and gives his marvelous Defense and Testimony to the Council. He also is rejected and then stoned to death outside the City.

And now Paul stands before the Sanhedrin to give witness to the Risen Christ. His witness will also be rejected. As noted earlier, within a few years, God will smash the whole of the Mosaic economy. The Temple will be destroyed; and the City will be razed to the ground.

God in His grace and longsuffering allows Paul to give a special final witness to the Sanhedrin.

a. Paul's Testimony to the Council. Verses 1-10.

1. He appeals to the Sanhedrin on the ground of a good conscience. Compare Acts 24:16.
2. He is smitten across the mouth at the command of the High Priest, Ananias. Verse 3.
3. Paul challenges him on the ground of violating their own Law while they

profess to be judging him on that Law. Verse 3.

Ananias was a corrupted High Priest, even as Annas and Caiaphas before him had been.

"Whited wall" — Compare John 18:19-23. Jesus Himself had also been smitten contrary to the Law when He stood before the Council.
I Peter 2:19, 23.

Matthew 23:27. Jesus called the Pharisees and Scribes, "Whited sepulchres."

These sepulchres were white-washed about the time of the Feast of Passover so that none would be ceremonially defiled and hindered from keeping the Feasts.

Within they were full of dead men's bones and rottenness.

They were 'white-washed,' but not 'washed white.' Outwardly appearing beautiful and white, but inwardly full of inner corruptions and filth, Matthew 23:27-39.

4. Paul is charged with reviling God's High Priest. Verses 4 and 5. He recognizes that he was wrong to speak in such a manner. Compare Exodus 22:28.
   Rulers were not to be evil spoken of.

   Even though King Saul was evil and corrupt, yet David would not touch the Lord's Anointed, even though the Spirit of the Lord had departed from him.

   The same principle is here also. The Spirit had departed from such a corrupted and Aaronic Priesthood. God Himself had introduced the new Priesthood after the Order of Melchisedek.
   There must always be respect for the powers that be.

   Paul had been away from Jerusalem a number of years, and it seems evident that the High Priest was not in his official High Priestly Garments or else Paul would have recognized this and known his office.

5. The Pharisees and the Sadducees are divided. Verses 6 to 10.
   It is evident that Paul 'perceived' by the Spirit the situation here as the Council consisted of High Priest and Pharisees and Sadducees.
   The Pharisees and Sadducees were Christ's greatest enemies.

   The Pharisees were the 'Fundamentalists' of the day, believing in the Inspiration of the Scriptures, and Miracles, etc.

   The Sadducees were the 'Modernists' of the day, denying the existence of Angel and spirit and miracles. Matthew 3:7.

   Paul hurls the challenge of his faith in "hope of the resurrection" out into the Court. Immediately it brought the Council into collision and dissension and the whole Council is divided.
   The Pharisees were forced to stand for the Doctrine of the Resurrection, and side with Paul against the Sadducees who denied this truth.

   God's method of battle and victory was to send confusion into the enemy ranks until they 'destroyed themselves.'
   The Pharisees admit they do not want to "fight against God." Compare Acts 5:39.

However they were more intent on defending their 'doctrine' than the Apostle Paul.
They had actually been fighting against God when they opposed Christ and His Church.

b. Paul is taken to the Castle before he is torn asunder in the fury of a divided Council. Verse 10.

c. The Lord Himself appears to Paul and re-assures him that he will also go to Rome and testify of the Lord, even as he had testified of Him at Jerusalem. Verse 11.
The Lord Himself had been through all the sufferings which Paul was enduring at the present time.
He had been scourged, falsely accused, denied before men, and His witness before the Sanhedrin and the Pharisees and Scribes had been rejected. He had been sent to Gentile Roman powers to be judged. So Paul was following in his Master's footprints.

d. The conspiracy to kill Paul. Verses 12 to 22.

In these verses we find more than 40 men who imposed on themselves a fast and a curse until they killed Paul.

In the providence and mercy and will of God, Paul's nephew overheard the plot against Paul's life and was able to tell him. Paul encouraged him to tell the Captian how the Jews had planned to have Paul brought down to trial before the Sanhedrin again and enroute there would slay him.

There is no miraculous deliverance from prison for Paul, as there had been for Peter and the other Apostles in the Acts. God had His plan and will for Paul to go to Rome and "all things were working together for good" in the situation at hand. Romans 8:28-30.

The Sovereignty of God is seen in so many little things.

For Daniel, it was a sleepless night for a King.
For Joseph, it was a couple of dreams from God given to Pharoah which needed interpretation.
For Moses, it was a few baby tears which preserved the life of the one called to bring about the downfall of Egypt and deliverance of a Nation from bondage.
For Esther, it was the touch of the golden sceptre and the change of the heart of a King to reward Mordecai, after reading a book in a sleepless night.

For Paul, it was his sister's son which 'overheard' the plot of the Jews to murder Paul.

> "God moves in a mysterious way,
> His wonders to perform,
> He plants His footsteps in the sea,
> And rides upon the storm."

e. Paul's journey to Caesarea. Verses 23 to 25.

The Lord here uses Roman justice, Roman horses, and Roman soldiers to escort Paul safely from Jerusalem to Caesarea to a Roman Court for judgment.
Note the 'escort' Paul is given. This was the Lord's protection for him from the Jews.

Thus we have —

Two Centurions,
Two hundred soldiers under them,
Seventy horsemen,
Two hundred spearmen,

Totalling 472 persons, at least, to accompany Paul safely to Caesarea.

This was not too bad an 'escort' for one man — God's man!

Even Paul had a beast to ride on! So different to all his travels by foot, etc.

f. The Letter of the Chief Captain Claudius Lysias sent to Felix the Governor. Verses 26-30.
Here he states why he has sent Paul to Felix.

g. Paul is conducted by night as far as Antipatris, from whence his guard mainly returns, and the horsemen accompany him to Caesarea.
Verses 31-33.

h. Felix reads the Letter, saying he will wait until Paul's accusers come and then he will hear the case. Paul is commanded to be kept in Herod's Judgment Hall. Verses 34-35.

This is the last Paul sees of Jerusalem. He has borne witness to the Lord Jesus Christ "before the Gentiles, and before the Children of Israel, and the Religious Rulers of the Sanhedrin."

Now he is going to bear witness "before Kings," and then finally is to go to Rome.

## PAUL'S WITNESS AT CAESAREA

Acts 24 — Acts 25 — Acts 26

AS NOTICED IN Acts 9:15, the 'order of witness' for Paul included:

1. Before the Gentiles,
2. Before the Children of Israel, and Sanhedrin,
3. Before Kings, or Rulers.

In these Chapters we have his witness "before Kings."

1. Before Felix. Acts 24.
2. Before Festus. Acts 25.
3. Before Agrippa. Acts 26.

1. **Paul's Testimony before Governor Felix.** Acts 24.

a. The High Priest, Ananias, with the Elders and an Orator named Tertullus, arrive in Caesarea after 5 days to inform Felix against Paul. Verse 1.

b. **The Accusation.** Verses 2-9 Cf. John 16; Luke 21:12-19; Matthew 10:16-35. After preliminary courtesies of Felix for his kindness to the Jews he brings the charge.

The Charge —

1. A pestilent fellow.
A perfect pest, a real plague. Amplified New Testament.

2. A mover of sedition among Jews throughout the world.
   An agitator and source of disturbance. Amplified New Testament.
3. A ring-leader of the Sect of the Nazarenes.
   A heretical, division-producing Sect. Amplified New Testament.
4. A Temple profaner. Desecrating and defiling the Temple at Jerusalem.
5. Would have been judged by Jewish Law had not the Chief Captain taken the matter out of their hands and placed Paul under Roman jurisdiction.
6. The Jews with Tertullus assent to these Charges.

c. **Paul's defense against the false accusation.** Verses 10-21.

1. Paul knew the Law of Moses, and these very men were violating the very Law they professed to uphold.
   They should have had their true witnesses. Exodus 20:16; Deuteronomy 17:6-7; 19:15-18; Mark 14:63.
2. He denies the charge that he was causing dispute in the Temple, or in the Synagogue, or in the City.
3. He states that they cannot prove these things are true which they accuse him of.
4. He brings in his witness.
   Paul admits that he does worship God after the way which they call 'heresy.'
   He believed in the Law of Moses and the Prophets in that they pointed to Christ Jesus. The Law and the Prophets witness of Him.
5. His hope is the resurrection. There will be a resurrection of (a) the just and (b) the unjust. Compare Revelation 20:1-10.
6. He testifies that he had gone to Jerusalem taking alms for his own people, and offerings. Compare Acts 11:29-30.
7. As he was in the Temple fulfilling vow of purification, Jews from Asia saw him and thus the uproar was caused by them, which led to Paul's arrest, falsely.
8. These Asian Jews should have been here to give evidence at the Court, if they had charges.
9. The High Priest and Elders present could not give any true charge against him, except it be that he caused dissension in the Sanhedrin when he brought in the faith of the Hope of Resurrection.
   Compare Acts 21:26.

d. **Felix defers Paul's judgment.** Verses 22-23.

Felix had more perfect knowledge and understanding of "The Way" and deferred Paul's case until the Chief Captain Lysias came down from Jerusalem to give further evidence in the case.

Paul is kept in custody. His friends are permitted to visit him.

e. **Paul before Felix and Drusilla.** Verses 24-25.

Paul is brought before Felix and his wife, Drusilla, who was a Jewess. Paul once again testifies of "The Faith" in Christ.

Compare Paul's condensed message here with John 16:7-14 and Jude 3. It was the Ministry of the Holy Spirit in operation.

Paul reasoned of:—

1. Righteousness, uprightness, purity of life.
   Romans 10:3-13; Romans 3:21-26.
2. Temperance, control of the passions, self-control.
   Romans 3:9-20.
3. Judgment to come.
   Hebrews 9:27; Revelation 20:11-15; Acts 17:31.

Felix procrastinates. "Procrastination is the thief of Time." He puts it off until a more convenient season.

Trembling with conviction, he became alarmed and terrified. Amplified N.T.

Convicted, but unconverted. He knew not that "TODAY is the Day of Salvation, NOW is the accepted time." II Corinthians 6:2.

TIME more convenient for him may not be given. TIME is in God's Hand. He gives to man 'now' only — not tomorrow!

In verse 26 we are told that he hoped that money would be given him to release Paul.
"The love of money is the root of all evil." I Timothy 6:10.

Judas sinned for money, Ananias and Sapphira sinned for money, Simon the Sorcerer tried to buy the power of God for money, and here Felix stakes his salvation off to a more convenient time and hopes for money!

Paul was "not for sale." None could bribe him.

Felix is a typical character study of the unregenerate man who:

1. Has knowledge of The Way.
2. Hears the Faith in Christ. The Word.
3. Is convicted of sin, of righteousness and judgment.
4. Trembles with guilt.
5. Yet procrastinates, looking for another more convenient season to call for the Word of God.
6. Has a hardened, covetous heart after the god of Mammon, which is money.
7. Yesterday is gone forever.
   Tomorrow for you may never come.
   God only gives you 'Today.'
   TODAY — if you will hear His voice. Hebrews 3:7.
   Proverbs 1:24-32.
   Felix communed with Paul often. His motive?
   He hoped for money!
   Eternity reveals that Felix will stand before another Throne of Judgment and will be judged, instead of having Paul before his Throne and judging him!

f. **Paul at Caesarea for 2 years.** Verse 27.

After 2 years Festus takes Felix' place and Felix wanting to maintain favor with the Jews left Paul bound.

Two years of grace shows Felix unrepentant! Leaving Paul bound in chains to please the Jews was outward evidence of his inner spiritual condition. Mark 15:15.

He left "the Word of God" (typified in Paul) bound to please the unbelieving and rebellious (typified in the Jewish Council.) For Paul it was not 'lost time,' but in God's plan.

2. **Paul's Testimony before Governor Festus.** Acts 25:1-27.

a. Festus goes to Jerusalem from Caesarea where the High Priest and the chief of the Jews informed him of Paul's case.
They hoped that he would bring Paul to Jerusalem to have his case dealt with there, intending to have him killed on the way there. A corrupted Sanhedrin. Verses 1-3. Compare Luke 23:14-15.

b. Festus stated that Paul would be kept at Caesarea and have his case judged under Roman Judgment. Roman justice.
He asks for them to bring witnesses to accuse Paul. Verses 4-5.

c. At Caesarea the Jews before Festus lay many grievous complaints against Paul which they could not prove.
Unproven accusations. Verses 7-8. Compare Acts 24:5, 13; Matthew 5:11-12; I Peter 4:12, 16.

Their repeated charges were:—

1. Charges against Paul, concerning the Law of Moses.
2. Charges against Paul in the Temple.
3. Added to this were charges against Paul concerning Caesar. Compare Romans 13:1-3.

d. Festus willing to give the Jews a pleasure asks Paul whether he would go to Jerusalem and be judged by Jewish Law as well as Roman Law before him. Verse 9.

e. **Paul appeals to Caesar.** Verses 10-12.

Compare Acts 23:11. The Lord had already told Paul that he was to bear witness of Him at Rome.
Now Paul sees the will of the Lord unfolding before him step by step. Acts 26:32; 27:24.

Once more Paul exercises his Roman Citizenship and his legal rights to proper justice.
After conferring with the Council, Festus agrees to send Paul to Rome and to Caesar.

f. **King Agrippa and Bernice come to Caesarea.** Verses 13-27.

Nothing happens by accident or coincidence in the purposes of God for His own.
King Agrippa and his wife Bernice came to Caesarea to salute Festus, and after many days Festus tells the King concerning Paul whom he has in bonds. Verses 13-14.

He speaks of Roman justice which could not condemn a man to death before the accusers faced the accused, and the accused is given license to answer for himself concerning the crime charged against him.
Verses 15-16.

He tells Agrippa of the case in which none of the things charged against Paul were found to be true; but simply involved certain questions about their own "superstition," or, literally, "their own demon-worship;" and about one called Jesus who Paul supposed to be raised from the dead.

Such is the concept in the mind of Festus about the Jewish Religion! Just the worship of another God; and further superstitions, even as the Greeks and Romans had numerous gods and religious superstitions.
Verses 17-19.

Festus admits his ignorance of such matters and tells how he asked Paul whether he would go to Jerusalem and be judged there. Paul had appealed to Caesar Augustus. Verses 20-21.

Agrippa desired to hear Paul for himself. Verses 22.

The next day came, and King Agrippa and Bernice enter into the place of hearing in great pomp and show, with Chief Captains and prominent citizens of the City.
Verse 23.
The Lord had a good 'congregation' ready for Paul's witnessing concerning his experience in Christ!

When all the host was assembled together, Festus stated before the King and all gathered that which concerned Paul. He admitted that he did not want to send a prisoner to Rome for appeal before Caesar without having definite 'crimes' signified.

Festus declares Paul's innocence but could not revoke Paul's appealing to Rome.

Unbeknown to him, "God was putting it in their hearts to fulfill His will." Revelation 17:17.

"The King's heart is in the hand of the Lord, as the Rivers of water: He turneth it whithersoever He will." Proverbs 21:1.

It was God's will for Paul to go to Rome! At Rome's expense!

Over all, through all and above all, Paul was being used as a Testimony to the Name of the Lord, before Rulers and Kings.

3. **Paul's Testimony before King Agrippa.** Acts 26:1-32.

Here we have the third main record of Paul's conversion to Christ.

1. Acts 9. His arrest by the Lord Jesus.
2. Acts 22. His witness to the Sanhedrin and Jewish people.
3. Acts 26. His witness before King Agrippa.

a. Agrippa gives permission to Paul to speak for himself. Verse 1.

b. Paul gives his remarkable testimony again. Verses 1-23.
The prominent points are as follows:-

1. He knows Agrippa is more familiar with the Jewish Religion and an expert in Jewish matters. Verses 1-3.
2. He declares his manner of life, as a Jew, and of the straitest Sect of Jewish Religion as a Pharisee, "a Separationist."
   He was well-known as such in his own Nation.
   Verses 4-5.
3. He is being judged for the Hope of the Promise made to the Fathers, which the 12 Tribes of Israel held to.
   This was the Hope of the Resurrection.
   In Paul's heart and mind, he knew this "Hope" was fulfilled in Christ Jesus the Lord.
   Verses 6-7.
4. Paul challenges Agrippa that it is not an incredible thing that GOD should raise the dead. Verse 8.
5. He tells once more of his persecution of the saints, and his utter hatred of "The Way."
   He elaborates on his part of giving voice in the death of many believers, his delegated authority to punish the Christians, how he compelled them to blaspheme, and how exceedingly mad he was against them, going to extreme measures in foreign Cities to kill them.

   What Paul had done to the believers was being done to him!
   Verses 9-11.
6. He tells of his conversion to Jesus on the Damascus Road.
   a. The Light at midday above the brightness of the noonday sun. Compare Revelation 1:16; Matthew 17:1-5.
      The Shekinah Glory in the Face of Christ.
   b. The prostration of all to the earth.
   c. The Heavenly voice of Jesus — the LORD.
   d. The Divine Commission and purpose of this appearing.
   e. His kicking like a stubborn ox against the pricks, or ox-goad.
      Verse 14.
   f. His ministry under Christ. Verses 15-18.
      1. To be a Minister.
      2. To be a Witness of all he sees and hears.
      3. The Lord will appear to him.
      4. To be delivered from the Jews.
      5. To be sent to the Gentiles and delivered from them.
      6. To open the eyes of the blind.
      7. To turn people from darkness to light.
      8. To turn people from the power of Satan to the power of God.
      9. To receive the forgiveness of sins.
      10. To receive an inheritance among the sanctified ones, by faith in Christ.

This was such a Commission. Compare Isaiah 61:1-4; Romans 16:20; Romans 3:23; Ezekiel 2:1-2; Isaiah 42:7, 16. The whole purpose of the Gospel of Jesus is to do all that which is listed above.

g. Paul was not disobedient to the Heavenly Vision. Verse 19. His whole life was the response and outworking of that Vision. Compare Numbers 12:6-8; I Samuel 3:1; Habakkuk 2:1-3. "Where there is no Vision, the people perish." Proverbs 29:18.

"Where there is no progressive vision, the people dwell carelessly."

h. Paul obeyed the Lord, witnessing in Damascus, then Jerusalem and then to the Gentiles. Verse 20.
He taught 1. Repentance and turning to God.
2. Works meet for repentance.
Romans 2:4; Hebrews 6:1-2; Matthew 3:1-2; 4:17; Acts 17:30; 20:21.

i. Because of all this, the Jews had taken Paul in the Temple and tried to kill him. Verse 21.

j. Paul praises the grace and mercy of God in preserving him through everything to that day.

He concludes his testimony with the basic facts of the Gospel.

1. The Law and the Prophets pointed to Christ.
2. Christ suffered on the Cross. His Death.
3. Christ rose from the dead. His Resurrection.
4. Christ is the Light of the world, to the Jews and also to the Gentiles. Verses 22-23; Acts 3:18; 17:3.

c. Festus declares Paul is mad. Verse 24.
Recognizing Paul's learning, Festus says that Paul has gone intellectually insane.
"Thy great learning is turning thee into raving madness."

They charged Jesus with this same charge. Mark 3:21. Compare II Corinthians 5:13.

d. Paul's final challenge to Agrippa. Verses 25-29.
Paul knew he was not mad, but speaking truth and soberness.
He challenges King Agrippa who knew the historical facts of these things, for it was not done in a secret corner.

King Agrippa believed in the Prophets and the Scriptures. But he did nothing about it. Compare James 2:19.

He says in front of all that assembly there, "Almost thou persuadest me to be a Christian." Verses 27-28.

With a little more persuasion Agrippa may have become a believer.

Only Eternity will reveal whether he ever did believe.

The last record is that King Agrippa was "almost persuaded . . ."

Almost persuaded . . . but lost!"

Paul could say: *"I am persuaded . . ."* Romans 8:38.

As King Agrippa and Bernice, and all the important people were in that Assembly, all heard the Gospel of Christ, leaving them without an excuse.

Paul was bound by chains, but was free!
They were free, but spiritually bound by the chains of sin!

e. The Case is closed at Caesarea. Verses 30-32.
Agrippa and Festus state that Paul has done nothing worthy of death or of prison and could have been set at liberty had he not appealed to Caesar.

The Lord desired Paul in Rome, and to Rome he must go!
Acts 23:11; 25:11.

One day the scene is to be changed and reversed.
Instead of Paul being the condemned and the accused, and Agrippa and Festus on the Throne of judgment, it will be Jesus Christ on the Throne, and Agrippa and Festus on trial.

Jesus Christ will do with them what they did with Him.

## PAUL'S JOURNEY TO ROME

Acts 27 — Acts 28

THESE FINAL CHAPTERS cover Paul's journey by ship to Rome and the last events in the Book of Acts.

1. **Paul's Voyage to Rome.** Acts 27:1-44.

There are several incidents in these Chapters which give us small cameo pictures of that which pertains to the Church, and the Ministries of the Lord moving in His will and purposes.

a. Paul is placed on a ship with other prisoners under Julius, a Centurion of Augustus' band.
With Paul is Aristarchus, a Macedonian of Thessalonica, and Luke, the Beloved Physician. Verses 1-2.
Compare Acts 19:29; 20:4; Colossians 4:10; Philemon 24.
What a comfort to Paul to have these brethren with him.

b. At Sidon Paul is refreshed by friends. Verse 3.
Even the Apostle Paul needed to be refreshed by the brethren.
Refreshing in the Spirit. Compare Isaiah 28:10-12.

c. During the first part of the Voyage there were 'contrary winds.' Verses 4-5.
Significant of the natural and the spiritual 'winds' which come the way of all who follow Christ.
The Lord Jesus had been in a Ship with His Disciples also when the 'contrary winds and storm' came.
He would be with Paul in this ship too.
Compare Matthew 14:24; Mark 6:48, John 6:16-21; Mark 4:35-41.
Jesus always comes in the storm unto His own.

d. Change of ships for Paul and the prisoners. Verse 6.

e. Paul foretells the coming storm and shipwreck. Verses 7-11.
After slow sailing for many days, through lack of the proper winds, and the time of the year was dangerous sailing, Paul steps forth telling the Ship-owner that the Voyage was to be greatly endangered.

Note verse 9. "The Fast" was The Great Day of Atonement, which took place on the 10th Day of the 7th Month in the Feast of Tabernacles. Leviticus 23:27.

The Centurion believed the Master and Owner of the ship more than Paul.

The Centurion knew the Master and Owner of the Ship!
Paul knew the Master and Owner of the seas!

The Centurion believed man!
Paul believed God!

The Ship-owner trusted the ability of his sailors and the make of the ship.

As usual, the majority rules. One man only had the mind of God. Verse 12. Compare Amos 3:7.

Perhaps it was suggested that a Tent-maker would not know too much about a ship in the sea?

f. The south winds blew softly. Verse 13.
They supposed they had gained their purpose, and off they sailed. Distant havens look like "Fair Havens" and peaceful to those who are full of self-confidence.
The sailors were deceived by the 'south winds blowing softly,' but God saw the coming storm.

The spiritual lesson is evident! It is easy to be deceived by soft south winds, or contrary winds. God knows the future and just when and where the storms will strike, testing the ability of the best sailor.

There are natural and spiritual lessons here.

g. The tempestuous wind called Euroclydon arose 'not long after.'
Verse 14. A typhoon.
Note the winds here:—

1. Contrary winds. Verse 4.
2. Little winds. Verse 7. Winds not suffer us.
3. South soft winds. Verse 13.
4. Tempestuous winds. Verse 14. Psalms 147:18; 148:8.
   Compare Revelation 7:1-4; Daniel 7:1-2; Ephesians 4:16-18.

Unexpected, but foretold by Paul.

h. The ability of men frustrated. Verses 15-20.

1. The ship caught in the wind, driven helplessly.
2. Ungirding the ship for fear of the quicksands.
3. Driven about in the storm and typhoon.
4. Tossed with the tempest. Ability of man frustrated.
   Helplessness. The power of the wind and the sea.
5. Ship's goods thrown overboard. Freight.
6. The ship's tackling apparatus also tossed into the sea.
7. No light of sun, moon or stars seen for many days.
   No source of guidance. No light.

8. All hope of being saved was taken away.
   God was permitting them to come to a place where they would believe and submit to His Word.

Note especially Psalm 107:23-30 in connection with this storm.

The Lord brought them to their "wit's end."

It is typical of the condition of the World. The World is in the winds and the storms, in a place of darkness, and things are being thrown overboard, but God has His man there at the right time.

i. Paul stands forth in faith. Verses 21-26.

After long abstinence, Paul stands forth reminding them of the Word of the Lord he had given before which they refused to heed.
They are more willing to listen to him now in the storm than when they were in the calm. Verses 9, 10.
How true of human nature.

Like the Disciples in the storm, it was the Lord's will for them to go to the other side, hence they could not go under for going over. Compare Luke 8:22-25.
No storm could defeat them.
It was the Lord's will for Paul to go to Rome in spite of storm or shipwreck.
Their hopelessness was met by a declaration of faith in God.

After reminding them of their unbelief and disobedience, Paul said, "I BELIEVE GOD."

In Verse 11, the Centurion believed the Owner of the Ship.
In verse 25, Paul said that he believed God. Compare Romans 1:16.

What they did not believe in time of peace they now believe in the storm.

The Angel of God was a ministering spirit sent to minister to Paul in the storm. Compare Hebrews 1:4, 14.

He assures Paul that he indeed will appear before Caesar and that all in the ship are given to Paul.
God will preserve all aboard the ship for Paul's sake.

The people in the world are blessed, whether they realize it or not, because of the people of the Lord.

Egypt was blessed because of Joseph. Geneses 39:5.
Laban was blessed because of Jacob. Genesis 30:30.
The ship's passengers and prisoners were blessed because of Paul.
The world is blessed because of the presence of the Church.

Paul tells them they would be cast on an Island.

j. **The Midnight Hour.** Verses 27-29.
After 14 days, about the Midnight hour the shipmen deemed they were near some land.
The Midnight Hour — always significant of the End of the Age.

| | |
|---|---|
| Matthew 25:1-13. | Virgins heard the Midnight cry. |
| Job 34:20. | The people shall be troubled at Midnight. |
| Psalms 119:62. | At Midnight will I rise to give thanks. |
| Acts 16:25. | At Midnight Paul and Silas prayed and sang. |

Mark 13:35. His coming may be at the Midnight Hour.

**The Fourteenth Day** — always significant of Passover.
Exodus 12:1-6; 11:4. The Feast of Passover took place on the 14th day, and at the Midnight Hour.

Here is the same spiritual significance in the storm at sea.

Deliverance would come to all on board the ship after the 14th Day, and the Midnight Hour.

k. Paul assumes responsibility of the ship. Verses 30-38.
As the Ship is tossed near the land and the rocks, the shipmen make as though they were lowering the anchors as they endeavour to escape in a boat.
Paul demands full obedience by all on board if all were to be saved. Compare verses 22 with 21.

The soldiers cut off the ropes of the boat and their last natural hope is gone. They have to trust God's Word through Paul now for salvation.

He took bread and gave thanks in the presence of them all, and encouraged them also to eat, saying not a hair of their heads would fall. Compare Matthew 10:30 and Luke 21:18.

There were 276 persons in all upon the ship.

l. The Ship totally wrecked. Verses 38-41.
In the morning they discovered a certain creek, and taking up anchors, hoisting up the mainsail to the wind, they let the ship run aground.
The forefront of the ship stuck fast and the hinder part was smashed to pieces with the violence of the waves.

m. All souls saved from the wreck. Verses 42-44.
The soldiers wanted to kill the prisoners lest any should escape but the Centurion desired to have Paul spared and suggested that all who could swim to shore do so, and others get there on broken pieces of the ship.

All escaped safely to the shore, according to the Word of the Lord — and Paul! Psalms 107:28-30; II Corinthians 11:23-26. This was another of Paul's shipwrecks in which the Lord delivered him.

"Thrice I suffered shipwreck . . ."

**TYPICAL SUMMARY:—**

The Holy Spirit has given much detail to the journey to Rome and the details of this shipwreck.

The natural first, then the spiritual.

The whole story in this Chapter can be likened to the World.

The World-system is like this old ship and is in the greatest storm of history as the End of the Age comes upon the earth. There is no hope of saving the ship (the World-system;) but God has His Witnesses in the winds and the storms who believe God and the only hope of escape and salvation from the wreck of the World-System is to believe God and the witness of His Servants.

The crash comes at the Midnight Hour, but those who trust God and the Word will be safe.

2. **Paul in Rome.** Acts 28:1-3.

a. **Paul on the Island of Melita.** Verses 1-6.

Paul and company find themselves on the Island of Melita which is the modern Island of Malta, located in the center of the Mediterranean Sea, 60 miles south of Sicily and in area about 95 square miles. Melita is not to be confused with the Island Meleda or Melitene which are located off the Dalmatian Coast. Melita had been occupied in the 10th century B.C. by Phoenicians. The name of the Island means "Refuge" in the Phoenician language (verse 1.) The sight of Paul's shipwreck is thought to have been "St. Paul's Bay," 8 miles northwest of modern Valletta. Verse 1. The barbarous (or Native) people were kind to them.

b. We find the great Apostle helping on the Island by gathering a bundle of sticks and laying them on the fire because of the rain and cold; ministering to the present, practical need. Verses 2-3.

c. During his helping, Paul is attacked by a venomous viper or serpent from the midst of the fire but is miraculously preserved from its bite. Mark 16:17. This is the only record in the New Testament of such a phenomenon. Notice that Paul did not take up the viper knowingly or willingly, to show that he was a "snake charmer or a snake handler," which he was not. Spiritually we take note of Satan, the Serpent or Viper, coming out of the fire or the heat at a time when the Ministry is labouring even at menial tasks, to try to destroy the work and workers of the Lord. But the Lord preserves His faithful remnant and continues to victoriously build His Kingdom. Satan is a DEFEATED foe, and his only weapon is deception. Verses 3-6.

Spiritually when God pours out the Latter Rain of His Spirit, and the Fire of the Lord is there, often the Serpent manifests himself to destroy the Ministry.

Note the reaction of the Natives when Paul escaped the deadly serpent.

1. When the snake came out they called him a Murderer. Verse 4.
   They thought he was under the vengeance of God.
2. When he was unharmed by the serpent, they said he was a god.

   Human nature is to decry you or deify you!

d. Paul's ministry of healing is shown by the laying on of hands. Verses 8-9. Mark 16:17.
Signs continue to follow the Apostle's work and all of his necessities are provided for. We note that the labourer is worthy of his hire and that God provides for the needs of His Ministry, Church, and people. Matthew 16:18; 6:28-34.

God brought blessing and healing in the Gospel of the Kingdom to this Island through the shipwreck. "All things (even shipwreck) work together for good to them that love the Lord." Romans 8:28.

Paul does not irresponsibly leave the work that the Lord may have begun on the Island of Melita, but rather stays for 3 months, watering and planting. We find that Paul did not request a special ship to carry him on to Rome as the great Apostle, but rather using, with the others, a ship "which had wintered in the isle." Verse 11b.

e. Follow all of Paul's journeys on a map. Verses 12-15.
In Puteoli, Italy, Paul finds some Christian brethren who desired him to

fellowship with them for seven days. The number 7 is significant of completeness, perfection, and wholeness. The Christian life is not complete or whole without the fellowship of the brethren. Notice that Paul desired to be with them. Here again we see the Apostle as one member of a "many-membered body." Paul did not associate exclusively with only the upper-class of Apostles, etc.; but enjoyed and appreciated all of the family of God — Jesus Christ being the Name and Center of all of their fellowship.

f. Paul thanked God when he saw the brethren coming to him. Paul knew that there was strength in fellowship, and thus "took courage" at the sight. Disunity, fear, and discouragement are the weapons of Satan. Verse 15. I Samuel 30:6. "David encouraged himself in the Lord." Not in his circumstances.

g. Paul's arrival in Rome. Verse 16.
Paul and the prisoners come to Rome and we note the outworking of God's will in relation to Rome from the following Scriptures:—

| | | |
|---|---|---|
| 1. | Acts 19:21. | Paul said, "I must see Rome." (Not as a tourist.) |
| 2. | Romans 1:10-15. | Paul wrote to the Romans, "I long to see you." |
| 3. | Acts 23:11. | Jesus said, "Thou must bear witness to Me also in Rome." |
| 4. | Acts 25:11, 16. | Paul said, "I appeal unto Caesar." |
| 5. | Acts 27:23, 24. | In the storm the Angel said, "Thou (Paul) must be brought before Caesar." |
| 6. | Acts 28:14, 16. | After the shipwreck, Paul said, ". . . we went toward Rome." |
| 7. | Finally, | "We came to Rome." |
| | | Christ was with Paul in the storm. |

h. After 3 days, Paul calls the chief of the Jews and testifies to them that it is because of "the Hope of Israel" in his Nation, that he is bound with the chain.

He testifies that he has done nothing against the people or the Customs of the fathers, but had been falsely accused. Hence he had appealed to Rome. Here he was in Rome now and once more desires to tell his brethren after the flesh concerning the Gospel of Christ. Verses 17-20.

Paul refers to the "Hope of Israel" in verses 20.
Compare Acts 26:6-7.

Colossians 1:27; Titus 1:2; 2:13; Hebrews 6:18.
The Messiah and the Resurrection was the Hope of Israel.

The Church looks forward to that "Blessed Hope" of Christ's appearing.

He is bound by a chain. Verse 20. When he writes his Epistle, he says that he is "A prisoner of Jesus Christ, — not a prisoner of Rome."
Ephesians 3:1; 6:20; II Timothy 1:10-12. He was not ashamed of this chain because he bore it for the Lord Jesus.

i. The enquiring Jews at Rome. Verses 21-24.
The Jews at Rome desire to hear about "This Sect which is everywhere spoken against."

This was no proof that it was not of God. Church History tells us that Christians were sometimes referred to as "Atheists" because they worshipped an Unseen God, whereas Pagans worshipped Nature; and the Emperor who could satisfy their temporal needs from his financial position in the Empire.

The Jews at Rome tell Paul they have no letters concerning him, nor have any Brethren come from Judea to witness against him.

Paul ministers and testifies to them out of the Law and the Prophets, which all pointed to the Lord Jesus as their Hope and Messiah.
Verse 23. Compare Luke 24:27, 44-46.

The results in Rome?

1. Some believed the things spoken. Believers.
2. Some believed not. Unbelievers.
   There is no neutral ground. Only two classes.

There will always be those that accept and those that reject the Gospel.

Satan would seek to discourage the Church by sighting that all the world is not accepting Jesus Christ and His Gospel.

God gives the increase. Evil doers will wax worse and worse, but the whole earth will be filled with the Glory of the Lord.

j. Paul turns to the Gentiles. Verses 25-29.
The Jews agreed not among themselves. Popular opinion is not the doorway to salvation.
Compare Acts 13:46; 18:6. Salvation only comes to the house through Christ.

In verses 25-27, we have Paul's final warning to Jewry, quoted from the Prophet Isaiah.
This verse is quoted several times in the New Testament, by the Lord Jesus and by the Apostles.
Isaiah 6:9; Matthew 13:14; Luke 8:10; John 12:40; Romans 11:8.

Spiritual blindness and spiritual deafness had finally settled upon Jewry, the House of Judah, as a whole.

It is worthy to remember Paul's pattern of Ministry as set forth in Acts.

"To the Jew first, and then to the Gentiles."

1. The Jew first.
2. The Gentile next.

Paul consistently followed this principle; and this Scripture was certainly fulfilled.
Note these Scriptures which show this.

1. He went to the Synagogues first in each City where there was one. Acts 13:5, 15; 14:1; 17:1, 17; 18:5; 19:8.

   There were thousands of Jews saved in the Early Church.
   Acts 2:4, 41; 4:4; 5:14; 6:7; 9:1, 22-23; 21:20-21; 11:19-21.
   At Pentecost there were 3000 souls, then later on another 5000, then multitudes.
   This was the "Remnant according to the Election of Grace." Romans 11:4-5.

   a. They were to be witnesses to Jerusalem, Judea, and then Samaria, and the Uttermost part of the earth. Acts 1:8.

b. They were to begin at Jerusalem. Luke 24:47-48, 49.

c. Paul said: "It was necessary that the Word of God should first have been spoken to you, but seeing you put it from you and judged yourselves unworthy of Eternal Life, we turn to the Gentiles." Acts 13:46.

d. The Gospel is the power of God unto salvation to every one that believeth, to the Jew first, and also to the Gentile.
Romans 1:13-16; Romans 2:9-10; 10:12.

e. Paul's main opposition however came from the Jews.
Acts 17:5, 10, 13-17; 18:12-14; 23:12, 20-23, 30; 24:5, 9; I Thessalonians 2:14-17.

2. After years of persistent opposition and rejection by the Jews as a whole, Paul turned to the Gentiles.
Even though he was sent to the Gentiles, he always went to the Jews first, and after rejection turned to the Gentiles. Note this in these Scriptures: Acts 9:15; 13:42-46, 47-48; 15:15-18; 14:2, 5, 27; 18:6; 21:11, 19-25; Romans 15:9-18, 27; 16:4.

God opened the Door of Faith to the Gentiles and they came into blessing in the Tabernacle of David in the Grace of the Lord Jesus Christ. God is visiting the Gentiles to take out of them a people for His Name, and Jerusalem will be trodden down until the Fulness of the Gentiles, and the Times of the Gentiles be fulfilled.
Romans 11:25; Luke 21:21-24.

The Jew and the Gentile can only be grafted into the Good Olive Tree by faith in Christ Jesus.
Hence Paul says: "Be it known unto you that the salvation of God is sent unto the Gentiles and that they will hear it." Acts 28:28.

k. Paul in Rome. Verses 30-31.
Paul dwelt in his own hired house in Rome and received all who came to him. Preached the Gospel of the Kingdom of God, and all that concerns the Lord Jesus Christ, unhindered.

"A Prisoner of Jesus Christ" — indeed!

**SUMMARY:—**

Thus the Book of Acts opens with the Outpouring of the Holy Spirit upon the Jewish Nation and closes with the rejction of the Gospel by that Nation, and Paul turning to the Gentiles.

Jewry as a Nation had rejected the Ministries of:—

1. John the Baptist,
2. The Lord Jesus Christ,
3. The Apostle Paul,
4. The Early Church believers consisting of both Jews and Gentiles.

The Gospel had spread from JERUSALEM TO ROME! From the Religious center of the then known world to the Political center of the world.

Both Rome and Jerusalem come into prominence in the Last Days before the Second Coming of the crucified-resurrected-ascended-glorified Son of the living God, Jesus Christ.

The Book of Acts can be described in these ways:

1. The Church in its beginning.
2. The Acts of the Holy Spirit.
3. The Seed-book of the Church.
4. The Divine Pattern for the New Testament Local Church.

Acts covers a period of about 30 years, from A.D. 34 to A.D. 64, approximately.

In A.D. 70, God permitted Rome to destroy the Temple at Jerusalem, making the Temple, Jerusalem, Jewry and the Land desolate, scattering Jewry to the four corners of the earth.

The Father God had rent the Veil in the Temple from top to bottom in connection with the death of His Son at Calvary, opening for all the Dispensation of Grace to Jew and Gentile.

The Natural Branches of Judah were cut off the Olive Tree because of unbelief. The Unnatural Branches of Gentiles were grafted in by faith.

Acts 1. The LORD JESUS CHRIST — The HEAD of the Church — His Body!

Acts 2. The CHURCH — THE BODY of Christ formed by the Holy Spirit!

Acts 3-28. THE BODY OF CHRIST — in operation, in manifestation.

The Book of Acts reveals the Lord Jesus Christ as the Head of the Church which is His Body, in whom all Fruit, Gifts, Grace, Ministries and all the Fulness of the Godhead dwells, as the Son of God.
Colossians 1:19; 2:9.

"A BODY hast Thou prepared . . . Lo I come to do thy will, O God." Hebrews 10:5-7.

He was prepared as A BODY in which God was able to fulfill His will in the earth.
And now the Church became THE BODY OF CHRIST, to continue doing that same will. The Fulness of the Son of God is to be manifested in this many-membered Body of Christ in the earth by the Spirit of God.

He said He would build HIS CHURCH, and the Gates of Hell (Hades) would not prevail against it. Matthew 16:16-18. The Book of Acts is the revelation of Him building His Church! A Victorious Church — A conquering Church — continuing the same Ministry of the ascended Head!

When He returns the second time from heaven, He will come for a GLORIOUS CHURCH without spot, or wrinkle, or blemish, or any such thing.
It will be a holy, and spotless Church — like unto Himself! Ephesians 5:23-32. This Church will be brought about by the Ministry of the Holy Spirit. It will be a Perfect Church!

The Ministry of Jesus Christ is God's Pattern to which this Church will be made, and fashioned. And every member in that Church will be 'according to the pattern in the heavenly Mount,' which is Jesus Christ!

The Early Glory of the Early Church was manifested under the Outpouring of the Holy Spirit in the Feast of Pentecost.
The Early Rain. James 5:7.

The Latter Glory of the Latter Church will be manifested under the Outpouring of the Holy Spirit in the Feast of Tabernacles.
The Latter Rain. Haggai 2:9.

May our prayer be "Lord, grant that Thy servants may with all boldness preach the Word, and that signs and wonders may be done in the Name of Thy Holy Child, Jesus," as we partake of that which God is doing in the Church in these Last Days.

**"Better is THE END of a thing than THE BEGINNING."**
Ecclesiastes 7:8.

## SUPPLEMENTARY

Through the Book of Acts flows a number of Bible Themes.
The following is a suggested list given for the benefit of the Student, along with some references to follow through.

1. **First Principles of the Doctrine of Christ.** Hebrews 6:1-2.
   a. **Repentance from dead works.**
   Acts 2:38; 5:31; 3:19; 8:22; 17:30; 26:20; 13:24; 19:4; 20:21.
   b. **Faith towards God.**
   Acts 3:16; 6:5, 7-8; 11:24; 13:8; 14:9, 22, 27; 15:9; 16:5; 20:21; 24:24; 26:18.
   c. **Doctrine of Baptisms.**
   Water Baptism and Holy Spirit Baptism.
   Acts 1:5; 2:38, 41; 8:12-16, 36-38; 11:16; 9:18; 10:47-48; 16:15, 33; 18:8; 19:3-5; 22:16.
   d. **Laying on of Hands.**
   Acts 4:30; 5:12; 6:6; 8:17, 18-19; 9:12, 17, 41; 11:21; 11:30; 13:3; 14:3; 19:6, 11; 28:8.
   e. **Eternal Judgment.**
   Acts 7:7; 8:33; 10:42; 13:46; 24:25; 1:15-26; 5:1-11; 13:6-12; 28:25-28.
   f. **Resurrection from the dead.**
   Acts 1:22; 2:31; 4:2, 33; 17:18, 32; 23:6, 8; 2:24, 30-32; 3:22, 26; 13:33-34, 22-23, 30, 37; 26:8; 7:37; 10:40; 17:31.
   The foundation of every sermon in Acts. The Resurrection of Christ and the sure resurrection unto judgment of all mankind.

2. **The Name of Jesus Christ.**
Acts 2:21, 38; 3:6, 16; 4:7, 10-12, 17, 18, 30; 5:28, 40-41; 8:12, 16; 9:14-16, 21, 27-29; 10:43, 48; 15:14, 17, 26; 16:18; 18:25; 19:5, 13, 17; 21:13; 22:16; 26:9.
All was done in the power and authority of the Name of the Lord Jesus Christ.

3. **The Word. Logos and Rhema.**
Acts 2:22, 20-41; 4:4, 29, 31; 5:5; 6:2, 4, 7; 7:22; 8:4, 14, 25; 10:36, 37, 44; 11:1, 19; 12:24; 13:5, 7 15, 26, 42-44; 15:6-7; 16:6, 32; 17:11; 18:11; 19:10, 20; 20:32, 35; 28:25.

5. **Ministry of Prayer.**
Acts 1:14, 24; 2:42; 3:1; 4:31; 6:4, 6; 8:15, 22, 24; 9:11, 40; 10:2, 4, 31; 12:5; 13:3; 14:23; 16:9, 13, 16, 25; 20:36; 21:5; 22:17; 28:8.

6 **Church Government — Local.**
Study Paul's Missionary Journeys and Establishment of Local Churches.

7. **The 5-Fold Ascension Gift Ministries.** Ephesians 4:1-16.
Deacons (Acts 6) Evangelists (Acts 8,) Apostles, Prophets and Teachers (Acts 13,) Elders (Acts 14:23.)

8. **Qualifications and Ministry of Elders and Deacons.** I Timothy 3; Titus 1.

9. **Divine Discipline.** Acts 5. Acts 8.

10. **The Fruit and Grace of the Spirit.** Galatians 5:22-23.

11. **The Operations of the Gifts of the Spirit.** I Corinthians 12:1-12.

12. **The Unity of the Church. One accord.**
Acts 1:14; 2:1, 46; 4:24; 15:25.

13. **Foreknowledge, Prophecy and Predestination.**
Acts 1:16, 20; 2:16-17, 25-31; 3:18-26; 4:28; 13:48.

14. **Ministry of Fasting.**
Acts 14:23; 10:30; 13:2-3; Luke 2:37; Matthew 9:14-15.

15. **Formation of the Body of Christ, of Jew and Gentile.**
I Corinthians 12:12-13; Acts 2. The Jews.
Acts 10-11. The Gentiles.
One Body in Christ.

16. **The Great Commission.**
Acts 1:8. Soul-saving commission of Christ outworked.

17. **Character Studies of Peter and Paul,** Apostles to the Jew and to the Gentile.
Acts 1-12 Peter. Acts 13-28 Paul.

18. **Law and Grace conflict.** Acts 15.

19. **God's Sovereignty and Man's Responsibility.**
Balance between both seen in the Book of Acts.

20. **Principles of Preaching** as seen in Apostolic Sermons.
Following are the most important Sermons or Witnesses given.

| | |
|---|---|
| Acts 2:14-36. | Peter on the Day of Pentecost. |
| Acts 3:11-26. | Peter before the people at the Temple. |
| Acts 4:5-22. | Peter's Witness before the Sanhedrin. |
| Acts 5:17-32. | Peter before the Council. |
| Acts 7:1-51. | Stephen's Defense before the Sanhedrin. |
| Acts 8:18-25. | Peter and Simon the Sorcerer. |
| Acts 8:26-40. | Philip and the Ethiopian. |
| Acts 10-11. | Peter and the Gentiles. |
| Acts 13-14. | Paul and Barnabas in the Synagogues and to the Gentiles. |
| Acts 15. | The Council at Jerusalem. |
| Acts 16-17. | Further Witness of Paul to the Gentiles. |
| Acts 20. | Paul's Word to the Elders of Ephesus. |
| Acts 22-23. | Paul's Testimony to the Jews and Sanhedrin. |
| Acts 24-25-26. | Paul's Witness before Felix, Festus, and Agrippa. |

To the Jews, Paul continually appealed to the Scriptures.
To the Gentiles, Paul preached the Gospel of God's Grace in Christ.

# Table of Scriptures on Water Baptism "IN THE NAME"

## SUPPLEMENTARY NOTES ON BAPTISM

Formulas of Water Baptism have been the cause of much dissension and division in the Church over the years, as Church History shows.

Believers have endeavoured to reconcile the apparent discrepancy between the Command of Jesus in the Gospels, the administration of baptism in the Acts, and the teachings on baptism in the Epistles.

The Gospels have been pitted against the Acts and the Acts against the Gospels, and both against the Epistles. The subject has become a theological issue over the Godhead as well as an issue over baptism formulas.

All Bible expositors recognize that no doctrine of Scripture can be built on one reference, but all references to any given subject should be brought together and compared, and then the answer is discovered. Hence, the writer has gone through the references to Baptism in the Gospels, the Acts and the Epistles. And it is in light of all these references and context that water baptism is administered in the formula of Scripture given here. Scripture must interpret Scripture.

— Kevin J. Conner

## FORMULA OF SCRIPTURE FOR BAPTISM

**TO THE CANDIDATE:**

"I baptize you into THE NAME
of the Father,
and of the Son,
and of the Holy Spirit:
into THE NAME of the LORD JESUS CHRIST;
into the likeness of His death,
that like as Christ was raised from the dead
by the glory of the Father, even so
you also shall rise to walk in newness of life."

This Formula composed of Scripture:

**QUOTES** the Command of Jesus in Matthew 28:19;

**INVOKES** the Triune Name of the Triune God, as in Acts 2:36;

**DECLARES** the spiritual truth of water baptism as in Romans 6:3-4.

Translations used:
- Authorized Version
- Revised Version
- Lamsa Translation
- Douay Version
- Amplified New Testament

For a complete treatment of this subject concerning the Name of the Eternal Godhead, the reader may purchase the text-book "THE NAME OF GOD", by the same author.

## BAPTISM IN THE GOSPELS

1. **The Command of Jesus** Matthew 28:19. A.V.

   Baptizing them in The Name:

   Of The Father,
   And of The Son,
   And of The Holy Spiritl

   Into The Name. R. V.

2. **Believer's Baptism** Mark 16:15. A.V.

   He that believeth, and is baptized, shall be saved.

## BAPTISM IN THE ACTS

1. **Jerusalem** — Acts 2:36-41. (Peter).
   Baptized in The Name of Jesus Christ. A.V.
   Baptized into The Name of Jesus Christ. R.V.
   Baptized in The Name of the Lord Jesus. L.
   Baptized in The Name of Jesus Christ. D.

2. **Samaria** — Acts 8;12-16, 35-38. (Philip)
   Baptized in The Name of the Lord Jesus.
   A.V., R.V. Into The Name of . . .
   L. D. (Note vs. 12 — Lamsa).

3. **Damascus** — Acts 9:5-18; 22:16. (Ananias)
   Baptized, calling on The Name of the Lord. A.V.
   calling on His Name. R.V. D.
   calling on The Name of the Lord. L.

4. **Ceasarea** — Acts 10:48. (Peter)
   Baptized in The Name of the Lord. A.V.
   Baptized in The Name of Jesus Christ. R.V.
   Baptized in The Name of our Lord Jesus Christ. L.
   Baptized in The Name of our Lord Jesus Christ. D.

5. **Philippi** — Acts 16:14-15, 31-34. (Paul)
   Believe on the Lord Jesus Christ and be saved. . .
   and was baptized . . . believing in God. A.V.

6. **Corinth** — Acts 18:8. (Paul) I Corinthians 1:10-17.
   Believe on the Lord . . . and were baptized. A.V.
   Were ye baptized in the name of Paul? A.V.

7. **Ephesus** — Acts 19:1-6. (Paul)
   Baptized in The Name of the Lord Jesus. A.V. R.V.
   Baptized in The Name of our Lord Jesus Christ. L.
   Baptized in The Name of the Lord Jesus Christ. D.

## BAPTISM IN THE EPISTLES

1. **Romans** — (Paul) — Romans 6:3-4.
   As many of us as were baptized into Jesus Christ were baptized into His death . . . buried with Him by baptism. A.V.

2. **Corinthians** — (Paul) I Corinthians 1:10-17
   Were ye baptized in the Name of Paul?
   Lest any should say I baptized in mine own name. A.V.
   Into the Name of Paul? R.V.
   All baptized unto Moses. A.V.
   Into Moses. R.V. I Corinthians 10:1-3.

3. **Galatians** — (Paul) — Galatians 3:27.
   As many as were baptized into Christ.
   A.V. Those of us . . . baptized in The Name of Christ . . . L.

4. **Ephesians** — (Paul) — Ephesians 4:4; Hebrews 6:2
   There is . . . One Baptism — ) Acts 19:5
   Doctrine of Baptism )

5. **Colossians** — (Paul) Colossians 2:12.
   Buried with Him in baptism. A.V.

6. **The Twelve Tribes** — (James) — James 2:7.
   That worthy Name by which ye are called. A.V.
   The precious Name by which you are distinguished and called (The Name of Christ invoked, in Baptism). Amp. New Testament.

7. **The Strangers** — (Peter) — I Peter 3:20-21. A.V.
   The like figure whereunto Baptism doth also now save us, not the putting away of the filth of the flesh . . . but the answer of a good conscience toward God by the resurrection of Jesus Christ.